INSPIRE / PLAN / DISCOVER / EXPERIENCE

NORTHERN
SPAIN

NORTHERN
SPAIN

CONTENTS

DISCOVER 6

EXPERIENCE 58

NEED TO KNOW 230

Left: The curving roof of Marqués de Riscal vineyard
Previous page: Verdant hills in the Basque Country
Front cover: San Juan de Gaztelugatxe, Costa Vasca

DISCOVER

The Bahía de La Concha, San Sebastián

WELCOME TO
NORTHERN
SPAIN

Wild, wind-whipped coasts and soaring green mountains. Pensive pilgrimage treks and prehistoric cave paintings. Whatever your dream trip to Northern Spain includes, this DK Eyewitness travel guide is the perfect companion.

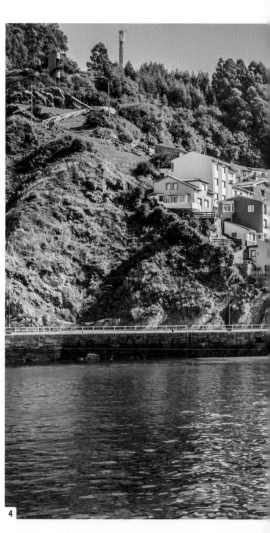

1 Cows grazing in the lush hills of the Picos de Europa.

2 A scallop shell marking the start of the pilgrim path.

3 Traditional Basque fiesta in the city of Vitoria-Gasteiz.

4 The harbour at Cudillero, an Asturian fishing village.

Radically different from the rest of the country, "Green Spain" is a land of striking emerald mountains and endless, varied coastlines dotted with traditional fishing villages. Outdoor pursuits abound, from hiking the teetering mountain trails in the Picos de Europa to relaxing on sun-kissed, surf-lashed beaches off the Biscay Coast.

Northern Spain's human history is ancient and evident. In Cantabria and the Basque Country, marvel at stunning cave art, painted over 30,000 years ago. Set off on the Camino de Santiago, and follow in the footsteps of medieval pilgrims; tracing ancient Roman paths along the Way of St James, you'll glimpse prehistoric houses, Romanesque churches and medieval stone crosses.

The beguiling cities of Northern Spain have their own special appeal: Bilbao is known for its glittering Guggenheim and cutting-edge art scene; San Sebastián for its world-leading cuisine and top tapas trails, plus prestigious jazz and film festivals. Inland, Pamplona and Vitoria-Gasteiz rejoice with traditional summer fiestas, and in wine country, Logroño seduces with sumptuous *pintxos* bars and *bodegas* brimming with fine riojas.

From the Pyrenees to the Rías Baixas and everything in between, we've broken Northern Spain down into easily navigable chapters, with detailed itineraries, expert local knowledge and colourful, comprehensive maps to help you plan the perfect visit. Whether you're staying for a weekend, a week or longer, this DK Eyewitness guide will ensure that you make the most of all that the region has to offer. Enjoy the book, and enjoy Northern Spain.

REASONS TO LOVE
NORTHERN SPAIN

Its cuisine is delightful. Its natural landscape is awe-inspiring. Its history pops up around every corner. There are endless reasons to love Northern Spain, but here are some of our favourites.

1 WORLDS OF DIFFERENCE

Northern Spain delights with its vibrant mix of Galician, Basque, Castilian and Catalan influences, all evident in the languages, foods, festivals and traditions across the region.

COOL CITIES 2

Its countryside is stunning, but Northern Spain's trendy cities are hard to beat: San Sebastián seduces with fine food and culture *(p156)* while just along the coast, Bilbao flaunts a chic contemporary art scene *(p150)*.

3 SEAFOOD

Fish-lovers eat like royalty across Atlantic-side Northern Spain, where deep-water vessels haul red tuna, bonito and silvery hake from the Bay of Biscay. In seaside villages and ocean-front resorts, sample marine treats like *pescaíto frito* (fried fish), seafood stew or classic Galician-style octopus.

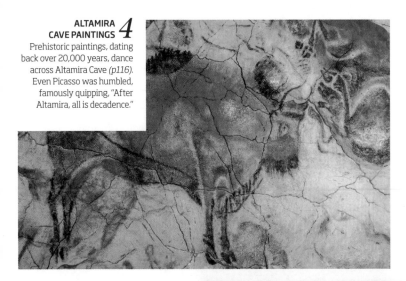

ALTAMIRA CAVE PAINTINGS 4

Prehistoric paintings, dating back over 20,000 years, dance across Altamira Cave *(p116)*. Even Picasso was humbled, famously quipping, "After Altamira, all is decadence."

POSTMODERN ARCHITECTURE 5

Frank Gehry left an indelible mark on Bilbao with his stunning Guggenheim *(p152)* and the Marqués de Riscal winery in the Basque Country *(p169)*. In Santander, Renzo Piano answered the challenge with his space-age Centro Botín art complex *(p112)*.

WALKING THE CAMINO DE SANTIAGO 6

You'll be presented with a coveted Compostela Certificate if you tackle the final 100 km (62 miles), or cycle the last 200 km (124 miles), of the celebrated pilgrim path *(p70)*.

SUN, SEA AND SURF *7*

Thousands of beaches beckon holiday-makers to catch some rays on the sand, snag the wind in their sails or snatch a long roller on a surfboard. Urban beaches like Santander's El Sardinero *(p113)* and San Sebastián's La Concha *(p158)* are among the finest.

WINNING WINERIES *8*

Sip aromatic *albariños* in Galicia *(p86)* and crisp *txakolí* in the Basque Country *(p169)*. In La Rioja and Navarra, quaff revered reds that rival their cousins across the Pyrenees in Bordeaux for richness and depth *(p198)*.

9 PINTXOS TRAILS

Spain's tastiest tradition is the *tapeo* – a stroll from bar to bar, sampling different tapas and *pintxos* *(p32)* at each. Join the locals in historic centres like Logroño on their hungry night-time hop *(p182)*.

10 MUSEO GUGGENHEIM

The radical design of Frank Gehry's colour-shifting titanium structure is intended to free the mind – all the better to appreciate the stunning contemporary art inside *(p152)*.

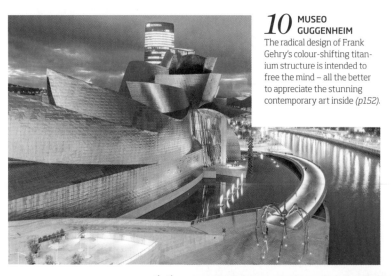

PICOS DE EUROPA 11

The deep gorges and verdant river valleys of this spectacular national park make for exceptional hiking, climbing, cycling and spelunking in every season, except winter – when you can ski, of course *(p102)*.

DRAMATIC COASTS 12

High cliffs and rocky outcrops punctuate much of the rugged, romantic Galician coast *(p82)*. The Basque Country is home to the loneliest crag of all, the mighty San Juan de Gaztelugatxe, joined to the mainland by a 231-step stone bridge *(p167)*.

EXPLORE
NORTHERN SPAIN

This guide divides Northern Spain into six colour-coded sightseeing areas, as shown on the map below. Find out more about each area on the following pages.

Atlantic Ocean

Ortigueira
Ferrol
Ribadeo
Avilés   Gijón
A Coruña
Vilalba
Santander
Carballo
Oviedo
ASTURIAS AND CANTABRIA
Mieres
p98
Santiago de
Lugo
Compostela
GALICIA
p60
Pontevedra
Carballiño
Ponferrada
León
Burgos
Vigo
Ourense
NORTHERN CASTILLA
AND LEÓN
Braga
p130
Benavente
Valladolid
Peñafiel
Vila Real
Zamora
Tordesillas
Porto
PORTUGAL
Salamanca
Segovia
Aveiro
Guarda
Ávila
Ciudad
Rodrigo
Madrid
Coimbra
Plasencia
Talavera de
la Reina
Toledo
Santarem
Trujillo
Ciudad Real
Lisbon
Mérida
Badajoz

Bay of
Biscay

Atlantic
Ocean

REP. OF
IRELAND
UNITED
KINGDOM
GERMANY
BELGIUM
CZECH
REP.
FRANCE
SWITZ.
AUSTRIA
NORTHERN
SPAIN
Bilbao
ITALY
Madrid
Barcelona
PORTUGAL
SPAIN
MOROCCO
ALGERIA
TUNISIA
LIBYA

WEST EUROPE & NORTH WEST AFRICA

Nantes

Niort

La Rochelle

Poitiers

Bordeaux

Arcachon

Villeneuve-sur-Lot

Rodez

FRANCE

Agen

Albi

Toulouse

Auch

San
Sebastián

Bayonne

Tarbes

Narbonne

Bilbao

**THE BASQUE
COUNTRY**
p146

P y r e n e e s

Pamplona

Perpignan

ANDORRA

Andorra la Vella

Vitoria-
Gasteiz

**NAVARRA
AND LA RIOJA**
p174

Jaca

La Seu
de Urgell

Figueres

Logroño

**CENTRAL AND
EASTERN PYRENEES**
p202

Girona

Huesca

Vic

Tudela

Manresa

Soria

Zaragoza

Lleida

Barcelona

Calatayud

SPAIN

Tarragona

Alcolea del Pinar

Amposta

Teruel

Vinaròs

Cuenca

*Mediterranean
Sea*

Mallorca

Tébar

Palma de Mallorca

Requena

Valencia

Albacete

Gandia

Almansa

0 kilometres   100

0 miles   100

N

GETTING TO KNOW
NORTHERN SPAIN

Countless visitors are drawn to the magnificent landscape of the north, with its sandy Atlantic beaches and intense blue waters, green mountains and verdant valleys. The cities, too, are enthralling: Santiago de Compostela, San Sebastián and Bilbao all give Barcelona and Madrid a run for their money.

PAGE 60

GALICIA

Tucked away in the northwest corner of the peninsula, Galicia is Spain's greenest region, and the heart of Spanish seafaring. Three of its four provinces have an Atlantic coastline and, inevitably, its cuisine is based around the daily catch. Inland, much of Galicia retains a medieval quality; the misty, emerald countryside is dotted with old granite villages and *pazos* – traditional stone manor houses. Those who brave the massive Camino de Santiago pilgrimage will experience this time-warped land at its finest as they journey to Santiago de Compostela, Galicia's capital.

Best for
Verdant landscapes and fresh seafood

Home to
Santiago de Compostela

Experience
Joining the pilgrims on the legendary Camino de Santiago

PAGE 98

ASTURIAS AND CANTABRIA

These two provinces are straddled by the Picos de Europa mountains, whose jagged peaks offer excellent rock-climbing and hiking opportunities. On the coast, you'll find the ancient seaside town of Santillana del Mar, as well as Santander and Oviedo, both busy university cities with a rich cultural life. Some of the earliest examples of art exist in Cantabria, most notably at Altamira, where the cave drawings and engravings are among the oldest to be found in Europe.

Best for
Outdoor activities and ancient art

Home to
Parque Nacional de los Picos de Europa

Experience
The ancient paintings in the Cueva de Tito Bustillo

PAGE 130

NORTHERN CASTILLA AND LEÓN

War and faith forged the northern tier of Castilla and León. The region's fortified towns and castle-like churches speak of the centuries-long war of the *reconquista*; and the medieval hero El Cid seems to haunt every corner of Burgos. The Camino de Santiago cuts through this region, slicing through Burgos, León and on into Galicia in a stolid parade of determined faith. Here you'll also find some of the richest late-medieval architecture in Spain.

Best for
Medieval and Renaissance architecture

Home to
León, Burgos

Experience
See the incredible stained glass and Gothic architecture of León Cathedral

→

PAGE 146

THE BASQUE COUNTRY

Stretching along the Bay of Biscay from the Cantabrian port of Castro Urdiales east to the French border, the Basque Country is a region of sprawling Atlantic beaches, backed by green hills and punctuated by picturesque rocky points. Home to avant-garde art and cutting-edge gastronomy, the region is further seasoned by the unique culture of the Basque people. Buzzing Bilbao has become an international model for the resurgent post-industrial city, while sleek San Sebastián remains a playground city of indulgent delight.

Best for
Unique culture and breathtaking coastlines

Home to
Bilbao, San Sebastián, Vitoria-Gasteiz

Experience
Relaxing on the beach of La Concha in glamorous San Sebastián

NAVARRA AND LA RIOJA

To the north, these mountainous regions brim with lush valleys and forests clustered with Medieval castles, Roman ruins and ancient monasteries and churches. At the end of the first millennium, Cistercian monks planted vines in both regions, and today La Rioja is renowned for its wine, with world-class *bodegas* scattered across its fertile hills. Meanwhile Navarra, the gateway to the Camino de Santiago, unfolds southwards into the badlands of Bárdenas Reales, a craggy dreamscape of rocky canyons and desert.

Best for
Wine tasting in La Rioja

Home to
Pamplona (Iruña), Logroño

Experience
Hiking through the Bosque de Irati forest

CENTRAL AND EASTERN PYRENEES

The Spanish Pyrenees skim the northern tier of Aragón and Catalonia. The highest and wildest terrain is found in Aragón, while in Catalonia the peaks become more accessible and the trails less rugged. Enjoy a gentler pace of life in the mountain villages, where old ways persist in the hearty cuisine and traditional festivals. Remote communities like Broto and Bielsa are enlivened by fiestas, a colourful hybrid of Christian and pagan carnivals.

Best for
Hiking in the rocky Pyrenees

Home to
Parque Nacional de Ordesa, Monasterio de San Juan de la Peña

Experience
Watching bearded vultures in the Parque Nacional de Ordesa

←

1 Playa de La Concha, framing San Sebastián.

2 The little island of Santa Clara rising in the bay.

3 Eduardo Chillida's *Comb of the Wind*, 1977.

4 Pouring *txakolí* at a *pintxos* bar in the Old Town.

Northern Spain offers endless options for exploration, from weekends discovering the charming cities to longer tours through dramatic landscapes. Wherever you choose to go, our handpicked itineraries will help you plan the perfect trip.

2 DAYS

in San Sebastián

Day 1

Morning Settle in at Juantxo Taberna (*www.juantxo.com*), a classic Spanish café in the heart of the charming Old Town, to savour a breakfast *bolintxe* (tortilla sandwich). Fortified, explore the maze of narrow streets that encircle the Plaza de la Constitución (*p156*) – you'll soon come across the Museo de San Telmo (*p158*), a former monastery transformed into the city's municipal museum. Lunch at a seafood restaurant rounds off the morning: the lovely, family-run Marinela overlooks the old port (*marinela-igeldo.com*).

Afternoon Walk off lunch by climbing tree-shaded paths up Monte Urgull (*p156*). At the top of this wooded hill you'll reach stunning viewing spots (*miradores*); the most spectacular is by the castle ruins at the summit, which overlooks gorgeous Playa de La Concha (*p158*). Back downhill, the New Town awaits. This elegant grid of wide avenues was laid out in the 19th century; today it's home to some of the city's chicest shops and galleries, along with the handsome, Neo-Gothic basilica (*p156*).

Evening A tapas tour around the Old Town is the best way to celebrate San Sebastián's miniature cuisine. Taste delicious *pintxos* at traditional bars Borda Berri and Gandarias in the heart of the Old Town (*p159*), and wash down traditional Basque snacks with a glass of chilled *txakolí*, the delightfully crisp local wine.

Day 2

Morning San Sebastián curves around one of the most beautiful bays in the world, the glorious Bahía de La Concha. Rise early to stroll around the bay to reach Eduardo Chillida's enormous sculpture, the *Comb of the Wind*. Pick a spot on the golden sand for some sunbathing. If you're feeling adventurous, take a boat out across the bay to reach the nearby rugged little island of Santa Clara. Once used to isolate plague victims, the islet is now a delightful spot for a walk and a swim at low tide.

Afternoon Back on dry land, there are plenty of great options for a beachfront lunch: for a treat, indulge in the excellent *menú del día* at the city's grandest hotel, the Hotel Londres y Inglaterra (*www. hlondres.com*). After lunch, make your way up Monte Igueldo, the 181-m- (593-ft-) high hill that juts up at the western end of the bay. Half way up, there's a charmingly creaky, century-old funicular which stops beside a delightful old-fashioned funfair. At the top, you'll reach the lighthouse; take in breathtaking sunset views, and watch as the elegant curve of the bayside city lights up at night.

Evening The glamorous Asador Alaia (*restaurantealaia.com*) makes an ideal dinner choice, especially if you can get a table on the terrace overlooking the twinkling lights below.

←

① *Puppy*, a floral sculpture beside the Guggenheim.

② The Puente de Viscaya, crossing the Nervión River.

③ *Pintxos* lined up in a Plaza Nueva bar.

④ Admiring a Baroque masterpiece by Van Dyck at the Museo de Bellas Artes.

2 DAYS
in Bilbao

Day 1

Morning Begin your visit at the world-famous Guggenheim Museum, a titanium vision from the future *(p152)*. Admire the gleaming curves of Frank Gehry's magnificent building, and say hello to Jeff Koons' flower-covered *Puppy* at the entrance. Inside, enjoy the spectacular interior and changing exhibitions. For lunch, snag a reservation at the museum's ultra-chic Michelin-starred restaurant Nerua *(www.nerua guggenheimbilbao.com)*.

Afternoon Explore the Siete Calles (Seven Streets), the medieval core that makes up the Casco Viejo *(p154)*, Bilbao's atmospheric old quarter. Scores of quirky shops and restaurants crowd the narrow streets, which are trimmed with traditional houses with plant-laden balconies. Don't miss out on the Museo Vasco *(p150)* for an insight into fascinating Basque traditions, or the nearby Catedral de Santiago, the city's oldest church. The wonderful waterside Ribera market is also worth a visit, chock-a-block with stalls of colourful produce.

Evening The Casco Viejo livens up at dusk, when the arcaded squares and streets fill with people savouring a *tapeo* – a *pintxos* tour from bar to bar. The Plaza Nueva is the epicentre of *pintxo* action, with a fabulous array of options. Try Gure Toki, which leads the pack when it comes to gourmet creations *(www.guretoki.com)*.

Day 2

Morning Spend a morning among the fine-art treasures of the Museo de Bellas Artes *(p150)*. Fascinating temporary collections complement excellent permanent exhibits, which include works by Goya, Zurbarán and Gauguin. Take a break on the terrace of the lovely café, overlooking the museum gardens. Before lunch, stroll around the elegant Ensanche Bilbaíno district, with its smart shops, delis and galleries. Pop into Azkuna Zentroa *(p151)*, a former wine warehouse transformed by Philippe Starck into a stunning cultural centre. Enjoy a delicious lunch in the stylish Bocadero *(bocaderobilbao.com)*.

Afternoon It's an enjoyable Metro ride out of town to the charming little seaside suburb of Getxo *(p167)*. As you are whisked along the edge of the Bilbao estuary, you'll pass Portugalete: catch a glimpse of the incredible Puente de Vizcaya, the world's oldest surviving transporter bridge, and one of few still in existence. You'll soon reach Gexto, where an amble through the tangle of narrow streets takes you to the old port, which bobs with colourful boats.

Evening Enjoy some early tapas and a glass of rioja at Arrantzale *(www.arrantzale. com)*, a typical fisherman's tavern with a terrace overlooking Getxo's port. Take a sunset sailing trip back to central Bilbao, and enjoy an unforgettable tour along the estuary as the sun turns the waters to gold.

1 Family-owned Bodegas Muga in the Rioja Alta.

2 Strolling the tree-shaded old centre of Pamplona.

3 Savouring a glass of wine and a bite to eat in Logroño.

4 The pretty village of Ochagavía, veiled in snow.

5 DAYS

in Navarra and La Rioja

Day 1

Start your trip in Pamplona, Navarra's enchanting capital *(p178)*. Explore the historic centre, still ringed by more than 5 km (3 miles) of medieval walls, and take time to admire the city's jewel, its magnificent cathedral *(p181)*. Here, exquisite 13th-century cloisters are an oasis of calm in the bustling capital. In the evening, join the locals on a *tapeo* for a taste of traditional tapas. Favourites on the tapas bar trail are Bar Gaucho *(p180)* and Bodegon Sarría *(www.bodegon sarria.com)* on Calle Estafeta, one of the principal streets of the *encierro* (bull-run).

Day 2

Make the 40-minute drive to Estella *(p190)*, a beguiling jumble of medieval churches, palaces and monasteries on the pilgrim route of Compostela. For lunch, try La Cepa on the arcaded main square amid townhouses adorned with ancient coats of arms *(restaurantecepa.com)*. Drive west to Logroño *(p182)*, capital of La Rioja, Spain's most celebrated wine region. Take a tour around the century-old Bodega Franco-Españolas *(www.francoespanolas.com)*. Back in the city centre, head down Calle Laurel for dinner at Soriano *(p183)*.

Day 3

Continue your exploration of wine country by driving to Haro *(p196)*, a bustling wine town with a well-preserved historic quarter. Dip into the excellent wine museum and explore the clutch of eminent *bodegas*, including Muga *(www.bodegasmuga.com)* and Bodegas Ramón Bilbao *(www.bodegasramonbilbao.es)*, for tours and tastings. After, lunch on succulent roast lamb baked in a brick oven at 150-year-old Terete *(terete.es)*. Then make for the tiny village of Santo Domingo de la Calzada, named after a medieval martyr whose relics are buried in a sumptuous 12th-century church *(p197)*.

Day 4

Rise early, and head east to Calahorra *(p195)* to stroll through the evocative Judería, home to a substantial Jewish community before the expulsion of the Jews in 1492. Continue to Olite, set amid a sea of vines, to wander ancient streets of fine mansions and churches, before exploring the splendid Palacio Real, the town's central medieval castle *(p190)*. Indulge in a luxurious lunch at the castle's impressive Parador de Olite *(p191)*. A 30-minute drive takes you to another medieval pilgrimage town, Sangüesa *(p189)*, nestled beside the River Aragón. The town's sinuous streets are lined with noble mansions and palaces; its star attraction is the stunning Romanesque church of Santa María La Real.

Day 5

On your final day, meander along the Valle de Salazar *(p185)*, a sylvan valley shaded with beech forest and scattered with charming villages. Stop at pretty Ochagavía for a stroll and a dip in the Piscina Natural, a natural swimming pool in the river. From Ochagavía, the mountain road winds upwards to the heart of the Bosque de Irati, Spain's largest primeval forest *(p185)*. Continue along the twisting road to Roncesvalles *(p187)*, an ancient pilgrim town on a mountain pass near the French border. Reward yourself with a hearty Navarrese dinner at the Posada de Roncesvalles *(laposada.roncesvalles.es)*.

7 DAYS
in the Pyrenees

Day 1

Start your journey in Jaca, a handsome town set against a sublime Pyrenean backdrop *(p214)*. Spend the morning exploring the town's 16th-century citadel and Romanesque cathedral, one of the oldest in Spain, and amble down to the river to admire the medieval Puente de San Miguel. For lunch, tuck into local specialities at Lilium *(restauranteliliumjaca.com)*. Then it's a 30-minute drive into the mountains to the Monasterio de San Juan de la Peña *(p210)*, a monastery perched under a craggy peak, said to have once guarded the Holy Grail. Back in Jaca, head to lively La Tasca de Ana for an evening of tapas and a glass or two of local wine *(p220)*.

Day 2

After a lie-in, make the leisurely drive south to reach the Castillo de Loarre *(p217)*, which hugs a rocky outcrop above the Ebro plain. Savour a locally sourced lunch at the Hospederia de Loarre *(www. hospederiasdearagon.com)* before driving east to Huesca *(p220)*. This charming town was once the Aragonese capital; its former

glory is evoked in the 12th-century royal palace and the Iglesia de San Pedro el Viejo, burial place of the Aragonese kings. In the evening, enjoy an elegant dinner at Michelin-starred Las Torres *(p220)*.

Day 3

Follow the narrow roads that snake eastward through the mountains to Alquézar *(p220)*, piled up steeply beneath a medieval castle. Meander the cobbled streets of the village before visiting the Iglesia de la Colegiata de Alquéza, where the walls are adorned with medieval frescoes. Stop in at family-run Casa Pardina for a bite to eat *(www.casa pardina.com)*. Hit the road again and continue to enchanting Aínsa *(p218)*, where steep, cobbled streets wind upward to the arcaded Plaza Mayor, the perfect spot for a romantic dinner at Callizo *(p220)*.

Day 4

Stock up on picnic supplies in Aínsa, and drive up to the Parque Nacional de Ordesa y Monte Perdido *(p206)* for a day's hiking

☐ The magnificent, star-shaped citadel at Jaca.

☐ Majestic Castillo de Loarre presiding over Aragón.

☐ Canoeing along the Noguera Pallaresa river.

☐ Brightly coloured mountain lodges in the village of Arties.

☐ Frescoes in the Iglesia de la Colegiata de Alquézar.

in one of the most stunning national parks in Spain. Keep an eye out for majestic bearded vultures soaring overhead, and for the delicate alpine flora that carpet the valley floors. Back in Aínsa, having worked up a big appetite, tuck into a hearty casserole at the Bodegon de Mallacán (bodegonmallacan.com).

Day 5

Head across the Catalan border to the Vall de Boí (p222). This remote valley is scattered with stone villages of slate-roofed houses and several exquisite churches filled with extraordinary murals that have earned them UNESCO World Heritage status. Most of the tiny villages have their own beautiful church, but the finest are in Taüll. Dinner is at the Hotel Santa Maria, a cosy mountain lodge overlooking the Taüll valley (www.taull.com).

Day 6

Press on north to Vielha, where grey stone and slate buildings are typical of the Val d'Aran (p221). Admire Vielha's fine churches and visit the little Museo Etnológico for a taste of the region's folk history. At lunch, sample Aranese cuisine at El Racó (www.braseriaelraco.com). In the afternoon, head on through the valley to the enchanting village of Arties, and the stylish hotel-restaurant Casa Irene, where you can indulge in a massage at the on-site spa (www.hotelcasairene.com).

Day 7

On your last day, rise early to drive south along another beautiful road which follows the Noguera Pallaresa river. After about an hour, you'll reach Sort (p222), a little town famous for its watersports. Head out on a thrilling whitewater excursion with Rafting Catalunya (raftingcatalunya.es) and take in the spectacular landscape of the Noguera Pallaresa river valley. After a fun-filled morning on the water, drive east to reach La Seu d'Urgell (p222), home to Catalonia's only Romanesque cathedral and a clutch of elegant mansions. End your trip with a well-earned and relaxing dinner on the lovely terrace of Hotel Andria (www.hotelandria.com).

$\longrightarrow$

1 The lighthouse, perched on a cliff edge, in Castro Urdiales.

2 The sweeping Playa el Sardinero, one of the beaches framing Santander.

3 Exploring the haunting El Monte Castillo cave system.

4 A cable car climbing to the heights of the Parque Nacional de los Picos de Europa.

10 DAYS
in the North

Day 1

Kick off with two of Cantabria's prettiest and most popular beach resorts, Castro Urdiales (*p128*) and Laredo (*p129*). Start with a stroll around Castro Urdiales' port, popping into its Gothic Iglesia de Santa María, which has a pinkish hue. Once you've worked up an appetite, order a seafood lunch at Arboleda (*www.restaurantelaarboleda.com*) and then spend an afternoon on the sand in Laredo. Although the town's beaches get busy in summer, you'll find breathtaking, emptier stretches the further you walk from the centre. After basking in the sun, head for dinner at La Marina Company (*www.lamarinacompany.es*).

Day 2

Next up is the Cantabrian capital Santander (*p112*), which was completely rebuilt in the 1940s after a devastating fire destroyed its historic heart. Still an atmospheric port city, it has good seafood restaurants and some wonderful beaches. Try the lively Marucho (*www.maruchorestaurante.es*) for lunch. In the afternoon, take in some of the city's cultural highlights, such as one of the exhibitions at the Centro Botín or the fishy delights at the Museo Marítimo, including a skeleton of a gargantuan whale. In the evening, some of the best tapas in town are to be found at Cañadío (*www.restaurantecanadio.com*).

Day 3

Drive southwest to Puente Viesgo for El Monte Castillo, a complex of caves (*p129*). They are not as well known as the nearby Cuevas de Altamira (*p116*), but they are just as impressive. From here, it's a 20-minute drive to Santillana del Mar (*p114*), which, despite its name, is not quite located on the coast. It's an enchanting and beautifully preserved town, paved with cobblestones and dotted with churches, palaces and mansions. Don't miss La Colegiata, the Romanesque monastery at the heart of the town. Good places for lunch or dinner include Los Blasones (*www.restaurante losblasones.es*) or Casa Uzquiza (*Calle Jesús Otero 5, 942 84 03 56*).

Day 4

It's around an hour's drive to the ancient little town of Potes (*p104*), which easily merits a couple of hours' strolling around, but also acts as a springboard for the stunning Parque Nacional de los Picos de Europa (*p102*). You could spend weeks here, but in one day you can at least enjoy a fantastic hike (visit the tourist office for suggested routes), some rock climbing, or simply pick up some picnic provisions in Potes and enjoy lunch among some of the most spectacular mountain scenery that Spain has to offer. On your return to Potes, have dinner in Casa Cayo (*www.casacayo.com*).

→

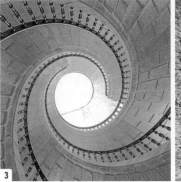

Day 5

Leave the Parque Nacional de los Picos de Europa via the Lagos de Covadonga, two picturesque lakes in the park's northwest corner, and continue to Covadonga *(p105)*, a charming mountain town that is worth a stroll. From here it's a ten-minute drive to the ancient Asturian capital of Cangas de Onís *(p105)*, which enjoys a spectacular mountain backdrop. After a scrumptious tapas lunch at Restaurant El Molin de la Pedrera *(www.elmolin.com)*, have a wander over the town's Romanesque bridge to the 8th-century chapel. Come evening, it's worth a detour from Cangas de Onís to the other side of Arriondas for the Michelin-starred Casa Marcial *(www.casamarcial.com)*, which showcases the finest of the region's hearty cuisine.

Day 6

Continue west to Gijón *(p118)*, a port city with a charming Old Town piled up on a narrow isthmus. While away the morning at the Palacio de Revillagigedo (Centro Cultural Cajastur), which hosts temporary exhibitions, and then wander along one of Gijón's long beaches, perhaps ending up at one or two of the tapas bars around Playa San Lorenzo. Once you've soaked up the sun here, head back into town to walk the Roman walls and explore Gijón's museums. End up at Auga *(www.restaurante auga.com)*, one of the finest eateries in town, for a decadent dinner.

Day 7

Spend a day in handsome Oviedo *(p106)*, a historic city gathered around a splendid Gothic cathedral. Check out the royal tombs and the 9th-century chapel, before lunch at Taberna Salcedo *(www.taberna salcedo.com)*. Famous across Spain for its vibrant cultural gems, Oviedo has pre-Romanesque churches located on the hills overlooking the city. The best preserved is Santa María del Naranco, a couple of miles northwest of the centre. Next, have a look at the superb art, including paintings by El Greco, Goya and Dalí, in the Museo de Bellas Artes *(p108)*. Afterwards, try the celebrated *fabada asturiana* (regional bean stew) at Casa Fermín *(www.casafermin.com)*.

① The Basílica de Santa María la Real de Covadonga.

② Surfers walking along Gijón's Playa San Lorenzo.

③ A spiral staircase in the Museo do Pobo Galego, Santiago de Compostela.

④ The pretty seaside town of Cudillero, on the Costa Verde.

⑤ Walking through the Puerta del Obispo Aguirre Izquierdo in Lugo.

⑥ *La Regenta* statue in Oviedo, dedicated to Leopoldo Alas y Ureña's novel.

Day 8

Head west along the coastal road that skirts the glorious Costa Verde (p127). With its cliffs and coves, verdant hills and picturesque villages, this is easily one of Spain's loveliest and least spoiled stretches of coastline. Stop off and explore charming towns such as Cudillero (p120), where you can dine on tapas at one of the outdoor cafés in the town's main square, Plaza Marina – try Bar Casa Julio at No 7 (617 43 82 54). Later head to Luarca (p121), for a mooch around its pretty harbour, perhaps ending up in Castropol (p120) for a seafood dinner on the waterfront at El Risón (Paseo del Muelle s/n, 985 63 50 65).

Day 9

Cross the border into Galicia and aim for the ancient city of Lugo (p76). Once an important Roman settlement, Lugo is still ringed by spectacular and remarkably intact Roman walls, which you can climb to enjoy fabulous views. First, have a hearty Galician lunch outside the city at charming Taberna do Labrego (www.tabernadolabrego.com). Once you breach the walls, you'll find that the old city is a jumble of narrow streets and pretty squares – perfect for a wander before visiting Lugo's Romanesque cathedral. Round off your day with dinner at Mesón de Alberto (p77).

Day 10

End your journey in the magical city of Santiago de Compostela – the culmination of the famous pilgrimage and a fitting finale to your trip (p64). An enchanting city built of cool grey stone, it is dominated by a magnificent cathedral, said to contain the bones of St James (Santiago). Allow plenty of time to visit the cathedral, before moving on to the Mercado de Abastos for a glass of wine and a plate of prawns at any of the bars in the market. Next, visit the Museo do Pobo Galego for an interesting look into local life over the centuries. In the evening, head for Dezaseis and be sure to try the city's star dishes – scallops or octopus (www.dezaseis.com). What better way to end your trip to the north coast than with a delicious plate of seafood?

Pintxos vs Tapas

You'll be served a *tapa* - a small snack to accompany your drink - at most bars in Spain. But along the Basque and Cantabrian coasts, tapas includes the exalted *pintxo*, haute cuisine in miniature, served on a slice of bread and skewered on a little stick. Think anchovy with pickled Guindilla peppers or grilled mushroom with shrimp on baguette. For the best variety, hop from bar to bar on a *tapeo* (tapas tour) in the side streets of San Sebastián *(p156)* and Logroño *(p182)*.

→

A tapas bar groaning with tasty dishes, San Sebastián

NORTHERN SPAIN FOR
FOODIES

Spain looks to the north for gastronomic greatness. Here at the source, feast on fresh seafood, or graze on tasty fresh tapas in traditional bars. For a meal of a lifetime, look to the cities, where glittering gourmet restaurants and Basque chefs are on the front line of foodie innovation.

Masters of Modern Cuisine

The revolutionaries of the New Basque cuisine continue their inventive ways in San Sebastián, a city with more Michelin stars per square metre than Paris or Lyon - second in the world only to Kyoto. Choose from a clutch of dazzling gourmet haunts: Arzak *(p159)*, Akelarre *(akelarre.net)* and Martín Berasategui *(martin berasategui.com)* are each lauded with three Michelin stars; and gastronomic giant Restaurante Mugaritz *(www.mugaritz.es)* has two Michelin stars. Be sure to reserve a table far in advance.

→

Chefs preparing cutting-edge dishes at Restaurante Mugaritz

Hearty Mountain Fare

After a strenuous hike across the Picos de Europa (p102) or a hilly stretch of the Camino de Santiago (p70), you'll have worked up a serious appetite. Tuck into rich mountain dishes such as pungent Cabrales blue cheese from Asturias (p105) or venison roasted over a traditional wood-fired grill (asador). Another classic favourite among experienced pilgrims is fabada, a rich savoury bean and chorizo stew (p125), best enjoyed at Asturian stalwart Los Arándanos (p121).

← Creamy Asturian blue cheese, served with quince and grapes

TOP 5 SEAFOOD SPECIALITIES

Polbo á Feira
A Galician paprika-spiced octopus dish.

Marmitako
A Cantabrian and Catalan seafood stew.

Percebes
Tubular shellfish, also known as goose barnacles, best steamed lightly in sea water.

Angulas
Once a Basque Christmas tradition, sautéed baby eels are now a pricey treat.

Txangurro
Basque spider crab is often served baked and stuffed as a main dish.

Fresh from the Sea

With endless wild coastlines brimming with abundant fresh fish and seafood, Northern Spain is pescatarian heaven. In the ports of A Guarda and Bermeo, deep-water vessels land red tuna, mackerel and silvery hake; on the cliffs of the Costa da Morte, harvesters gather sweet percebes; and on the flats of O Grove foragers dig for fresh clams. This glorious marine bounty appears on tables across the land, from traditional Spanish seaside haunts like Coruña's Restaurante O Fado (p73) to Japanese sushi restaurants like Umami in Oviedo (p106).

↑ The brightly coloured fishing port of A Guarda in Pontevedra

Traditional Spirits

From 50 per cent proof Galician brandy, *orujo*, to the plum-based Navarrese liqueur, *patxaran*, every region has its own traditional spirit. An aniseed-scented Anís makes a popular after-dinner tipple, as does *queimada*, a Galician witches' brew of *orujo* mixed with lemon or orange slices, sugar and coffee beans.

←

Setting *queimada*, the witches brew, aflame in a traditional clay pot

NORTHERN SPAIN
RAISE A GLASS

Socializing over drinks and snacks is a way of life in Spain, with savoury tapas accompanying wine, beer or cider, and a biscuit complementing coffee, chocolate or milky horchata. Ask about the local tipple, as each region has its own wines and ciders.

A World of Wine

Spain's most famous wine is produced in La Rioja and the Basque Country, where you'll find stunning vineyards like the modern Ysios *(p172)* and the Marqués de Riscal *(p169)*, which offers tastings and wine-based spa treatments. Be sure to taste your way across the Galician and Basque coasts: sample aromatic *albariños* at Bodegas Martín Códax in Pontevedra *(martincodax.com)*, and in Zaurutz, make sure to try the lightly sparkling local *txakolí (p169)*.

→

The modern exterior of the Marqués de Riscal and *(inset)* wide-ranging tasting sessions at its vineyard

Exceptional Cider

When Asturian bartenders pour *sidra* from a bottle raised nearly a metre above the glass, they're not just being dramatic – the technique aerates the cider and releases its unique aromas. Fermented from local apples, traditional bone-dry, low-alcohol *sidra* is enjoyed across Northern Spain. Some of the best sipping spots are found in the countryside surrounding San Sebastián, like the cool Zelaia *(zelaia.eus)* and 450-year-old cider house Lizeaga *(lizeaga.eus)*.

→

Pouring a refreshing glass of Asturian *sidra* the traditional way

Crafty Draughts

Spain's small-scale craft brewers have an annual output measured in dozens rather than thousands of barrels of beer. But an increasing number of bars place a local craft beer on tap, and increasingly well-known breweries like Basqueland *(basquebeer. com)* and Laugar *(laugarbrewery. com)* offer tours and tastings. Look for the liveliest craft scenes in student neighbourhoods. In Bilbao, trendy little Bihotz Café *(Calle de Arechaga, 6)* is always buzzing, with a good selection of beers to choose from.

→

Sampling local craft ales in Laugar's tap room, near Bilbao

Bilbao's Modern Monuments

When Frank Gehry's abstract titanium-skinned Museo Guggenheim Bilbao *(p152)* opened in 1997, it transformed the city into a champion of adventurous architecture. Cross Santiago Calatrava's exuberant Zubzuri Bridge to get a better view of the museum, known as "the titanium flower". In this cool contemporary city, you can shop, dine or swim in the Azkuna Zentroa, a wine warehouse sleekly reimagined by French design giant Philippe Starck. Even Bilbao's Metro system has had a modern makeover – it's entered through a glass tube created by Sir Norman Foster, and known locally as the *"Fosterito"*.

$\rightarrow$

Titanium curves of the Guggenheim ripple along the Nervión river, Bilbao

NORTHERN SPAIN FOR
ARCHITECTURE

Northern Spain's architecture speaks of faith across the centuries. Simple piety informs the ancient Romanesque churches of Asturias, while soaring Gothic cathedrals in Burgos and León reach for the heavens. Bilbao's Postmodern landmarks recast heroic-scale structures in secular terms.

Renaissance Landmarks

Fine Renaissance structures can be found all along the Camino de Santiago. The 1515 Convento de San Marcos in León was a royal gift to the knights of the Order of Santiago *(p135)*. The Hostal dos Reis Católicos *(p65)* was built by Isabel and Fernando in 1499 beside Santiago Cathedral for noble pilgrims who had reached the end of their trek.

$\leftarrow$

The lovely cloisters of the 16th-century Convento de San Marcos, León

Pillars of Faith

Oviedo's Romanesque churches (p110) merge geometry and nature-inspired Visigothic forms to stunning effect. The Romanesque style arrived in Catalonia in the 11th century; you'll see many stunning surviving examples on a drive through the Vall de Boí (p222). Topped with lofty bell towers, the valley's churches are adorned with iron-work and replicas of their original frescoes.

←

The squat Romanesque
Church of Santa Cristina
de Lena, near Oviedo

Gothic Glories

Grand flying buttresses, pointed arches and ribbed vaults all characterize Northern Spain's Gothic architecture. Seek out the pair of flamboyant spires that top majestic Burgos Cathedral (p140) or head to León, where the vast, elegant cathedral is known as the "House of Light" because its huge windows fill the space with glowing colour (p136). In Santander, the vast cathedral's carved Gothic cloisters embody rhythmic serenity in stone (p112).

→

Majestic León Cathedral,
a great example
of the Gothic style

The Great Outdoors

From meandering coasts to a forested, mountainous interior, Northern Spain's landscapes beg to be explored. Ride the Fuente Dé cable car up to stunning Picos de Europa mountain trails (p102) or scamper through the treetops and slide down ziplines at Santander's Forestal Park (www.forestalpark.com). In the colder months, the Pyrenees afford winter sports galore (p222) and in summer, the beaches are great for surfing, snorkelling and sailing (p44).

$\rightarrow$

Climbing through the woods on a Forestal Park treetop adventure

NORTHERN SPAIN FOR
FAMILIES

Natural parks laced with trails; a lighthouse-dotted coast of broad beaches; ancient ruins and dinosaur footprints that inspire inquisitive minds. There are plenty of reasons Northern Spain continues to attract families year after year.

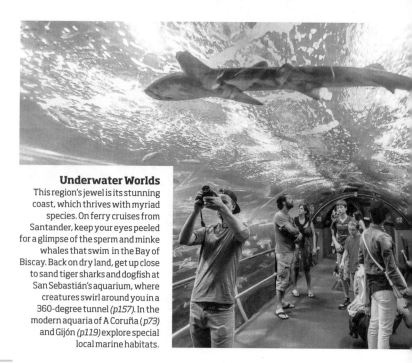

Underwater Worlds

This region's jewel is its stunning coast, which thrives with myriad species. On ferry cruises from Santander, keep your eyes peeled for a glimpse of the sperm and minke whales that swim in the Bay of Biscay. Back on dry land, get up close to sand tiger sharks and dogfish at San Sebastián's aquarium, where creatures swirl around you in a 360-degree tunnel (p157). In the modern aquaria of A Coruña (p73) and Gijón (p119) explore special local marine habitats.

Epic Natural History

La Rioja is Spain's "Jurassic Park", where 100 million years ago dinosaurs roamed the marshy plains. Today, dinosaur enthusiasts can trace these prehistoric beasts on a trail at El Barranco Perdido, where there are also models, fossil workshops, an adventure playground and a Cretaceous beach for swimming (p194). Follow in the footprints of thunder lizards at the Museo Jurásico in Colunga, where replica skeletons with massive claws and teeth give the attraction an edge – as do the looming replicas of 16 different dinosaurs (p124).

← Posing with a dinosaur at the Museo Jurásico in Colunga

TOP 4 FAMILY FRIENDLY FESTIVALS

La Tamborrada
A raucous fiesta of pipe-and-drum parades and fireworks (p50).

Fiesta de la Arribada
Medieval reenactments recall Columbus's 1492 arrival in America (p51).

Aste Nagusia
An exhuberant nine-day August fest celebrating all things Basque in Bilbao.

Regatas de La Concha
On the first two Sundays of September, thousands of rowers race across San Sebastián's bay.

↑ The 360-degree tunnel at the San Sebastián Aquarium

Park Amusements

On hot days, head for A Coruña's Aquapark Cerceda, to make a splash on the water slides and jet fountains (aquaparkcerceda. es). For a more relaxing afternoon, take a ride on the carousel in Santander's Jardines de Pereda, or enjoy the old-fashioned Monte Igueldo amusement park, reached from San Sebastián by cable railway.

↑ Riding beside Bahia Concha at the Monte Igueldo amusement Park

Among the Celts

Celtic culture spread across the Iberian Peninsula from the Miño River valley during the Bronze Age. At Castro de Coaña, survey remnants of an ancient fort that rise from a hilltop *(p120)*, and near A Guarda, explore circular foundations of a Celtic village *(p88)*. In A Coruña *(p72)*, admire the Celtic artistry of Cícere metalwork displayed at the Museo Arqueológico.

→

The mysterious circular foundations of a Celtic village, A Guarda

UNEARTHING THE PAST

Antiquity seems close at hand in Northern Spain – at every turn, you'll find vestiges of the Basque, Roman and Celtic cultures that shaped the region. Marvel at prehistoric art, explore ancient ruins, and walk in the footsteps of pilgrims to trace the history of the north.

Legendary Cultures

The Basques have a history of self-government stretching back to before Roman times, a language like no other and a body of unique sports and traditions. Also set apart from the rest of Spain by a language closer to Portuguese than Spanish, Galicia draws on Celtic roots in its folklore, literature and music. Explore this nuanced cultural history at the Museo de San Telmo in San Sebastián *(p158)*, which tells the tale of Basque identity from the Middle Ages to the modern independence movement. At the Museo do Pobo Galego in Santiago de Compostela *(p64)*, delve into Galicia's seafaring history and learn about the traditional dress, music and crafts of the Galician people.

→

Works of art on display at the Museo de San Telmo in San Sebastián

Pilgrims' Footsteps

The route to Santiago (p64), the supposed resting place of St James, is certainly well-trodden (p70). The main path follows a Roman trading route, walked by half a million pilgrims each year during the Middle Ages. The pilgrims would stay in simple shelters or at monasteries along the way, and would return with a scallop shell as a souvenir. Set off on this challenging trek and join the 300,000 people who take the Way of St James each year.

→

Hiking along the Way of St James, towards Santiago de Compostela

Ancient Art

The Palaeolithic hunters of Northern Spain literally left their mark on the walls of caves through Asturias, Cantabria and the Basque Country. Study splendid replicas of hand paintings and lively depictions of animals at the Museo de Altamira (p116), or see originals underground at El Castillo (p129).

←

Expressive prehistoric cave painting in the caves of Altamira

Roman Remains

The Roman Legions left their stamp across the north in settlements like the gold-mining town of Astorga (p144) and in Lugo (p76), where Roman fortifications still encircle the Old Town. In A Coruña, climb the Torre de Hércules, the oldest Roman lighthouse still in operation (p72), and near Gijón (p118) visit the baths in Campo Valdés, which chronicle daily Roman life.

→

Ancient Roman walls encircling Lugo's Old Town

Wild Mountains

The ridges of the Picos de Europa (p102), and the Pyrenean national park of Ordesa (p206) are cut across with challenging hiking trails. Trek through the mountains and gaze over breathtaking landscapes of deep gorges, snowy peaks and lush canyons. This is the realm of rare alpine creatures – look out for chamois pattering across the peaks and vultures circling high overhead (p209).

→

Crossing a mountain pass in the snowcapped Picos de Europa

NORTHERN SPAIN FOR
RUGGED LANDSCAPES

Bounded by snowcapped mountains, craggy canyons and wind-whipped coasts, this is the wild corner of Spain. Hike amid the dramatic peaks of the Picos de Europa, explore the glorious coastlines and get lost in the verdant forests of "Green Spain".

Spectacular Sea Cliffs

Along the northern coasts, mountains greet the sea with high cliffs and giant granite and slate headlands. The Galician coast, in particular, has striking views from the rocks across the estuaries of the Rías Baixas. On the Costa da Morte, drive the corniche roads to see the dramatic "end of the earth", as the Romans called the cliffs around Fisterra (p83).

←

A lighthouse marking the rock-bound Cabo Vilán on the Costa da Morte

The Grandest Geology

The north is peppered with geological wonders. In Navarra, dusty desert canyons and monolithic rock formations make up the Bárdenas Reales *(p192)*, a craggy dreamscape which served as the Dothraki Sea in TV epic *Game of Thrones*. At El Soplao, a vast cave system dazzles underground explorers, its subterranean chambers forming a natural cathedral of crystalline formations *(p127)*.

→

Astonishing rock formations adorning the El Soplao caves

Majestic Forests

Great swathes of the damp, mountainous north are shrouded by Europe's oldest forests. Hike through the mist-wreathed Bosque de Irati *(p185)* or the Parque Nacional de Ordesa *(p206)*, where beech and Pyrenean oak trees are a refuge for rare birds, boar and brown bears. In November, make for the woodside villages of Galicia to catch the scent of sweet chestnuts roasting on bonfires as Os Magostos marks the turning of the seasons.

←

Autumn colour flaring across the forest in the Parque Nacional de Ordesa

On the Water

Sailing enthusiasts will find boats for hire in all the major resorts, like Santander *(p112)* and San Sebastián *(p156)*. If your interest leans towards sport fishing, head to the main docks of any resort town and haggle with the fishing charter boats. Some captains also offer sightseeing excursions and party trips.

Sailing yacht
entering calm waters
around Santander

NORTHERN SPAIN
ON THE COAST

All along the Atlantic coast, golden sands unfurl between green mountains and blue sea. These Bay of Biscay beaches are some of Spain's best for sunbathing and strolling and the waters offshore are top for surfing and sailing.

TOP 4 SURFING BEACHES

Playa de Razo, Carballo, Galicia
Plenty of A-frame waves make this a perfect spot for learners.

Salinas, Asturias
This urban beach bustles in July with the Salinas Longboard Fest.

Loredo/Somo, Cantabria
Twin beach breaks across a Santander peninsula give way to an exhilarating offshore reef break near Isla de Santa Marina.

Mundaka, Basque Country
Spain's most famous surfing beach has a left-hand rivermouth break.

Surveying the sandy expanse of Playa el Sardinero, Santander ↓

Brave the Swell

Surfers of all stripes love the wave-lashed northern coasts, and some of the best spots for wind- and kitesurfing are found in Galicia. Try the Port of Bares for windsurfing, and San Jorge for off-shore kitesurfing – KiteboardinGalicia is one of the top schools *(kiteboardin galicia.com)*. In the Basque Country, keen surfers can master Costa Vasca waves with Mundaka Surf Shop Surf School *(mundakasurfshop.com/surf-school)*.

→

Windsurfing around the Galician coast, and *(inset)* heading out to sea on the Costa Vasca

Sun-Kissed Strands

Despite its reputation as wild and rugged, the north has plenty of spots for sun, sea and sand. The beachside cities of Santander and San Sebastián preside over the elegant crescents of El Sardinero *(p113)* and La Concha *(p158)*, offering ample opportunities for swimming and sunbathing. To the west, the Rías Baixas are home to little coves and sandy stretches, like the Praia da Lanzada, a spit of fine white sand *(p86)*. Out to sea, the pristine Illas Cíes *(p87)* promise dreamy seclusion.

Heading Downriver

Paddle through La Rioja on the Ebro as it meanders through vineyards, or descend the Sella *(p124)* – in summer this route is so popular that bars pop up on the riverbanks. For some adrenaline, try white-water rafting on Galicia's Río Miño *(p94)*, where the national rafting championships are held each spring.

Canoeing down the River Sella, one of the most popular paddling routes

NORTHERN SPAIN FOR
OUTDOOR ACTIVITIES

With its glorious coastline and magnificent mountains, every corner of Northern Spain offers a wealth of outdoor activities. Surf Atlantic rollers, ski in the Pyrenees or hike the famed Camino de Santiago: the choice is yours.

On Two Wheels

With spectacular, varied terrain, and a milder climate than the rest of the country, Northern Spain is a great place to explore by bicycle. The north is crisscrossed by sweeping Vías Verdes (Green Ways), a system of converted disused railway lines that grant cyclists and hikers easy access to stunning scenic countryside *(viasverdes.com)*. Two excellent routes are the Basque Plazaola circuit (40 km/ 25 miles), which runs through old railway tunnels, and the Río Oja route, following the Riojan riverbanks (28 km/17 miles).

→

Cycling through Unha, a Pyrenean mountain village

Walk This Way

From gentle coastal trails to remote Picos de Europa paths *(p102)*, a host of hikes pepper Northern Spain. There are plenty of long-distance GR *(Gran Recorrido)* routes, including the stunning GR11 which tracks the breadth of the Pyrenees. Then, of course, there's the Camino de Santiago – the snaking route which takes in the region's most religious sites before reaching Santiago de Compostela's grand cathedral *(p70)*.

→

Trekking through Navarrese countryside on the Camino de Santiago

Hit the Slopes

Snowbunnies are spoilt for choice when it comes to skiing in the north. Plenty of top resorts are located in the Pyrenees, including the chichi Baqueira-Beret *(p223)*, family-favourite La Molina *(lamolina.cat)* and budget-friendly El Formigal *(formigal-panticosa.com)*. Beginners might prefer the resort of Valgrande-Pajares, in the Picos de Europa *(p102)*, with its gentle slopes, wide runs and a ski school.

←

Skier jumping over powdery snow at the prestigious resort of Baqueira-Beret

Perfect Paragliding

Northern Spain's cinematic landscape is really best enjoyed from the air. Near Bilbao, Sopelana's cliffs and beaches are the ideal environment for learner gliders; while in the Pyrenees, thermals over Organya's high valley support long flights on sunny days – perfect for practising aerial acrobatics.

→

Paragliding over the dramatic valley of Organya in the Pyrenees

Astonishing Art

The jewel of the north, Bilbao's gargantuan Guggenheim sets the city apart as a great centre for contemporary art *(p152)*. The Museo de Bellas Artes de Bilbao houses equally edgy work, mainly by Basque artists *(p150)*. In San Sebastián, modern sculpture covers the city itself: explore monumental works by the late Basque sculptors Eduardo Chillida and Jorge Oteiza on a walking tour *(p156)*. Over in Santiago, catch the Galician avantgarde at the Centro Galego de Arte Contemporánea *(p65)*.

→

Construcción Vacía (Empty Construction) by Jorge Oteiza, San Sebastián

NORTHERN SPAIN'S
CAPTIVATING CITIES

Northern Spain seduces with astonishing countryside, but its urban centres hold their own special appeal. Make for the dazzling northern cities and embrace avant-garde art, eclectic shopping, fantastic film and - most of all - stellar gastronomy.

For Late Nights

Spain comes alive after dark, and you can enjoy a buzzing nightlife in almost every big northern city. Catch live bands at the Playa Club in A Coruña *(playaclub.club)*; dance the night away at Shake! in Bilbao *(635 31 89 19)*; or party from midnight until dawn at Discoteca Bataplan on San Sebastián's Playa de La Concha *(bataplan disco.com)*.

←

Musician performing at Shake! nightclub in Bilbao

On the Big Screen

Film buffs should seek out film fests to catch the best in new Spanish and international cinema. San Sebastián's Film Festival is the most prestigious (p157), but Bilbao's ZINEBI Festival of Documentary and Short Film (zinebi.eus) and Santander's International Film Week (late April to early May) are equally enticing.

$\rightarrow$

Movie star Chris Hemsworth taking a selfie with fans at the San Sebastián Film Festival

Shopping Spots

Northern cities are perfect for a bit of retail therapy. In Bilbao, the Calle de Mayo comes alive with its Saturday flea market, where locals come to chat and browse vintage wares, and on Sundays, the Plaza Nueva bustles with a weekly antiques market. In San Sebastián, too, a lively Sunday craft fair takes over the city's historic food market. Don't underestimate pint-sized Gijón (p118), which is chock-a-block with boutiques.

$\rightarrow$

Browsing at a second-hand bookshop on Bilbao's Plaza Nueva

Social Snacking

The north has a reputation for great gastronomy, and here great snacking is part of everyday life. Strike out on a *tapeo (p12)* in the old quarters of Bilbao (p150) and Pamplona (p178), where busy bars buzz with diners sampling mini dishes. In San Sebastián, a guided *pintxos* tour with local foodie, Mimo, gives visitors a taste of the action (sansebastian.mimofood.com).

$\leftarrow$

Eating and drinking with friends at a tapas bar in Pamplona

A YEAR IN
NORTHERN
SPAIN

JANUARY

△ **New Year's Day** (1 Jan). Fiestas, concerts and spectacular light shows illuminate Northern Spain's towns and cities.

La Tamborrada (19–20 Jan). San Sebastián resounds with the beats of hundreds of drums.

FEBRUARY

△ **Carnival** (late Feb or Mar). Towns across Northern Spain erupt in colourful celebrations and parades.

Os Peliqueiros (Sun and Mon of Carnival, late Feb or Mar). In Laza (Ourense) the townspeople don flamboyant costumes and parade.

MAY

△ **El Santo Fiesta** (10–15 May). Processions, feasts and music honour La Rioja's patron saint, Santo Domingo de la Calzada.

Día das Letras Gallegas (17 May). Celebration of Galician language, literature and culture.

JUNE

Azkena Rock Festival (late Jun). Vitoria-Gasteiz hosts big-name musicians at this iconic rock fest, one of the best in the country.

△ **Wine Battle** (29 Jun). Thousands squirt wine at each other during this manic Haro fiesta.

SEPTEMBER

△ **San Sebastián Film Festival** (last 2 weeks Sep). Since 1953, San Sebastián has hosted one of the world's top film festivals.

Fiesta San Mateo (late Sep). Logroño celebrates the wine harvest with traditional foot-crushing of grapes, parades, music and food.

OCTOBER

△ **Fiestas de San Froilán** (early Oct). This centuries-old fair in Lugo features religious ceremonies, a medieval market and a puppet festival.

Seafood Festival (first and second week Oct). Fresh seafood tasting and traditional Galician music and dance in O Grove.

MARCH

△ **Fiesta de la Arribada** (*first weekend*). In Baiona the re-enactment of the 1493 return of the *Pinta* from America is accompanied by a medieval fair.

Semana Santa (*Mar–Apr*). Large processions led by religious brotherhoods take place in Northern Castilla y León and Navarra.

Pasión Viviente (*Good Friday*). Residents of Castro Urdiales (Cantabria) re-enact the last days in the life of Christ.

APRIL

Aberri Eguna (*Easter Sunday*). Basque National Day is celebrated with music, sports, food and drink.

△ **Güevos Pintos** (*Tue after Easter Sun*). In Pola de Siero, this Easter festival is marked by colourful displays of painted eggs.

La Folía (*Sun after Easter*). Illuminated boats carry a statue of the Virgin across the harbour in San Vicente de la Barquera.

JULY

International Jazz Festivals (*Jul*). Enjoy the music of jazz legends at venues across the Basque Country.

△ **BBK Festival** (*early Jul*). Bilbao's Mount Cobetas plays host to this cool rock, pop and indie music festival.

Festival de la Sidra (*mid-Jul*). Nava's three-day festival celebrates fine Asturian cider.

Feast of St James (*24 Jul*). A massive firework display in Santiago de Compostela.

AUGUST

△ **Fiestas de María Pita** (*Aug*). A month of concerts and events honours war heroine, María Pita.

Festival Internacional de Santander (*Aug*). Dance, music, and theatre take over the city of Santander (Cantabria).

La Romería do Naseiro (*late Aug*). Each day of this five-day festival in Viveiro is dedicated to a different Galician food speciality.

Batalla de Flores (*last Fri*). A jubilant parade of flower-covered floats, street markets and music in Laredo (Cantabria).

NOVEMBER

△ **All Saints' Day** (*1 Nov*). Families throughout Spain honour deceased relatives with cemetery visits and floral displays.

Gijón Film Festival (*late Nov*). Gijón hosts an international festival of films made for, and by, young people.

DECEMBER

△ **Santo Tomás** (*21 Dec*). The people of San Sebastián and Bilbao dress up and hold festive markets.

Santos Inocentes (*28 Dec*). Spain's April Fools' Day revolves around pranks and good food.

Nochevieja (*31 Dec*). Revellers make the rounds of tapas bars and toast the New Year.

1

A BRIEF
HISTORY

Northern Spain's history is beleaguered by power struggles: it was the cradle of the *reconquista*, battleground of the Carlist Wars and a Republican stronghold during the Spanish Civil War. Today, the region celebrates its disparate past and the myriad cultures that have shaped it.

Prehistoric Spain

Tribes of early humans first settled on the Iberian Peninsula in around 800,000 BC. In 5000 BC, these hunter-gatherers were usurped by Neolithic farmers, and it was around this time that ancesters of the Basques settled in the region. In around 1200 BC, the Celts began to arrive. Over the following centuries they mixed with Iberian tribes, laying the foundations of Celtiberian culture. Next, merchants arrived from across the Mediterranean, starting with the Phoenicians in around 1100 BC. This melting pot of cultures coexisted harmoniously until the Romans invaded.

Did You Know?

The Phoenicians gave Spain its name, *Ispania*, meaning "land of the rabbits".

Timeline of events

800,000 BC

Early human presence in Atapuerca caves, near Burgos.

5000 BC

Neolithic farmers usurp early humans, and begin to cultivate the Iberian Peninsula.

219–201 BC

The Second Punic War marks the start of Roman control of the peninsula.

18,000–12,000 BC

Cave art painted at Altamira, Cantabria.

61 BC

Roman emperor Julius Caesar begins his final conquest of Galicia and northern Lusitania.

Roman Spain and the Visigoths

The Romans entered Spain as part of the Punic Wars, capturing Cartagena from the Carthaginians in the south in 209 BC. It took the Romans around 200 years to subdue the entire peninsula, with Cantabrian tribes in the north resisting the longest. The new conquerors named the land Hispania and divided it into three provinces: Tarraconensis, Lusitania and Baetica. After centuries of prosperity and development, the fall of the Western Roman Empire in 476 left Hispania in the hands of the Visigoths, a nomadic Germanic tribe.

Al Andalus

In 711 North African Arabs and Berbers, known as the Moors, invaded the Iberian Peninsula, overthrowing the Visigoths. The caliphate of al Andalus was established in Córdoba and the city became the epicentre of the Moorish territory. At its height, the rich and powerful caliphate included part of southern France. The northern kingdoms of Spain, with their inhospitable mountainous terrain, severe climate and fiercely resistant inhabitants, remained unconquered.

1 A map showing the Roman settlements in the northern Spanish region of Cantabria. ↑

2 An ancient human skull from Atapuerca, one of the earliest prehistoric settlements, near Burgos.

3 Ancient Roman mosaic, displayed at Girona's archaeological museum.

4 Baths at Ronda, dating back to the time of al Andalus.

AD 476	589	711	756
Western Roman Empire falls, leaving Hispania under the control of the Visigoths.	King Reccared I embraces Christianity, and Toledo becomes the capital of Visigothic Spain.	Moors begin their conquest of the Iberian Peninsula, seizing control from the Visigoths.	Caliphate of Córdoba is established.

19 BC

Agrippa conquers Cantabria and Asturias, completing the Roman conquest.

The Reconquista

The Reconquest *(reconquista)* of Moorish Spain by Christian fighters started almost as soon as the Moors took control. Led by the Visigoth nobleman Pelayo *(p103)*, the Christian resistance won its first battle in Covadonga in 722, which saw the establishment of the Kingdom of Asturias. By the 11th century, the peninsula was split into the Christian north – comprising the five kingdoms of León (formerly Asturias), Castile, Navarra, Aragón and Catalonia – and the Muslim south of al Andalus. When the Christians captured Seville in 1248, the southern city of Granada became the last remaining Moorish enclave in Spain.

The Age of Discovery

The marriage of Isabel I of Castile and Fernando II of Aragón saw their two kingdoms united in diplomatic and religious matters. The "Catholic Monarchs" instigated the Spanish Inquisition, a brutal religious purge which sought to spread Catholicism and rid the country of the Protestants, Jews and Muslims. Their reign also saw the completion of the *reconquista*, when Granada was taken in 1492. Later that same year, explorer

SANTIAGO

One of the 12 apostles, St James (Santiago in Spanish) is the patron saint of Spain and his remains are supposedly held in the cathedral at Santiago de Compostela. It is said that St James miraculously appeared to fight for the Christian army at the Battle of Clavijo in 844 and was subsequently known as Santiago Matamoros (St James the Moor-slayer), an emblem of the *reconquista*.

Timeline of events

c 810
St James's tomb supposedly discovered at Santiago de Compostela.

905
Sancho I founds the Kingdom of Navarra.

1013
Caliphate of Córdoba disintegrates into various emirates.

1492
Granada falls to Christian forces. Columbus sails to the Americas.

Christopher Columbus, under the patronage of Isabel and Fernando, landed in the Americas, marking the beginning of Spain's overseas expansion. The discovery voyages led to growth in trade, which encouraged the development of northern coastal towns. Prosperity did not last: the Spanish Empire engaged in constant wars, fighting variously the French, Turkish, Dutch and English.

Bourbons to First Republic

When Carlos II died without an heir in 1700, the Habsburgs and Bourbons fought for his crown. Bourbon King Felipe V was victorious, and made Spain into a centralized state, abolishing the local rights of Catalonia and Aragón. In return for their loyalty, the Basque Country and Navarra were allowed to keep their rights.

The 19th century was marked by wars and civil conflict: Napoleon invaded Spain in 1807; and between 1833 and 1876, the country was beleaguered by the Carlist Wars. In 1873, the Carlists were defeated, and the monarchy was abolished altogether during the short-lived First Republic.

[1] Christian forces attacking Moorish soldiers during the *reconquista*. ↑

[2] A statue of King Pelayo of Asturias, Covadonga.

[3] The Spanish Armada sails against England in 1588.

[4] King Felipe V of the French Bourbon dynasty.

[5] Prisoners being taken through the mountains during the Carlist Wars.

1512
Annexation of Navarra completes the unification of Spain.

1521
Basque seaman Juan Sebastián Elcano navigates the globe.

1702–14
War of the Spanish Succession.

1807–14
Napoleon leads the Peninsular War against Bourbon Spain.

1873–74
First Spanish Republic.

Primo de Rivera and the Second Republic

A tumultuous period of social unrest, violence and political uncertainty followed the collapse of the First Republic. In 1874, the monarchy was restored, but corruption fostered anarchism. The country's increasing instability was briefly checked by Primo de Rivera, who seized power in 1923, but he lost the support of the king and army in 1930 and resigned. Following a public vote, King Alfonso XIII was forced to abdicate and the Second Republic was declared in 1931. Reforms proved ineffective and the country was rocked by outbreaks of anticlericalism, while unemployment rose.

The Civil War and Francoist Spain

The Second Republic implemented liberal measures but the conservative Confederación Española de Derechas Autónomas won the 1933 elections. In response, anarchists and socialists rose up in 1934. Another election in 1936 saw the liberal Popular Front narrowly defeat the right-wing National Front. Political tensions came to a head and Civil War broke out. The Nationalists, led by General Franco, took control of swathes of Spain, but were

1 Declaration of a siege state in Madrid as Primo de Rivera leads a military coup on 23 September 1923.

2 Manuel Azana Días, the first prime minister of the Second Republic.

3 Republican poster from the start of the Civil War, 1936.

4 International Women's Day march in 2019.

Timeline of events

1923–30
Dictatorship of Primo de Rivera.

1934
Revolution in Asturias suppressed by Franco.

1936–39
Spanish Civil War.

1975
Following Franco's death, Juan Carlos is proclaimed king.

HEMOS SALIDO DE LA JAULA

halted outside Madrid. Support from Hitler and Mussolini helped them to take the capital in 1939, and Franco installed himself as a dictator. Under Franco, Spain was a fascist state, ruled by a single party. All cultural diversity was banned in an attempt to make the country homogenized, and the use of the Basque, Catalan and Galician languages was banned. The Basques reacted particularly fiercely, and the 1960s saw the emergence of the violent campaign of the Basque separatist group, ETA.

Northern Spain Today

Franco named Juan Carlos, Alfonso XIII's grandson, as his heir. He inherited Franco's absolute power, but chose not to exercise it, instead installing himself as a constitutional monarch and considerable power was devolved to the regions. Moving away from the isolating policies of Francoism, Spain looked outward once more – in 1985 it joined NATO, and the following year became a member of what would become the European Union. In 2018, ETA disbanded, bringing an end to their decades-long campaign of violence.

↑ The Tree of Gernika, an ancient Basque symbol of freedom

1977
Spain holds its first general election since its return to democracy.

2002
Spain adopts the Euro as its currency.

2014
Juan Carlos I abdicates; his son Felipe VI accedes to the throne.

2018
ETA disbands.

2019
On 8 March, International Women's Day, over 5 million women walk out of work to march through the streets.

EXPERIENCE

Walking in the Picos de Europa, Asturias

GALICIA

The oldest evidence of early humans in Galicia dates back around 120,000 years. By the time the Roman conquerors arrived in the 2nd century BC, the area was inhabited by the Celtic Gallaeci, from whom the region takes its name. After the fall of the Western Roman Empire, Galicia existed as an independent kingdom, first under the Suevi people (whose conversion to Christianity saw Galicia officially adopt the religion) and then the Visigoths. Following a brief occupation by the Moors, Galicia was reconquered by Christian forces and subsumed into the Kingdom of Asturias, which was itself later absorbed into the Kingdom of Castile.

The discovery of the supposed tomb of St James the Apostle in the 9th century AD confirmed medieval Santiago de Compostela as Europe's most important religious shrine, after St Peter's in Rome. Pilgrims from beyond the Pyrenees first flocked to this holy site along what became the Camino de Santiago in the 11th century, following the scallop shells that line the route.

The establishment of a central Spanish state in the 15th century saw Galicia's distinct culture and language (galego) sidelined. This erosion persisted until the 19th century, when the Rexurdimento (revival) of all things Galician began in earnest, particularly the use of galego as a literary language. Franco's regime suppressed this resurgence until his death, after which Galicia regained its autonomy in 1981, and its culture was fiercely celebrated once more. Today, galego is an everyday language, spoken fluently by over half of Galicians.

GALICIA

Must Sees

1 Santiago de Compostela
2 A Coruña
3 Pontevedra
4 Lugo
5 Reserva Nacional de Os Ancares

Experience More

6 Ribadeo
7 Viveiro
8 Ortigueira
9 Mondoñedo
10 Cedeira
11 Ferrol
12 Betanzos
13 Malpica
14 Camariñas
15 Cabo Fisterra
16 Padrón
17 Noia
18 Sanxenxo
19 A Toxa
20 Vigo
21 Cambados
22 Illas Cíes
23 A Guarda
24 Baiona
25 Tui
26 Ribadavia
27 Ourense
28 Celanova
29 Verín
30 Monasterio de Ribas de Sil
31 Monforte de Lemos
32 Mosteiro de Santa María de Oseira
33 Allariz
34 O Cebreiro
35 Vilar de Donas
36 Santa Eulalia de la Bóveda
37 Sarria

↑ The terracotta roofs of the sprawling Mosteiro de San Martiño Pinario

1

SANTIAGO DE COMPOSTELA

🗺A2 ✈A Coruña 🚉10 km (6 miles) north 🚌🚆 ℹ️Calle Rúa do Vilar 63; www.santiagoturismo.com

Santiago de Compostela was Christendom's third most important place of pilgrimage in the Middle Ages, after Jerusalem and Rome. Today, more than 200,000 pilgrims journey to the city every year.

①

Museo das Peregrinacións e de Santiago

📍Praza das Praterías 2
📞881 86 73 15 🕐9:30am-8pm Tue-Fri, 11am-7:30pm Sat, 10:15am-2:45pm Sun
🗓1 & 6 Jan, 1 May, 16 Aug, 24-25 & 31 Dec

This museum, founded in 1951, has three main focuses. It considers pilgrimage as a general concept, the Camino de Santiago in particular, and the city of Santiago de Compostela – the pilgrimage's end point. It also hosts temporary exhibitions about pilgrimages from elsewhere in the world. Entry is free after 2:30pm on Saturdays, all day Sunday and on some holidays throughout the year.

②

Mosteiro de San Martiño Pinario

📍Praza da Inmaculada 5
⛪Church: Jun-Oct: 10am-8pm daily; Nov-May: 10am-7pm daily 🌐espacio culturalsmpinario.com

This huge monastery, the second largest in Spain, dominates Santiago de Compostela's Praza a Inmaculada. It is now home to a theological school and is not open to the public. Visitors can enter the impressive Baroque church, however, which has a huge double altar and an ornate Plateresque façade with carved figures of saints and bishops.

③

Museo do Pobo Galego

📍Costa de San Domingos s/n 🕐10am-2pm & 4-7:30pm Tue-Sat, 11am-2pm Sun & public hols
🌐museodopobo.gal

Housed in a former convent, this museum tells the story of Galicia's history and culture.

📷 PICTURE PERFECT
Spiral Staircase

Within the Museo do Pobo Galego, photographers shouldn't miss the chance to snap a shot of the triple-helix staircase, with its branches twirling elegantly upwards to wrap themselves around a circle of sunlight.

The building alone is worth a visit, with its most intriguing features being the triple-helix staircase and the adjoining church, admission to which is included in the price of entry to the museum. Most of the signage around the museum is in *galego* and Castilian only, but there is some English-language information available from reception.

---

④

Hostal dos Reis Católicos

⌂ Praza do Obradoiro 1
ⓦ parador.es

Built by the Catholic monarchs in the late 15th century as an inn and hospital for sick pilgrims, this magnificent building sits proudly on the Praza do Obradoiro. Now a parador, it is thought to be one of the oldest hotels in the world. Parts of it remain open to the general public, such as its courtyards. A stand-out feature is its elaborate Plateresque doorway.

⑤

Centro Galego de Arte Contemporánea (CGAC)

⌂ Rúa Valle Inclán 2
◷ 11am–8pm Tue–Sun
ⓦ cgac.xunta.gal

This impressive collection of contemporary art is housed in a stark granite building, which was designed by Portuguese architect and Pritzker-prize-winner Álvaro Siza between 1988 and 1993. The museum was established to promote local contemporary artists but, alongside Galician works, you'll find artists from the rest of Spain, Portugal and South America well represented here.

There are some 1,200 works on show, including some pieces that were created specifically for this space. Alongside the permanent collection, the light-flooded gallery also hosts temporary exhibitions and workshops for both adults and children.

Outside, Siza collaborated with the Galician landscape gardener Isabel Aguirre to preserve an orchard, which was once attached to the convent that borders the site. Siza painstakingly designed the building to make it look as though it is part of the wall surrounding this garden. It's a lovely place to sit and relax after exploring the museum, or enjoy great views across the city from the terrace.

EAT

Casa Marcelo
An affordable spot to enjoy a Michelin-starred menu. If you simply can't decide, the chef will be happy to select and prepare a tasting menu for you.

⌂ Rúa Hortas 1
ⓦ casamarcelo.net

€€€

O Curro da Parra
Situated right next to the market, this trendy restaurant uses only fresh local produce to create Galician dishes with gourmet twists.

⌂ Rúa Traversa 20
ⓦ ocurrodaparra.com

€€€

Abastos 2.0
Make the most of being near the ocean by sampling the delicious seafood on offer at this small but impressive venue. Tasting menus are available, so you can try as many tapas as possible.

⌂ Praza Abastos, Caestas 13-18 ◷ Sun ⓦ abastos douspuntocero.com

€€€

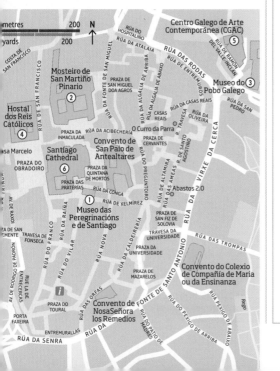

(6) 🏛 🎟

SANTIAGO CATHEDRAL

🏠 Praza do Obradoiro ⏰ Cathedral: 9am–7pm daily;
Museum: Apr–Oct: 9am–8pm daily; Nov–Mar: 10am–8pm
daily 🚫 1 & 6 Jan, 25 Jul, 25 Dec 🌐 catedraldesantiago.es

With its twin Baroque towers soaring high over the
Praza do Obradoiro, this monument to St James is a
majestic sight, as befits the finishing line of the
Camino de Santiago *(p70)*.

Constructed between the 11th and 13th centuries,
the cathedral stands on the site of a 9th-century
basilica built by Alfonso II. The resulting melting
pot of architectural styles only serves to remind
visitors of this building's status as one of the
greatest shrines in Christendom. As you walk
through the famous Pórtico da Gloria, you'll be
greeted by the same interior that met pilgrims
in medieval times.

Did You Know?

The scallop shells
marking the Camino
symbolize the fact that
St James was once
a fisherman.

The twin towers
are 74 m
(243 ft) high.

Statue of St James

The richly sculpted
Baroque Obradoiro
façade was added
in the 18th century.

Pazo de Xelmírez, the
old archbishop's palace

The Pórtico da
Gloria is sculpted
with statues of
the apostles.

Touching the Santo dos
Croques (Saint of Bumps)
with the forehead is said to
impart luck and wisdom.

← A fountain in the shadow
of Santiago Cathedral's
clock tower

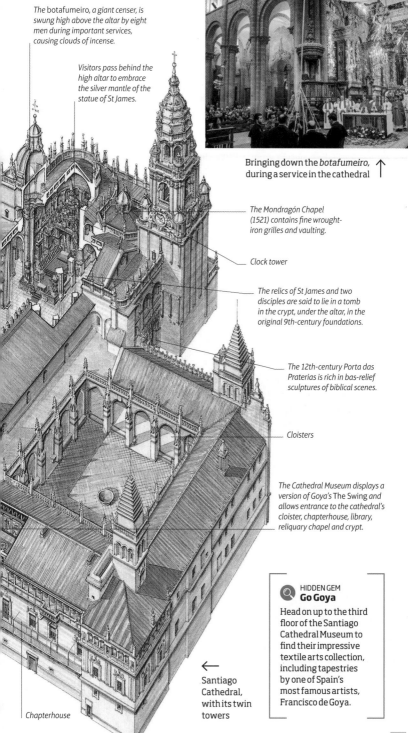

The *botafumeiro, a giant censer,* is swung high above the altar by eight men during important services, causing clouds of incense.

Visitors pass behind the high altar to embrace the silver mantle of the statue of St James.

Bringing down the *botafumeiro,* during a service in the cathedral ↑

The Mondragón Chapel (1521) contains fine wrought-iron grilles and vaulting.

Clock tower

The relics of St James and two disciples are said to lie in a tomb in the crypt, under the altar, in the original 9th-century foundations.

The 12th-century Porta das Praterías is rich in bas-relief sculptures of biblical scenes.

Cloisters

The Cathedral Museum displays a version of Goya's The Swing and allows entrance to the cathedral's cloister, chapterhouse, library, reliquary chapel and crypt.

← Santiago Cathedral, with its twin towers

Chapterhouse

🔍 HIDDEN GEM
Go Goya

Head on up to the third floor of the Santiago Cathedral Museum to find their impressive textile arts collection, including tapestries by one of Spain's most famous artists, Francisco de Goya.

A SHORT WALK

SANTIAGO DE COMPOSTELA

Distance 1 km (0.5 miles) **Nearest train station**
Santiago de Compostela **Time** 15 minutes

With its narrow streets and old squares, the city centre is compact enough to explore on foot. So, if the Camino de Santiago sounds completely overwhelming, why not take this gentle stroll through the city to get a tapas-size taste of the famous pilgrimage instead? The route even finishes at the Praza do Obradoiro, where the Camino also reaches its climax. Around this grand square is an ensemble of historic buildings that has few equals in Europe. The local granite gives a harmonious unity to the mixture of architectural styles. And, of course, the hallowed Santiago Cathedral looms over them all.

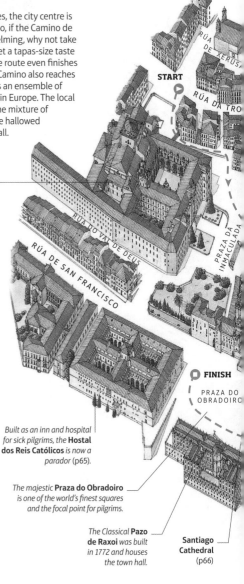

The Baroque church of the **Mosteiro de San Martiño Pinario** has a huge double altar and an ornate Plateresque façade with carved figures of saints and bishops (p64).

RÚA DE XERUSA

START

RÚA DA TRO

RÚA DO VAL DE DEUS

RÚA DE SAN FRANCISCO

PRAZA DA INMACULADA

FINISH

PRAZA DO OBRADOIRO

Built as an inn and hospital for sick pilgrims, the **Hostal dos Reis Católicos** is now a parador (p65).

The majestic **Praza do Obradoiro** is one of the world's finest squares and the focal point for pilgrims.

The Classical **Pazo de Raxoi** was built in 1772 and houses the town hall.

Santiago Cathedral (p66)

↑ Santiago Cathedral, dominating the Praza do Obradoiro, at dusk

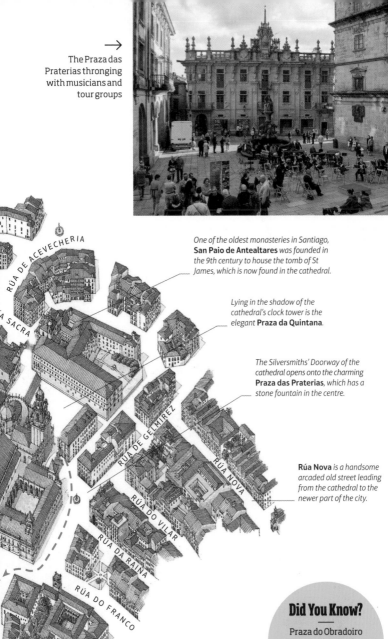

The Praza das Praterias thronging with musicians and tour groups

One of the oldest monasteries in Santiago, **San Paio de Antealtares** *was founded in the 9th century to house the tomb of St James, which is now found in the cathedral.*

Lying in the shadow of the cathedral's clock tower is the elegant **Praza da Quintana**.

The Silversmiths' Doorway of the cathedral opens onto the charming **Praza das Praterias**, *which has a stone fountain in the centre.*

Rúa Nova *is a handsome arcaded old street leading from the cathedral to the newer part of the city.*

RÚA DE ACEVECHERIA

RÚA SACRA

RÚA DE GELMIREZ

RÚA NOVA

RÚA DO VILAR

RÚA DA RAINA

RÚA DO FRANCO

Colegio de San Jerónimo

Did You Know?

Praza do Obradoiro (Square of Workshops) earned its name from the cathedral's stonemasons.

0 metres	100
0 yards	100

N

A LONG WALK

CAMINO DE SANTIAGO

Distance About 770 km (480 miles) **Walking time** Four weeks **Difficulty** The route begins with a steep climb through the Pyrenees and there are several other challenging parts

According to legend, the body of Christ's apostle James was brought to Galicia. In AD 813 the relics were supposedly discovered at Santiago de Compostela, where a cathedral was built in his honour *(p66)*. In the Middle Ages half a million pilgrims a year flocked there from all over Europe, crossing the Pyrenees at Roncesvalles *(p187)* or via the Somport Pass *(p215)*. They often donned the traditional garb of cape, long staff and curling felt hat adorned with scallop shells, the symbol of the saint. The various routes, marked by the cathedrals, churches and hospitals built along them, are still used by travellers today. Here, we guide you on the Way of St James.

Atlantic Ocean

End your walk as pilgrims have for centuries – at the door of **Santiago Cathedral** *(p66).*

You need to walk the last 100 km (62 miles) – from **Sarria** *to Santiago de Compostela (p64) – to be eligible for a Compostela Certificate.*

One of the main pilgrim stops, **León Cathedral** *(p136) contains one of Spain's finest collections of stained glass.*

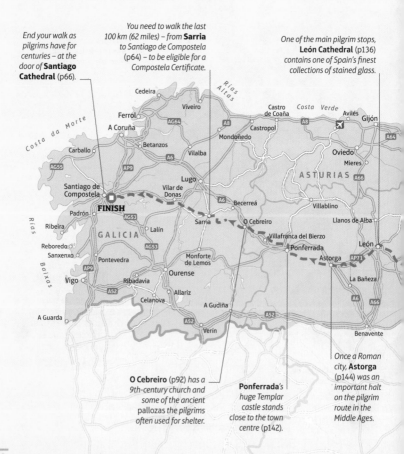

O Cebreiro (p92) has a 9th-century church and some of the ancient pallozas the pilgrims often used for shelter.

Ponferrada's huge Templar castle stands close to the town centre (p142).

Once a Roman city, **Astorga** *(p144) was an important halt on the pilgrim route in the Middle Ages.*

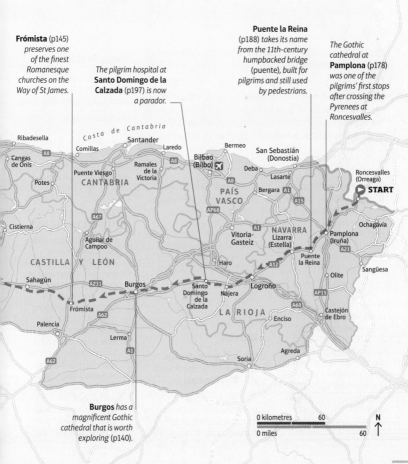

Locator Map
*For more detail see p62,
p132 and p176*

GALICIA

Camino de Santiago

← Walking along pretty
Calle del Carmen, on
the approach to the
centre of Pamplona

Frómista (p145)
*preserves one
of the finest
Romanesque
churches on the
Way of St James.*

The pilgrim hospital at
**Santo Domingo de la
Calzada** (p197) *is now
a parador.*

Puente la Reina
(p188) *takes its name
from the 11th-century
humpbacked bridge
(puente), built for
pilgrims and still used
by pedestrians.*

*The Gothic
cathedral at*
Pamplona (p178)
*was one of the
pilgrims' first stops
after crossing the
Pyrenees at
Roncesvalles.*

Bay of Biscay

Costa de Cantabria

Ribadesella
Cangas
de Onís
Comillas
Santander
Laredo
Bermeo
San Sebastián
(Donostia)
Roncesvalles
(Orreaga)
▶ START
Potes
Puente Viesgo
Ramales
de la
Victoria
Bilbao
(Bilbo)
Deba
Lasarte
Ochagavía
CANTABRIA
PAÍS
VASCO
Bergara
Pamplona
(Iruña)
Cistierna
Aguilar de
Campoo
Vitoria-
Gasteiz
NAVARRA
Lizarra
(Estella)
Sangüesa
CASTILLA Y LEÓN
Haro
Puente
la Reina
Olite
Sahagún
Burgos
Santo
Domingo
de la
Calzada
Nájera
Logroño
Castejón
de Ebro
Frómista
LA RIOJA
Palencia
Lerma
Enciso
Agreda
Soria

Burgos *has a
magnificent Gothic
cathedral that is worth
exploring (p140).*

0 kilometres 60

0 miles 60

N ↑

↑ Fishing boats lining the marina in A Coruña

2

A CORUÑA

AB1 **✈**10 km (6 miles) S ▣➤➤ **ⓘ**Plaza María Pita 6; www.turismocoruna.com

This proud city and busy port has played a sizable role in Spanish maritime history. Felipe II's doomed Armada sailed from here to England in 1588. Today, the sprawling, industrial suburbs contrast with the elegant city centre, which is laid out on an isthmus.

①

Plaza María Pita

This harmoniously designed square bears the name of Galicia's national heroine. In 1589, María Pita defended the town (her birthplace) against the English, who were led by the navigator and buccaneer Francis Drake.

There is a statue honouring María in the plaza , which is today a popular spot for pavement cafés, surrounded by arcaded houses offering protection against the elements. Here, too, is the huge Neo-Renaissance town hall (Palacio Municipal), with three huge domes. Spain's finest clock museum is housed within it. Beside the town hall rises the 17th-century Baroque Iglesia de San Jorge.

②

Jardines San Carlos

These Romantic gardens are laid out on the site of a fortress whose walls have survived to this day. Buried at their centre is the Scottish General John Moore, killed by the French at the Battle of Elviña (1809).

③

Domus

ARúa Ángel Rebollo 91 **⏱**Times vary, check website **ⓦ**coruna.gal

This interactive museum is devoted entirely to the study of mankind. Exhibits on genetics, evolution and neurology are housed in a futuristic museum designed by the Japanese architect Arata Isozaki.

④

Torre de Hércules

AAvenida de Navarra **☎**981 22 37 30 **⏱**10am–6pm daily (to 9pm Jun-Sep)

The Tower of Hercules is the world's oldest working lighthouse, built during the reign of the Emperor Trajan in the 2nd century AD. Its current appearance is the result of 18th-century renovations.

THE CITY OF GLASS

Houses with large glass balconies (galerías), glistening in the sun, are common all over Galicia, but the most famous ones are found here, leading visiting sailors to dub A Coruña the "City of Glass". The galerías were designed to face the harbour, and so are located at the back of the buildings. Those lining the harbourfront promenade, the Avenida de la Marina, are best viewed from the Real Club Náutico.

EAT

Restaurante O Fado
The stand-out dish at this fish restaurant is the *arroces* - a creamy seafood risotto.

⬙ Estrada Circunvalación ⬙ ofado restaurante.com

€ ⟨€⟩ €

↑ A bull shark floats past in the Aquarium Finisterrae

⑤

Iglesia de Santiago

⬙ Calle del Parrote 1
⬙ 11:30am-1:30pm & 5:30-6:30pm Mon-Fri (6:30-7:30pm in summer)

Stone from the Torre de Hércules was used to build this Romanesque-Gothic hall church (12th–15th century) where, in the Middle Ages, the town council met. It is the oldest church in A Coruña.

⑥

Aquarium Finisterrae

⬙ Paseo Alcade Francisco Vázquez 34 ⬙ Times vary, check website ⬙ coruna. gal/mc2/gl

At the edge of the ocean, this modern aquarium has viewing platforms for watching the waves. The circling sharks are a highlight.

⑦

Avenida de la Marina

This harbourfront promenade is one of A Coruña's great landmarks. Glass-balconied houses run along its length and at one end is a memorial obelisk topped by a clock.

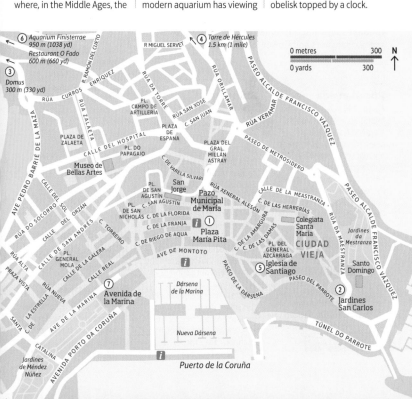

↑ Looking out across the terracotta rooftops of Pontevedra's Old Town

❸
PONTEVEDRA

🅰A3 🚉Pontevedra 🚌🚐 🛈Marqués de Riestra 30; www.visit-pontvedra.com

The provicial capital, Pontevedra lies inland at the head of a long *ría* backed by green hills. The delightful Old Town is typically Galician, with its network of cobbled alleys and tiny squares punctuated with granite calvaries and flower-filled balconies.

①
Rúa Alameda

A tour of Pontevedra is best begun on the town's grand Alameda boulevard. Set along this green promenade are many 19th-century buildings, attended by numerous statues of notable figures such as Christopher Columbus and Rosalía de Castro (*p84*).

> **Did You Know?**
>
> The Church of Santo Domingo was founded by Dominican nuns in 1281.

②
Ruinas do Santo Domingo

🅰Avenida Montero Rios 1
🕙15 Mar-Oct: 10am-2pm & 4-7:30pm Tue-Sat, 11am-2pm Sun; Nov-14 Mar: email gabinetedidactico.museo@depo.es 🌐museo.depo.es

The impressive Gothic ruins of the Church of Santo Domingo form the oldest part of the Museo de Pontevedra. Of the church buildings, only the main apse, south wall and the convent entrance survive. Before it was declared a National Monument in 1895, and saved from demolition, the site hosted variously a hospice, women's prison and a school. Today there is a collection of Roman steles

and medieval coats of arms and tombs.

③
Museo de Pontevedra

🅰Calle Pasantería 2-12
🕙10am-9pm Tue-Sat, 11am-2pm Sun
🌐museo.depo.es

On the Praza de la Leña, two 18th-century mansions, along with two other buildings in the adjacent streets, make up the Museo de Pontevedra, which is regarded as one of the best museums in Galicia. The superb collections include Celtic gold bracelets and necklaces, and particularly fascinating locally found Bronze Age treasures.

Among the paintings on display are 15th-century Spanish primitives, canvases by Zurbarán and Goya, and on the top floor a collection by Alfonso Castelao, a Galician artist and nationalist who forcefully depicted the misery endured by his people during the Spanish Civil War.

Basilica de Santa María la Mayor

⌂ Avda Santa María 24
🌐 santamarialamayor.org

The greatest monument of the Galician Renaissance style is the 16th-century Basilica de Santa María la Mayor. Its Plateresque west façade, which features a richly sculpted portico resembling a reredos, was funded by the sailors' guild. Next to the basilica is the Jewish Quarter and a cemetery.

PONTE DO BURGO BRIDGE

According to legend, Pontevedra was founded by Teucro, one of the heroes of the Trojan War, but in reality it was the Romans who constructed a bridge across the Lérez river, around which the town developed. Today, the restored medieval bridge - Ponte do Burgo - remains one of the town's landmarks, dating back to the 12th century. Part of the "Portuguese way" on the Camino de Santiago, its magnificent wide arches span the river.

Capela da Peregrina

⌂ Praza da Peregrina

This lovely church dedicated to Pontevedra's patron saint – the Virgen de la Peregrina – is a stop on the pilgrim trail to Santiago de Compostela. It is built to a circular plan and features a bow-fronted façade. The footprint of the building is in the shape of a scallop shell, the symbol of pilgrimage (*p70*).

Praza da Ferraría

Near to the tiny Praza das Cinco, sporting an 18th-century *cruceiro* (*p85*), is the huge, tree-lined Praza da Ferraría, with a beautiful fountain. This busy town square is actually made up of three smaller plazas, where you will find plenty of lively pavement cafés and bars. Worthy of mention here is the Renaissance Casa das Caras, decorated with sculpted faces.

Iglesia de San Francisco

⌂ Praza da Estrela, s/n

This 14th-century church looks out on the busy Praza da Ferraría. Its exterior is not particularly noteworthy, but within the church's serene interior visitors can admire attractive stained glass, 16th- and 18th-century murals, and tombs dating back to the 16th century.

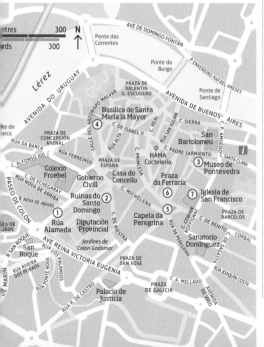

The Catedral de Santa María presiding over Lugo's Roman walls ↑

4

LUGO

 📍C2 🚉 🚌 ℹ️ Praza do Campo 11; 982 25 16 58; Tue & Fri

Lugo is the oldest of Galicia's provincial capitals. A settlement already existed here 2,000 years ago, and its name is probably Celtic in origin (*Lugh* means "God of the Light"). Attracted to the settlement by its thermal springs, Romans built a wall here, which today encircles the Old Town. Apart from the fortifications in Ávila, Lugo's is the best-preserved old town wall in Spain.

① Town Walls

The 1st- to 2nd-century AD Roman fortifications are 2 km (1.2 miles) long, 4–7 m (13–22 ft) thick, and up to 12 m (39 ft) high. Over the centuries, the walls have defended the city against the Suevi, the Moors and Norman pirates.

Today they are among the best-preserved town walls in Spain, with ten gates (five old and five new) as well as 71 towers. On A Mosquera tower, two broad windows have survived. Visitors can walk along the top of the fortifications, which form an unbroken circle around the Old Town, to enjoy stunning vistas of Lugo.

② Catedral de Santa María

📍 Praza Santa María 1
🕐 8am-8:30pm daily

The Romanesque-Gothic cathedral dates from the 12th century and was modelled on the cathedral in Santiago de Compostela (*p66*). Over the centuries, it acquired elements of other styles, including a Neo-Classical façade and Baroque cloisters, alongside its distinctive Gothic flying buttresses. The cathedral has a Renaissance chancel and altars and a series of ornate chapels. There is a collection of religious art within the cloisters.

③ Casa dos Mosaicos

📍 Rúa Doutor Castro 20-22
📞 982 25 48 15 🕐 Mid-Jun-mid-Oct: 11am-1:30pm & 4-7:30pm Tue-Sat, 11am-2pm Sun; mid-Oct-mid-Jun: 11:30am-1:30pm Thu-Sat, 11:30am-1:30pm Sun

The remnants of a 3rd- to 4th-century AD Roman villa, which probably belonged to a wealthy nobleman, have been converted into an excellent contemporary museum. An audiovisual guide describes the history behind the superb mosaics, still dazzling after almost two millennia.

④ Museo Provincial

📍 Praza da Soidade
🕐 9am-9pm Mon-Fri, 10:30am-2pm & 4:30-8pm Sat, 11am-2pm Sun
🌐 museolugo.org

The museum is housed in the former monastery of San Francisco. The museum's main aim is to present Galician art. Exhibits include Celtic and

Roman jewellery, coins, traditional Galician ceramics, sundials and paintings.

⑤ Iglesia de Santo Domingo

🏛 Praza de Santo Domingo
🕐 6pm daily for mass only

Dating from the 13th century, this monastery was built in Romanesque and Gothic styles (this can be seen in the three apses with tall windows). The façade is hidden behind the monastery wall, which has 18th-century arcades. The chapel and altars are Baroque.

Of note are the tomb slabs framed by decorated arches, in particular that of Fernando Díaz Rivadeneyra, which features a figure of the knight.

⑥ Praza Maior

In Roman times, there was probably an amphitheatre on Praza Maior; a market was later established here. The square is popular with locals, who come to relax in the nearby cafés. The tree-lined boulevard is guarded by two stone lions that once decorated Praza Maior's now vanished fountain.

EAT

Mesón de Alberto
Seafood is the order of the day at this two-storey restaurant. There's a smaller bistro-style menu on the lower floor and more elaborate fare on offer upstairs.

🏛 Rua Cruz 4 📞 982 22 83 10

€€€

Porta Nova was the main northern gate, through which people would enter and leave the town.

A statue of a Roman eagle in Praza Santo Domingo commemorates Augustus's capture of Lugo from the Celts in the 1st century BC.

Built in 1738, the town hall acquired its clock tower a few decades later.

The semicircular towers in the town walls would once have been topped by windows, examples of which can be seen at the tower of A Mosquera.

The Galician city of Lugo, encircled by Roman walls

5

RESERVA NACIONAL DE OS ANCARES

A C2 **W** osancares.org

Straddling the provinces of Lugo and León, Os Ancares is a mountainous nature reserve of outstanding wild beauty. The park's many hiking trails cut through a landscape of snowy mountains, undulating hills, deep glacial valleys, winding rivers and verdant forest, punctuated by ancient villages.

Thanks to its varied landscape, the region features an abundance of plants and wildlife, including such rare species as the capercaillie, deer and wild boar. Once inhabited by ancient Celtic tribes, thought to have sought refuge among the mountains from Roman invaders, the valleys abound with charming villages where the rustic way of life still reigns supreme.

A ramblers' paradise, the reserve has hiking trails that wind up Alto del Obispo's 2,000-m- (6,500-ft-) high peaks and down into villages such as Piornedo, where you'll see examples of *pallozas*, the traditional dwellings that pepper the valley settlements. Os Ancares was declared a Biosphere Reserve by UNESCO in 2006, and the commitment to preserving the reserve's magnificently diverse ecosystem is paramount.

DEGRADA TRACK

The most impressive of the park's many trails, this 18-km (11-mile) circular hike crosses the Cabana Vella woods, taking in Os Ancares' tallest peaks – Tres Obispos, Pena Rubia and Mustallar.

Morning mists rising over the undulating hills of Os Ancares ↑

Must See

→ Iconic pre-Roman *pallozas* in Piornedo, the best-preserved such dwellings in Europe

↓ Ancient dwelling in Santa María do Castro

TOP 5 OS ANCARES VILLAGES

Navia
Here you'll find a picturesque single-span bridge, several *castros* (fortified settlements) and the castle of the Altamira family.

Piornedo
This little village, with its pre-Roman thatched huts *(pallozas)*, can only be reached on foot.

O Cebreiro
According to legend, this little village on the pilgrim path was once the setting for many miracles *(p92)*.

Santa María do Castro
Home to the historic *castro* of Santa María de Cervantes and the Santa María church.

Becerreá
Nestled between steep hills and valleys, this is the starting point of most trails into the park. There are several bridges here, along with the 17th-century Monasterio de Santa María. Look out for wildlife, like red foxes.

EXPERIENCE MORE

6 Ribadeo

C1 Lugo Rúa
Dionisio Gamallo Fierros 7;
www.ribadeo.org

Galicia's north coast, between
Ribadeo and Ferrol, is an area
of natural beauty known as
the Rías Altas, formed from
ría (estuary) inlets and beautiful bays characterized by high
waves, beaches with fine
white sand and an abundance
of fish. The characterful fishing town of Ribadeo, with its
attractive harbour, occupies
a picturesque setting on the
banks of the Ría de Ribadeo.
Among the many observation
points here are the hill of
Santa Cruz, with its monument of a piper, and La
Atalaya, formerly a bastion.

The expansive beach at Praia
das Catedrais is known for its
rock formations that recall
Gothic arches. The waters of
the *ría* can be explored by
pleasure boat from the
nearby haven of Porcillán.

The town itself is home to
the 18th-century Colegiata de
Santa María del Campo, with
two Baroque altarpieces.
Inside are earlier elements –
Romanesque arches and two
Gothic portals with plant
ornamentation. Another
attraction is the Modernist
residence of the brothers
Moreno, which recalls the
work of Antoni Gaudí.

North of Ribadeo lies the
18th-century fort of San
Damián, which once defended
the mouth of the *ría*. It is now
a municipal exhibition space.
About 10 km (6 miles) west of
Ribadeo is the fishing town
of Foz, which also has fine
beaches. Nearby is the
Romanesque Iglesia de San
Martín de Mondoñedo.

Ribadeo's dramatic
Praia das Catedrais,
and *(inset)* arching
↓ rock formations

7 Viveiro

C1 Lugo Avda
Ramón Canosa s/n;
www.viveiro.es

Situated on the beautiful *ría*
of the same name, Viveiro is
the prettiest and most popular town in the Rías Altas,
with good hotels and res-
taurants. Fragments of its
medieval walls survive – their
most beautiful feature is the
Plateresque Gate of Carlos I,
by Maestro Pedro Poderoso.
It is decorated with coats of
arms, medallions and an
image of St Roch, the town's
patron saint. Facing the gate
is the 15th-century bridge,
Ponte de la Misericordia.

Of note is the Romanesque
Iglesia de Santa María del
Campo, with a Baroque belfry
and a 19th-century clock
tower. The Romanesque-
Gothic Iglesia de San
Francisco has a beautiful
apse. On the Praza Maior,
where a cheese and vegetable
market is held each Thursday,
stands the town hall, with
a sundial and 17th- and
19th-century houses.

↑ Gothic and Baroque touches in the sacristy of Mondoñedo's Romanesque cathedral

Nearby rises the Renaissance Casa de los Leones, with lions on the coat of arms.

Viveiro's district of Covas borders a long white beach, while to the west of the town, the hill of San Roque offers fine views across the estuary. The Ría de Viveiro constitutes the mouth of the Landro river. In the 19th century, two ships – the *Magdalena* and the *Paloma* – sank here during a violent storm.

---

⑧

Ortigueira

 ▲B1 **▲** A Coruña
ℹ Avda Escola de Gaitas, A Lagarea; www.turismo ortigueira.com

This little fishing town is set within a diverse landscape of fertile valleys, hills and steep cliffs, with fantastic beaches nearby. The town's neat white houses date mainly from the 19th and 20th centuries, although the area has a rich prehistory, including the oldest Galician megaliths (4400 BC). North of town lie the ruins of Punta dos Prados – a settlement dating from the 4th to the 1st centuries BC.

On a hill overlooking the town is a fully restored, working 19th-century windmill, the Molino de Viento de Campo da Torre.

⑨

Mondoñedo

 ▲C1 **▲** Lugo **ℹ** Plaza de la Catedral 34; www.mondonedo.net

This small valley town was the provincial capital for nearly four centuries. There are an unusual number of fine buildings here, the oldest is the 13th-century Romanesque Catedral de la Asunción, which features 14th-century murals. Its Museo Diocesano has works by Zurbarán and El Greco, and the 18th-century Palacio Episcopal contains a Neo-Gothic chapel. Nearby is the Fonte Vella, a 16th-century fountain decorated with the coat of arms of Carlos I; beyond it extends the old Jewish quarter.

Museo Diocesano
⊘ ⊘ **▲** Plaza de la Catedral **☎** 982 52 10 06 **☉** 10am–2pm & 4–6pm daily

Did You Know?

Mondoñedo cathedral's figure of the Virgin was brought here from St Paul's Cathedral in London.

EAT & DRINK

Bar Puerto Restarantes
This restaurant right next to the port of Vigo serves seafood bought daily from the local market. The owners pride themselves on their traditional Galician menu.

▲ A3 **▲** Rúa República Argentina 15, Vigo **ⓦ** barpuerto restaurante.es

---

Cienfuegos Bar
The chilled-out atmosphere makes this a perfect spot for a drink or two, with delicious *pintxos* (tasty little bar snacks) to graze on.

▲ C1 **▲** Plaza José María López, Ribadeo **☎** 661 43 15 53 **☉** Mon

---

Don Paco Café
Perfectly located just a few steps from Malpica's pretty harbour, this café makes a lovely place for a pit-stop coffee, or something stronger.

▲ A1 **▲** Praza Cruceiro 1, Malpica **☎** 981 72 00 32

O Semaforo de Fisterra
The café-bar of this elegant hotel is a delightful place for a drink with stunning coastal vistas and views of Fisterra's magnificent lighthouse.

▲ A2 **▲** Faro de Finisterre, Fisterra **ⓦ** hotelsemaforode fisterra.com

10

Cedeira

 B1 **A Coruña** **Av de Castelao; 981 48 21 87**

One of the prettiest villages in the Rías Altas, Cedeira spans the river Condomiñas, and has excellent beaches, exquisite seafood, a tiny fishing harbour and good conditions for watersports. The surrounding area is ideal for fishing. In the medieval Old Town, fragments of the town walls are preserved. The parish Iglesia de Nuestra Señora del Mar de Cedeira dates from the 15th century.

Some 12 km (8 miles) from Cedeira is the 12th-century Monasterio de San Andrés de Teixido, set amid wild, windswept countryside. Perched above the Atlantic atop sheer surf-battered cliffs, this Galician shrine once belonged to the Knights of Malta. The earliest preserved fragments in the monastery are the late-Gothic north portal, and the murals depicting the martyrdom of St Andrew. It is customary for pilgrims to throw breadcrumbs into the nearby spring, which flows from

beneath the church's altar. Legend has it that if a crumb floats in the water, your wish will be fulfilled.

11

Ferrol

B1 **A Coruña** **Rúa Magdalena 56; www.turferrol.com**

Ferrol has strong links with the sea – in the 16th century some of the ships in the Spanish Armada set sail from its port. It wasn't until the 18th century, however, that the town became an important naval base, acquiring an arsenal, shipyards and the castle of San Felipe, which defended the local ría. Ferrol's Magdalena district was laid out in symmetrical Neo-Classical style in the 18th century. It features many houses with glass balconies, plus the 18th-century Iglesia de San Xulián with Mannerist elements, designed by military engineer Julián Sánchez Bort.

Lying 10 km (6 miles) south of Ferrol is Pontedeume, an attractive medieval town that features a tower with a huge coat of arms, built in the 14th century in honour of Count

→ Dramatic cliffscape of Cabo Vilán near Camariñas

Andrade. There is also an old bridge, in the middle of which once stood a hostel for pilgrims and a hermitage. The impressive ruins of Andrade's castle are perched on a hilltop 5 km (3 miles) to the south of Pontedeume, affording expansive views of the surrounding countryside.

12

Betanzos

B2 **A Coruña** **Praza de Galicia; 981 77 66 66** **betanzos.es**

At the heart of this fascinating town is the Praza García Hermanos, an elegant 18th-century square. The steep streets are lined with old houses and Gothic churches.

PICTURE PERFECT
To the Lighthouse

Drive 11 km (7 miles) west from Malpica to the Faro de Punta Nariga to snap panoramas of this impressive ship-shaped lighthouse and the craggy cliffs that surround it.

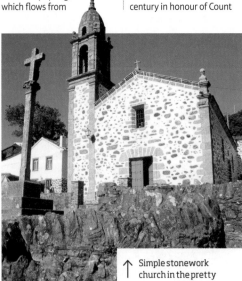

↑ Simple stonework church in the pretty village of Cedeira

The interior of the 15th-century Iglesia de Santiago is decorated with an equestrian figure of St James. Within the 14th-century Iglesia de San Francisco are beautiful tombs, supported on figures of a wild boar and a bear. The Iglesia de Santa María de Azogue, with a beautiful façade and rose window, has a 15th-century Flemish reredos.

Malpica

🅰 A1 🅰 A Coruña 🛈 Avda Emilio González 1; www.concellomalpica.com

The most northerly point on the Coste da Morte, this small fishing town has good beaches and enchanting views of the nearby Sisargas islands – an important nature reserve. Of particular interest is the Romanesque Iglesia de Santiago de Mens; legend has it that the church was linked with Mens castle by an underground tunnel. Near Malpica is the partially destroyed Cerqueda dolmen, a prehistoric tomb.

Visit in August, when Nuestra Señora del Mar (Our Lady of the Sea) is honoured with processions and fireworks.

Camariñas

🅰 A2 🅰 A Coruña 🔳 🛈 Paseo Marítimo; www.camarinas.net

This pretty fishing town is known for the bobbin lace that is manufactured and sold here. In the town's 18th-century Iglesia de San Jorge is a valuable reredos sculpted by José Ferreiro bearing images of saints.

On the wild and rugged Cabo Vilán headland, 5 km (3 miles) north of Camariñas, stands a lighthouse with the longest beam of all Galician lighthouses. Here, too, are wind turbines for electricity.

Cabo Fisterra

🅰 A2 🅰 A Coruña 🔳 🔳 🛈 Rúa Real 2; www.concellofisterra.com

Known in English as Finisterre, and translated as "World's End", this cape was long considered to be Continental Europe's most westerly point, though in fact that distinction belongs to Portugal. This is the last part of the Camino

---

COSTA DA MORTE

This stretch of coastline extends from Malpica in the north east to Cabo Fisterra in the south west. It is known as the "Coast of Death" because of the many ships lost in storms or smashed on the rocks over the centuries. The landscape here has a wild beauty; the steep cliffs, iconic Galician lighthouses, *cruceiros* and gigantic *hórreos* (p85) will long remain in the memory. At great risk, fishermen scour the coast for barnacles for use in local cuisine.

---

de Santiago (p70). Here pilgrims traditionally burn the clothes that they have worn during their long pilgrimage.

The village of Cabo Fisterra lies 3 km (2 miles) from the cape. A highlight here is the Romanesque Iglesia de Santa María de las Arenas, with a figure of the Santo Cristo da Barba Dourada (Christ of the Golden Beard). Beside the church, there is a striking 15th-century *cruceiro* (stone cross).

Strolling Noia's old-world streets in the cool of the evening ↑

⓰ Padrón

🅰A2 🅰A Coruña 🚊🚌
ℹ Avda de Compostela; www.concellodepadron.es

This quiet town, famed for its piquant green peppers, was a major seaport until it silted up. Legend has it the boat carrying the body of St James to Galicia *(p61)* arrived here. The supposed mooring stone, or *padrón*, lies below the altar of the church. The leafy avenue beside the church features in the poems of Rosalia de Castro (1837–85). Trace her steps at the **Museo Rosalia de Castro**. Another lauded Galician author, the Nobel prize winner, Camilo José Cela, is celebrated at the **Fundacion Camilo José Cela**.

Casa-Museo Rosalía de Castro

🚫 🅰La Matanza (Retén)
📞 981 81 12 04 ⏱ Tue–Sun

> 💬 **INSIDER TIP**
> **Play Pepper Roulette**
>
> If you're a bit of a risk-taker, be sure to sample some of Padrón's famous green peppers. More often than not, they are quite mild, but one pepper in every few platefuls will pack a spicy punch.

ROSALÍA DE CASTRO

Rosalía de Castro (1837–85), a Galician national icon, was the foremost figure of the 19th-century renaissance in the Galician language, with such works as *Cantares Gallegos*. Her poetry is coloured by her difficult life, marked by a deep sense of nostalgia and melancholy. De Castro is celebrated in Galicia with the festival of Día das Letras Galegas (Galician Literature Day) on 17 May each year.

Fundación Camilo José Cela

🅰🅰 🅰C/Santa María 22
📞 981 81 24 25 ⏱ Mon–Fri

⓱ Noia

🅰A2 🅰A Coruña
ℹ Alameda s/n; 981 84 21 00

According to legend, this town was founded by the great-grandson of Noah; hence Noia's coat of arms features a dove with an olive sprig in its beak. The town's golden age was in the 15th century, when it was one of Galicia's main ports. The medieval town plan and houses bearing coats of arms survive from that period.

Worth seeing is the late-Romanesque Iglesia de San Martino; its portal is richly decorated with saints and biblical figures. Santa María a Nova, dating from the 14th century, stands in the middle of the Quintana dos Muertos, an exceptionally interesting cemetery. In its northern part rises Cristo de Humilladoiro, a conical stone chapel that contains a 16th-century cross. The four columns supporting it are finely decorated with the phases of the moon and injured animals fleeing from hunters and hounds. In the southern part of the cemetery many gravestones show the symbol of the guild to which the deceased belonged.

REGIONAL GALICIAN ARCHITECTURE

Galicia's wealth of distinctive traditional buildings reflects the region's long history of Celtic and Roman settlement. Aside from the many pilgrimage churches dotting the route to Santiago, there are Celtic houses, medieval grain stores, stately stone palaces and ancient crosses. While in A Coruña, glass *galerías* are a common sight, villages like Pontevedra are peppered with narrow, two-storey fishermen's cottages.

PALLOZAS
These thick-walled thatched houses are among the oldest structures in Europe, dating from Celtic times. The inhabitants used to divide the space into living quarters, animal stables and a food store.

HÓRREOS
Built as far back as Roman times, *hórreos* are wooden granaries that stand on stone stilts to protect the grain from damp and pests. The cross is often used as a decorative motif. Hundreds can be found in the area surrounding Vigo *(p86)*.

PAZOS
These traditional stone mansions housed nobility in the 17th and 18th centuries. Nowadays many have been converted into hotels. Piornedo *(p79)* is home to the most famous examples.

FISHERMEN'S COTTAGES
In fishing villages along the Galician coast, narrow two-storey houses with glass-enclosed balconies are common. Their functional plan creates living space on the upper floor, with storage for fishing equipment on the ground floor.

CRUCEIROS
Distinctive *cruceiros* (stone crosses) can be spotted throughout Galicia, beside churches, next to cemetery gates, by the Stations of the Cross (as in A Guarda) and on roadsides where accidents have occurred. They are said to protect travellers from harm.

Traditional Galician wooden *hórreo*, raised high off the ground ↑

18

Sanxenxo

A3 **Pontevedra**
Puerto Deportivo Juan Carlos I; www.sanxenxo.es

With its good restaurants, lively nightlife, promenade and attractive beaches, Sanxenxo is one of the most popular resorts in the Rías Baixas. One of the best-known local beaches is Praia da Lanzada – a superb sandy strand that's a favourite with windsurfers. Silgar beach has the most modern sports harbour in Galicia. Just 2 km (1.2 miles) west of Sanxenxo town is Portonovo, known for the beautiful beaches of Caneliñas and Canelas, and its quirky seaside sculptures, which include a giant taking a siesta beside the marina.

Sanxenxo's Old Town features the 17th-century Iglesia de San Xinés as well as the 16th–18th-century Pazo de los Patino, with a tower, the coats of arms of its former inhabitants, and stone steps leading out onto a terrace. The Sanxenxo area also

↓ Sanxenxo beach, a perfect place for rock-pooling

enjoys a good reputation for its *albariño* white wine, which can be enjoyed on a bar hop around the town's many seaside bars and cafés.

19

A Toxa

A3 **Pontevedra**
Ayuntamiento, Praza do Corgo, O Grove; www. turismogrove.es

A tiny pine-covered island joined to the mainland by a bridge, A Toxa is one of the most stylish resorts in Galicia. The belle époque palace-hotel and luxury villas add to the island's elegant atmosphere. Its small church is covered with scallop shells. Across the bridge is O Grove, a thriving family resort and fishing port on a peninsula, with glorious beaches.

20

Vigo

A3 **Pontevedra**
Estación Marítima de Ría, C/Cánovas del Castillo 3; www.turismodevigo.org

Galicia's largest town is also the biggest fishing port in

FISHING IN SPAIN

The Spanish eat more seafood than any other European nation except Portugal. Each year, some 61,000 fishermen and 16,000 boats land over a million tonnes of hake, tuna, lobster and other species popular in Spanish cuisine. Nearly half of the fish and shellfish caught in Spain is supplied by the modern Galician fishing fleet, one of the largest in the EU, but because fish stocks in the seas around Europe have become depleted through overfishing, deep-sea trawlers have been forced to look for new fishing grounds as far away as Canada or Iceland.

Spain. Vigo is not noted for its buildings but does have striking modern sculptures such as Juan José Oliveira's statue of horses in the Praza de España.

The oldest part of the town, Barrio del Berbes, is near the port and used to be the sailors' quarter. Its cobbled alleys are full of bars and cafés

↑ Baroque bell towers added to the Romanesque church of San Benito, Cambados, in 1784

where you can find some of the finest tapas.

In the surrounding area there are up to 1,700 *hórreos* and 30 *cruceiros (p85)*, as well as dolmens and the remnants of Celtic settlements *(p120)*.

 Cambados

🅰A3 📍Pontevedra
ℹ️Praza do Concello; www.cambados.es

In Cambados' historic centre is the Pazo de Bazán, a manor house built in the 17th century by the ancestors of renowned 19th-century writer Emilia Pardo Bazán. Today it is a parador. A century older is the Pazo de Fefiñáns, decorated with Baroque coats of arms, in which one of the town's oldest *bodegas* has been established; the estate also comprises the late 16th-century Iglesia de San Benito. In the Santo Tomé district, visit the ruins of the 10th-century San Sadurnino tower. Just over half a kilometer (0.4 miles) east of the town centre, the roofless ruins of Iglesia de Santa Mariña de Dozo stand beside the hill of A Pastora. Close by is the **Museo Etnográfico e do Viño**, where there are exhibits on the region's history and culture, along with the traditions of wine production in the Rías Baixas. This area's excellent

white wine, *albariño*, is well-known throughout Europe. Cambados celebrates it with a festival on the first weekend of August each year, and as the wine's renown has spread it has become quite a substantial affair. Music, folkloric displays, street entertainment and merrymaking fill the town over some four or five days, during which time thousands of corks are pulled.

Museo Etnográfico e do Viño

🌐🏛️ 📍Avenida da Pastora, 104 📞986 52 61 19 🕙10am-2pm & 4:30-7:30pm Tue-Sat (till 8pm in summer), 10am-2pm Sun

 Illas Cíes

🅰A3 📍Pontevedra 🚢
ℹ️Estación Marítima de Ría, C/Cánovas del Castillo 3, Vigo; 986 22 47 57

The three islands of Cíes (Mondeagudo, Faro and San Martiño) are uninhabited, if you don't count the lighthouse keeper and guards. The archipelago is a national park and a paradise for waterfowl. A pristine area of natural beauty, the islands offer a range of breathtaking landscapes, spectacular sandy beaches, the ruins of a Celtic *castro*, and an ancient Suevi monastery that was plun-

Parador de Baiona

Beautifully set in an old fortress looking out to the sea, this parador is a luxurious place on which to splash out.

🅰A3 📍Rua Arquitecto Jesus Valverde, Baiona 🌐parador.es

€€€

Hotel Puerta Gamboa

Ideally located near Vigo's port, this hotel's quaint rooms, many with exposed stonework, offer a comfortable and cosy atmosphere.

🅰A3 📍Rua Gamboa 12, Vigo 🌐en.hotelpuerta gamboa.com

€€€

Hotel Talaso Louxo La Toja

This four-star hotel on A Toxa island offers luxury without the price tag. There's a pool and a chic restaurant.

🅰A3 📍A Toja, O Grove 🌐louxo latoja.com

€€€

dered by the Vikings and later by English pirates. The Illa Mondeagudo is joined to the Illa do Faro by a sandbar and an artificial embankment along which runs the road. There is a campsite on Faro, Camping de Illas Cíes, which must be booked in advance. The islands also have a first-aid post, café and police station. Boats arrive at the improvised port on the Illa Mondeagudo from Vigo, and from Baiona in summer.

Reconstruction at the Celtic settlement site at A Guarda ↑

A Guarda

🅰A3 🔵Pontevedra 🚍
🛈Praza do Reloxo 1; 986 61 45 46

The little fishing port of A Guarda is famous for seafood and is particularly well known for its lobsters.

Overlooking the town is the Monte de Santa Tregra, home to the remains of one of Galicia's most complete Celtic *castros* (fortified settlements), dating from the 1st century BC.

THE GALEGO LANGUAGE

Galicia has its own language, known locally as *galego*. Although related to Castilian – both descend from Latin – it is closer to Portuguese, with which it is for the most part mutually intelligible. It is an official language in Galicia, along with Castilian, and is spoken by around half the Galician people. Local initiatives in place aim to improve this statistic.

The **Museo Arqueológico de Santa Trega** explores the ancient settlement.

Some 13 km (8 miles) north the tiny Baroque Monasterio de Santa María stands by the beach at Oia.

Museo Arqueológico de Santa Trega

 🄌Monte Santa Tegra, A Guarda 🄲690 01 70 38 🄍Tue–Sun 🄍Jan

Baiona

🅰A3 🔵Pontevedra 🚍
🛈Paseo da Ribeira; 986 68 70 67

The *Pinta*, one of the caravels from Columbus's fleet, arrived back at this small port in 1493, bringing the first news of the "discovery" of the Americas. This event is commemorated in the Festa da Arribada, on the first weekend in March.

Today Baiona, which is sited on a broad bay, is a popular summer resort, its harbour filled with pleasure and fishing boats. There are lovely beaches here, especially the long Praia America.

A royal fortress once stood on the Monterreal promontory,

north of the town. Sections of its defensive walls remain, but inside it has been converted into a smart parador. There are superb views from here.

Tui

🅰A3 🔵Pontevedra 🚉🚍
🛈Praza de San Fernando; www.tui.gal

As the inhabitants of Tui like to say, their small city is history carved in stone. It lies on the Miño river, on the border with Portugal. The old quarter, with its narrow streets and secret passageways, has arcaded houses with coats of arms, churches and former manor houses. Rising above this is the fortress-like 12th-century Catedral de Santa María.

The town's defensive walls and battlements lend it the appearance of a fortress, and indeed it performed this role due to its border location. The Soutomaior tower affords a magnificent view over Tui, the river and the Portuguese town of Valença do Minho. The banks of the Miño are linked by the iron Puente Internacional (1884), a bridge by Gustave Eiffel, and by a modern

motorway bridge. Not far from Tui is the hill of Aloia – a park with a wide variety of flora and fauna. Many archaeological finds have been made here, including Roman walls. The hill has good observation points of the Miño river valley.

 26

Ribadavia

🅰B3 🏛Ourense
🚌 ⓘ **Praza Maior 7; www.ribadavia.net**

Set in a fertile valley, Ribadavia has for centuries produced Ribeiro wines. The town was also once home to a Sephardic community, and a walk through the Jewish quarter today is like stepping back in time. The modest houses, with perfectly preserved façades, conceal former *bodegas* within their walls. The Jewish Information Centre, housed above the tourist information office, has information and exhibitions. Located on Praza Maior are houses with characteristic arcades, a town hall with a wrought-iron belfry and 16th-century tower bearing a sundial, and the Baroque Pazo de los Condes de Ribadavia.

Also preserved is the 15th-century Sarmiento castle, which offers audio-guided tours on Monday to Saturday. Important elements of the castle complex are the 9th-century rock-hewn tombs whose outlines reflect those of human figures, and fragments of the Old Town walls. The Gothic Casa de Inquisición – an 11th-century House of Inquisition – bears on its façade as many as five coats of arms of families connected with the Holy Office.

By the road leading out of town stands the Monasterio de Santo Domingo. This 14th-century monastery church, the best example of local Gothic style, contains medieval tombs.

 27

Ourense

🅰B3 🏛Ourense 🚉🚌
ⓘ **C/Isabel la Católica 2; www.turismode ourense.com**

The old quarter of Ourense was built around the thermal springs of As Burgas. Even today, these spout water at a temperature of 65° C (150° F). In Roman times, visitors were also drawn by the abundance of gold in the Miño river.

The city's old quarter is its most interesting district,

> **Ourense was built around the thermal springs of As Burgas. Even today, these spout water at a temperature of 65° C (150° F).**

particularly the small area around the arcaded Praza Maior. The main square is lined with 18th- and 19th-century buildings, including the town hall and the former bishop's palace. Also located on the square is the Catedral de San Martín, founded in AD 572 and rebuilt in the 12th–13th centuries. The cathedral's main entrance (the Pórtico del Paraiso) has partially preserved polychrome decoration. By the high altar is a huge 16th-century Gothic-Renaissance reredos by Cornelis de Holanda.

Nearby is the Baroque Iglesia de Santa María Madre. Built on the site of a Seuvi temple, the medieval church building incorporates 1st-century columns.

Another important landmark is the Puente Romano, a seven-arched 307-m (1,007-ft) bridge that crosses the Río Miño, north of town. Built on Roman foundations, it is now pedestrianized.

↑ Historic buildings in the Praza Maior, Ourense

㉘ Celanova

🅰B3 📍Ourense
ℹ️ Praza Maior 1; www.
concellodecelanova.com

This village is known for its grand Praza Maior, where you'll find the Benedictine Monasterio de San Salvador. Also known as the Monasterio de San Rosendo, after its founder, the monastery was established in the 10th century. Much of the current church dates from the 18th century and is mostly Baroque in style, with an ornate altarpiece and Gothic choir stalls. There are guided tours of the church. In the garden is the well-preserved 10th-century Mozarabic Capilla de San Miguel.

In nearby Bande, 26 km (16 miles) south of Celanova, is the 7th-century Iglesia de Santa Comba, one of the few surviving Visigothic shrines in Europe. Built on the plan of a Greek cross, with thick walls, the barrel-vaulted church contains the tomb of St Torcuato.

㉙ Verín

🅰C3 📍Ourense 🚌 ℹ️ Rua Imans da Salle; 988 41 16 14

Set amid vineyards on the southern edge of Galicia, Verín is noted for its fine wines. The town grew up around thermal and mineral springs, which are reputed to have therapeutic powers, and have given it a thriving bottled water industry.

In the Old Town, there are 17th-century arcaded houses with glass-encased balconies (*galerías*). The area's biggest attraction is **Castillo de Monterrei**, some 3 km (2 miles) to the west. Now a parador, it was built to defend the border during the wars with Portugal; within its three rings of walls is a 15th-century square keep, an arcaded courtyard and a 13th-century church. The castle once housed a monastery and hospital. It can be visited on a guided tour.

Castillo de Monterrei
 📞 988 02 92 30

940

—

The year that Celanova's Capilla de San Miguel, one of Spain's oldest chapels, was built.

㉚ Monasterio de Ribas de Sil

🅰B3 📍Ourense
🚉 San Esteban de Sil
(15 km/9 miles away)
🚌 From Ourense (then 15-minute drive)
📞 988 01 01 10 🕐 Daily

Near its confluence with the Miño, the Sil river carves an exceptionally deep gorge in which dams form two reservoirs. A hairpin road winds to the top of the gorge, where the Romanesque-Gothic Monasterio de Santo Estevo de Ribas de Sil is situated high above the river. Some elements of the monastery exhibit different architectural styles, such as the Renaissance cloisters and Baroque façade. The building has been restored and modernized (with a glass wall in the cloisters), and is now home to an exclusive parador.

㉛ Monforte de Lemos

🅰C3 📍Lugo 🚉 🚌
ℹ️ Rúa Comercio 8; www.
monfortedelemos.es

On a hill overlooking the town of Monforte de Lemos are the remnants of a fortress – fragments of the massive walls, the palace of the Lemos family and the Mosteiro de

←
The cloisters of Celanova's Monasterio de San Salvador

San Vicente do Pino are preserved here. The monastery's Renaissance façade conceals a Gothic interior. Of note is the 30-m (98-ft) 13th-century tower.

The Cabe river runs through the town's centre, spanned by a number of bridges including the Ponte Vella: originally Roman, the current structure dates from the 16th century. Overlooking this stretch of the river, the Convento de Santa Clara, dating from the 17th century, accommodates a museum of religious art with some fine Italian reliquaries.

In the suburbs of Monforte stands the Colexio de Nosa Señora da Antiga, a Piarist college in the Herrera style, dating from the early 16th century. The small picture gallery within displays two paintings by El Greco and five works by the Mannerist painter Andrea del Sarto.

32

Mosteiro de Santa María de Oseira

🅰B3 🏛Oseira, Ourense
🕐For tours only, check website 🌐mosteirode oseira.org

The Cistercian Mosteiro de Santa María de Oseira, one of many monasteries in the area, was founded in the 12th century. Its name derives from the word *oso* (bear), as bears once roamed the remote area where it was built. The complex includes a Gothic church, remodelled during the Baroque period, with two huge towers; its construction was based on the cathedral in Santiago de Compostela *(p66)*. The chapterhouse rooms have columns with twisted shafts and capitals resembling palm leaves. The monastery also features a well-preserved staircase in the Herrera style and three cloisters – the Knights', Medallions' and Pinnacles' cloisters – which date from the 16th century. Medicinal liqueurs are produced by the monks who live here.

33

Allariz

🅰B3 🏛Ourense
🚉 🚍 ℹ️Paseo da Alameda; www.allariz.com

The most attractive feature of Allariz is its location by the Arnoia river, crossed by a medieval stone bridge next to which you can swim and hire rowing boats. The town is built on a medieval plan, with narrow streets and old houses decorated with coats of arms.

↑ Mosteiro de Santa María de Oseira, with its manicured gardens

In the centre of the town is the Real Monasterio de Santa Clara, where visitors can admire a Gothic ivory figure of the Virgin and a crystal cross dating from the same period. Also worth visiting is the shrine of San Benito, with a lofty 17th- to 19th-century tower, and the **Parque Etnográfico do Río Arnoia**, in which there are museums of leather crafts and textiles as well as a mill.

Parque Etnográfico do Río Arnoia

🕐🎫♿ 🏛Casa da Cultura, Rúa do Castelo, s/n 🕐Times vary, check website for details 🌐museos.xunta.gal/en/rio-arnoia

> 💬 INSIDER TIP
> **August Empanadas**
>
> On the last weekend of August be sure to catch the Allariz Empanada Festival. Sample tasty Galician pies and enjoy the live music, dances and sporting events.

❸❹
O Cebreiro

C2 🏛Lugo
📞 982 36 70 25

High up in wild, windswept mountain countryside, famous for its volatile weather and with wonderful mountain views, is tiny O Cebreiro. Here you'll find several *pallozas* – oval or rectangular Celtic thatched stone huts.

Many pilgrims begin the last stage of the Camino de Santiago (*p70*) from here; the local church is one of the oldest monuments on the route. According to legend, the 9th-century pre-Romanesque Iglesia de Santa María La Real was the scene of a miracle involving the transformation of bread and wine into the flesh and blood of Christ. Inside the church is a 12th-century chalice, known as the Holy Grail, in which the transformation is said to have taken place.

One of the *pallozas* contains the **Museo Etnográfico**, which presents the daily life of the settlement's former inhabitants.

Museo Etnográfico
🏛O Cebreiro ⏰Tue–Sat; winter: 11am–6pm; summer: 8:30am–2:30pm 🌐museos. xunta.gal/en/cebreiro

❸❺
Vilar de Donas

🅰B2 🏛Lugo 🅸Palas de Rei; 982 38 00 01

In this hamlet on the road to Santiago stands the small, aisleless Romanesque **Iglesia de San Salvador**, dating from the early 13th century and built on the plan of a cross. Initially, it belonged to a convent, inhabited first by nuns (hence the name – Donas) and later by the Knights of the Order of St James. The Knights' Chapter would meet here each year. Tombs of the knights are preserved inside the church, as are 14th-century Gothic murals depicting biblical scenes and the figures of King Juan II and his wife with melancholy expressions. The external ornamentation comprises plant motifs, birds, figures that are half human and half bird, griffins and angels. The doors of the church bear the elegant original Romanesque fittings. Notable, too, is the tower (a later addition) that is visible from afar, and the remnants of the portico, which stands in front of the main western entrance. The church was built of granite, which in places has now become covered with weeds.

West of Vilar de Donas, the village of Palas de Rei has an abundance of Romanesque churches and chapels; there are also several dolmens and *castros* here.

Iglesia de San Salvador
🕤 🏛27216 Palas de Rei 📞 669 54 40 ⏰Easter–Oct: 11am–2pm & 3–6pm Tue–Sun; Nov–Easter: ask priest for key

↑ The Romanesque entrance of the Iglesia de San Salvador

❸❻
Santa Eulalia de la Bóveda

🅰B2 🏛Santalla de Bóveda s/n, Lugo 📞982 16 01 24 ⏰Winter: Mon–Fri 8am–3pm, Sat 10am–2pm; summer: Tue–Fri 8:30am–2:30pm, Sat 10am–2pm

Situated 14 km (9 miles) from Lugo (*p76*), this small temple was originally pagan, before being put into use by early Christians, and then forgotten until its rediscovery in 1962. One of the great mysteries of Lugo province, the building probably dates from the 3rd or 4th century AD, and its purpose has been the subject of various interpretations. Some suggest that Santa Eulalia was built as a bath-house, others say it was a temple to the Phrygian goddess Cybele (the Roman

Did You Know?

Galicia's tipple of choice – *queimada* – is known as "witches' brew" as it is set on fire.

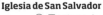

← Cross inside the Iglesia de Santa María La Real in O Cebreiro

> **Some suggest that Santa Eulalia was built as a bathhouse, others say it was a temple to the Phrygian goddess Cybele.**

equivalent of he Greek goddess Rea, the mother of all the gods). It is possible that sacrificial bulls and rams were slaughtered here, their blood being collected in a special shallow basin. Centuries later, the temple was used as a church for christenings.

Originally, the church had two storeys, but only the lower one has survived – an almost perfectly preserved square crypt, whose vaulting was damaged during the demolition of the chapel that had been added to the upper floor. Three sides of the crypt are covered with earth; the fourth has two small windows providing the only source of light, apart from the entrance.

Inside the church you can see the atrium leading to the semicircular entrance, the basin, a few columns, various bas-reliefs and, above all, the barrel vaults covered with murals of birds. The symbolism of birds seemingly points to the cult of Cybele, but it also facilitated the Christianization of the temple, since St Eulalia is the patron saint of birds.

37

Sarria

A C2 **Q** Lugo
i Rúa Vigo de Sarria 15;
www.sarriaturismo.com

Sarria is a common starting point for pilgrimages to Santiago de Compostela, which lies 111 km (69 miles) away (100 km is the minimum distance required to receive the certificate of completion of the pilgrimage). The town

was established by Alfonso IX, who died en route to Santiago. Due to its location, Sarria has many hostels for pilgrims. Of particular note is the beautiful 13th-century hostel near the church and monastery of La Magdalena, which has been transformed into a youth hostel, **Albergue Monasterio La Magdalena**. The monastery has a Renaissance façade and a late-Gothic cloister.

Another building spanning the Romanesque and Gothic styles is the 13th-century Iglesia de San Salvador, beside the fortress of the same period, of which only the tower remains. The town also has four medieval bridges. In the surrounding area there are many more attractive Romanesque churches.

Albergue Monasterio La Magdalena
⌂ Avda La Merced 60
☎ 982 533 568

TOP 4 GALICIAN FIESTAS

Os Peliqueiros
On Carnival Sunday (p50) Laza is overtaken by masked characters.

Flower Pavements
Ponteareas' streets, along which the Corpus Christi procession passes in May or June, are carpeted with petals.

A Rapa das Bestas
Semi-wild horses are rounded up in Oia in May or June for their manes and tails to be cut.

St James's Day
On the night before 25 July, there is a firework display in Praza do Obradoiro in Santiago de Compostela.

↑ Pilgrims beginning the Camino de Santiago in the town of Sarria

A DRIVING TOUR
THE MIÑO RIVER VALLEY

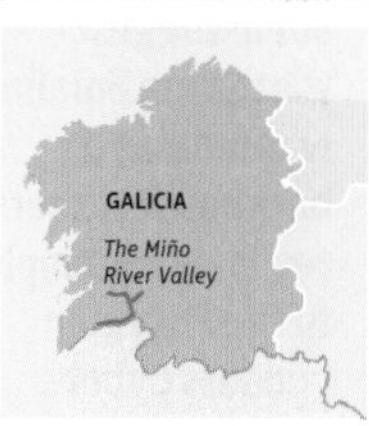

Length 75 km (47 miles) **Stopping-off points** Crecente; Melón; A Cañiza **Terrain** Some steep, winding roads to Melón, but generally easy

Covering 307 km (190 miles), the Miño is Galicia's longest river. Its source is in the Sierra de Meira; it flows through the towns of Lugo and Ourense, entering the Atlantic Ocean at A Guarda. The final stretch is along the Portuguese border. This drive follows the river through Galicia, as it cuts through a landscape of steep valleys and farmland as well as vineyards, where crisp Ribeiro white wines are produced.

GALICIA
The Miño River Valley

Locator Map
For more detail see p62

*Stop off in **Melón**, where the ruins of the Monasterio de Santa María de Melón, including the original 12th-century chancel, cloisters and aisles, survive.*

*End this drive in **Mondariz**. Known for the mineral waters spouting from Troncoso spring, this has been a popular meeting place for centuries. The Mondariz Balneario hotel offers a variety of spa treatments.*

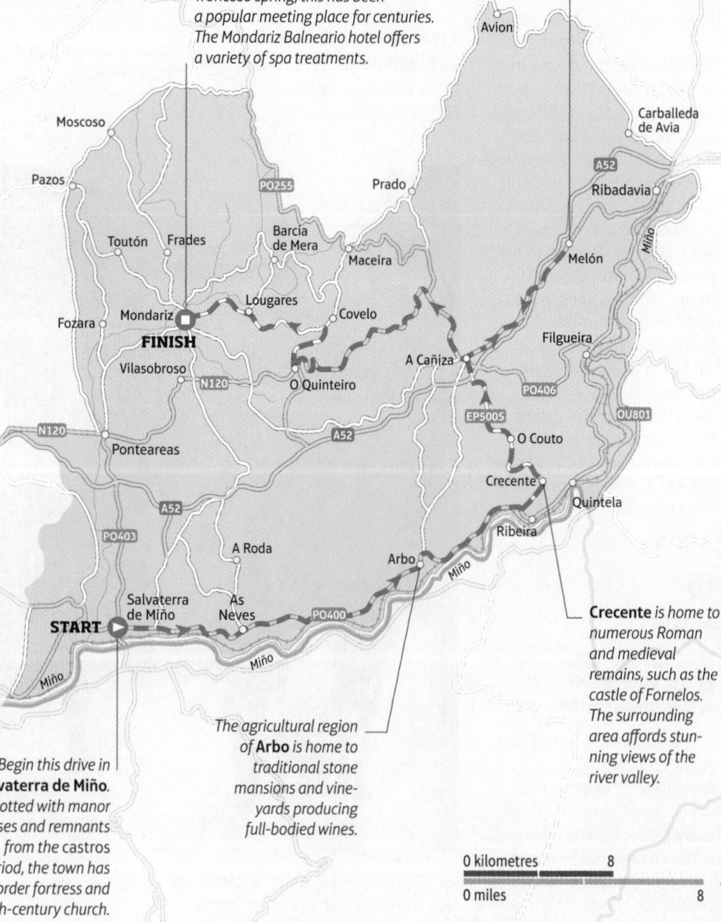

Crecente is home to numerous Roman and medieval remains, such as the castle of Fornelos. The surrounding area affords stunning views of the river valley.

*The agricultural region of **Arbo** is home to traditional stone mansions and vineyards producing full-bodied wines.*

*Begin this drive in **Salvaterra de Miño**. Dotted with manor houses and remnants from the castros period, the town has a border fortress and 16th-century church.*

0 kilometres 8
0 miles 8

N ↑

↑ Ruins of the Cistercian
Monasterio de Santa
María de Melón

A DRIVING TOUR
THE SIL RIVER VALLEY

Length 70 km (43 miles) **Stopping-off points** Ourense; Esgos; Castro Caldelas **Terrain** Steep, winding and sometimes narrow roads

The picturesque Sil river valley, replete with chestnut and oak trees, is part of the wine-producing region of Ribeira Sacra. The region owes its name to the local monasteries – for centuries, the monks were involved in the cultivation of vines. The Sil valley and its branches are often extraordinarily steep, with vineyards seeming to climb up near-sheer valley sides. This makes for a challenging drive, but it's well worth it for dramatic views of vertiginous gorges, sweeping valleys and remote monasteries surrounded by dense woodland.

*Begin this drive at the majestic **Sil Canyon**, where the river flows through a deep gorge with walls rising 300 m (984 ft).*

*You'll pass through the outskirts of **Ourense** (p89), which developed as a settlement around thermal springs in Roman times.*

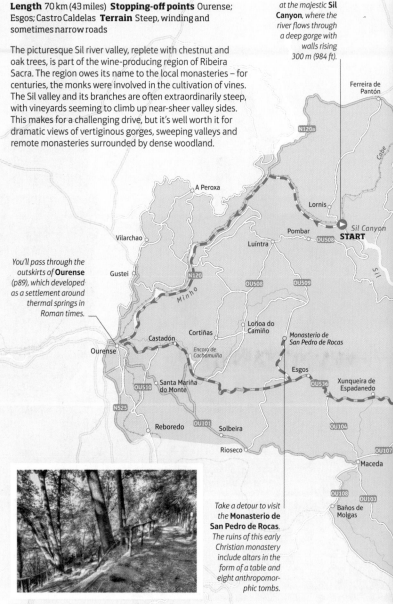

Ferreira de Pantón

N120a

Cabe

A Peroxa

Lornis

Pombar

Sil Canyon
START

OU508

Vilarchao

Luintra

Sil

Gustei

N120

OU508

OU509

Minho

Loñoa do Camiño

Monasterio de San Pedro de Rocas

Cortiñas

Castadón

Encoro de Cachamuíña

Esgos

Xunqueira de Espadanedo

OU536

Ourense

Santa Mariña do Monte

OU510

OU104

N525

Reboredo

OU101

Solbeira

OU107

Rioseco

Maceda

OU108

OU103

Baños de Molgas

*Take a detour to visit the **Monasterio de San Pedro de Rocas**. The ruins of this early Christian monastery include altars in the form of a table and eight anthropomorphic tombs.*

↑ Beech-dappled paths in the woods surrounding San Pedro de Rocas

End this tour at **Parada de Sil**, where you'll find the spectacular Monasterio de Ribas de Sil (p90). Enjoy stunning views over the Sil at the Balcones de Madrid observation point.

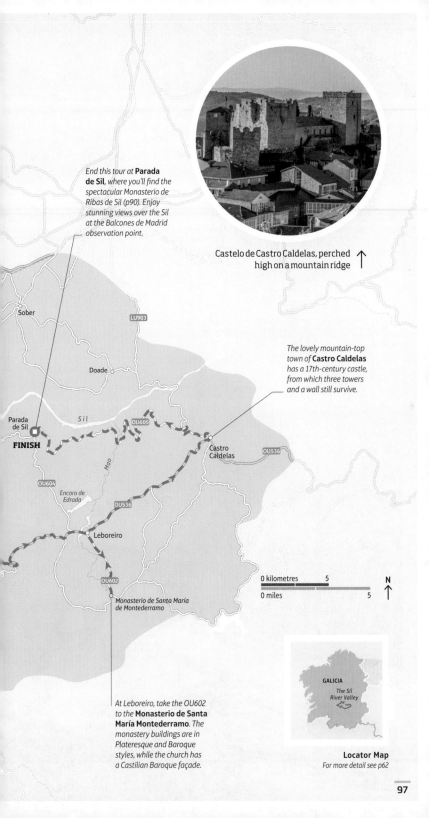

Castelo de Castro Caldelas, perched high on a mountain ridge ↑

The lovely mountain-top town of **Castro Caldelas** has a 17th-century castle, from which three towers and a wall still survive.

Sober

LU903

Doade

Parada de Sil
FINISH

Sil

OU605

Castro Caldelas

OU536

OU604

Encoro de Edrada

OU536

Leboreiro

OU602

Monasterio de Santa María de Montederramo

| 0 kilometres | 5 |
| 0 miles | 5 |

N ↑

At Leboreiro, take the OU602 to the **Monasterio de Santa María Montederramo**. The monastery buildings are in Plateresque and Baroque styles, while the church has a Castilian Baroque façade.

GALICIA
The Sil River Valley

Locator Map
For more detail see p62

ASTURIAS AND CANTABRIA

Asturias, helped by its mountainous terrain, has a long history of resisting invasion. Although the Romans did conquer the area, they failed to fully subdue the native inhabitants. The *reconquista* (Reconquest) is said to have begun in Asturias around AD 722, when a Moorish force was defeated by the Christians at Covadonga. The Christian Kingdom of Asturias was founded in the 8th century, eventually stretching from the Basque Country down to what is now northern Portugal as Asturias conquered more and more Moorish-held land. Uniting with the Kingdom of Castile in 1230, the area now known as Asturias was declared a principality in the 14th century, and put under the patronage of the heir to the Spanish throne. To this day, the region's official name is the Principality of Asturias, and Spain's heir is known as the Prince or Princess of Asturias.

Cantabria also fell to the Romans, and came close to defeat by the Moors, who were pushed back after Cantabria entered into an alliance with neighbouring Asturias. In the late 19th century, numerous smaller areas were amalgamated to create the Province of Cantabria. Its capital, Santander, has a long history as a Roman settlement, medieval town and later a major port of trade with the New World. However, traces of its illustrious past are scarce due to a huge fire in 1941 that destroyed more than 400 buildings in the Old Town.

ASTURIAS AND CANTABRIA

Must Sees

1. Parque Nacional de los Picos de Europa
2. Oviedo
3. Santander
4. Santillana del Mar
5. Museo de Altamira
6. Gijón

Experience More

7. Castro de Coaña
8. Castropol
9. Cudillero
10. Taramundi
11. Luarca
12. Parque Natural de Somiedo
13. Valle de Teverga
14. Salas and Valle del Narcea
15. Avilés
16. Bárzana and Bermiego
17. Valdediós
18. Villaviciosa
19. Ribadesella
20. Comillas
21. Alto Campoo
22. Valle de Cabuérniga
23. San Vicente de la Barquera
24. Castro Urdiales
25. Valle del Besaya
26. Laredo
27. Soba and Ramales de la Victoria
28. Puente Viesgo

ASTURIAS AND CANTABRIA

Atlantic Ocean

Bay of Biscay

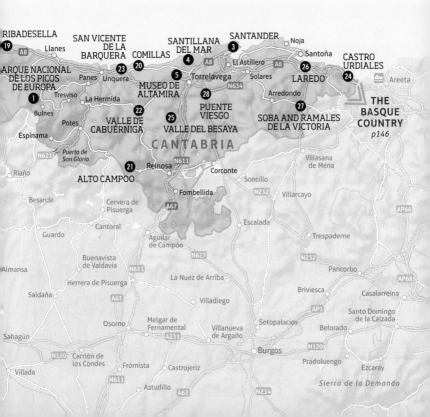

RIBADESELLA
19 A8 Llanes

SAN VICENTE
DE LA
BARQUERA
COMILLAS
23 20
SANTILLANA
DEL MAR
4

SANTANDER
3 Noja
Santoña
El Astillero A8 26 LAREDO
Solares 27
CASTRO
URDIALES
24 Areeta

PARQUE NACIONAL
DE LOS PICOS
DE EUROPA
1 Tresviso
Bulnes
Potes
Espinama
N621
Puerto de
San Glorio
Riaño
Besande
Panes Unquera
La Hermida
MUSEO DE
ALTAMIRA
5 Torrelavega
N634
28
PUENTE
VIESGO
VALLE DE
CABUÉRNIGA
22
25
VALLE DEL BESAYA
Arredondo
SOBA AND RAMALES
DE LA VICTORIA

THE
BASQUE
COUNTRY
p146

CANTABRIA
21 Reinosa
ALTO CAMPOO
N611
Corconte
Fombellida
Villasana
de Mena
Soncillo
N232 Villarcayo
AP68

Cervera de
Pisuerga
Cantoral
Escalada
Trespaderne
N232

Guardo
Buenavista
de Valdavia
N611
Aguilar
de Campóo
A67
La Nuez de Arriba
Villadiego
Briviesca
Pancorbo
AP68
Casalarreina

Almansa
Herrera de Pisuerga
A67
Saldaña
Osorno
Melgar de
Fernamental
A231
Villanueva
de Argaño
Sotopalacios
AP1
Santo Domingo
de la Calzada
Belorado

Sahagún
N120 Carrión de
los Condes
Frómista
Castrojeriz
Villada
N611
Astudillo
A62
Burgos
N120
Pradoluengo
N234
Ezcaray
Sierra de la Demanda

Verdant plains surrounding
the Lago de la Ercina, fringed ↑
by the Picos de Europa

①

PARQUE NACIONAL DE LOS PICOS DE EUROPA

🅐E2 🏠Asturias, Cantabria and Castilla y León 🚌Oviedo to Cangas de Onís
ℹ️Avenida Covadonga 43, Cangas de Onís; www.parquenacionalpicoseuropa.es

Stretching for 647 sq km (250 sq miles), this national park straddles three regions and is crowned by the Picos de Europa. These beautiful mountains were reputedly christened the "Peaks of Europe" by returning sailors for whom this was often the first sight of their homeland.

Encompassing deep winding gorges and verdant valleys, the Parque Nacional de los Picos de Europa is rich walking territory. A dramatic footpath follows the Desfiladero del Río Cares gorge in the heart of the Picos, passing through tunnels and across high bridges. If this sounds too energetic, a cable car makes the steep ascent from Fuente Dé to a wild rocky plateau pitted with craters and offering a spectacular panorama of the Picos' peaks and valleys. Other highlights include the Naranjo de Bulnes (a tooth-like crest), the sparkling Lago de la Ercina and the town of Covadonga, the site of Pelayo's historic victory.

Did You Know?

The Picos de Europa includes more than 200 mountain peaks over 2,000 m (6,560 ft) high.

← Riding the Fuente Décable car to the peaks

Walking along the dramatic Río Cares gorge ↓

PELAYO THE WARRIOR

A statue *(below)* of this Visigothic nobleman who became king of Asturias guards the basilica at Covadonga. It was close to this site, in AD 718, that Pelayo and a band of men – though vastly outnumbered – are said to have defeated a Moorish army. The victory inspired Christians in the north of Spain to reconquer the peninsula. The tomb of the warrior is in a cave which has become a shrine.

 Cangas de Onís, Covadonga

EXPLORING THE PICOS DE EUROPA

① Fuente Dé

🏛 **Asturias** 🌐 **cantur.com**

The cable car in Fuente Dé takes visitors up to an altitude of 1,900 m (6,234 ft) above sea level. As it ascends 750 m (2,461 ft) up the steep mountain, panoramic views of the wild surrounding landscape are gradually revealed. From the Mirador del Cable, the observation point at the

summit, ambitious walkers can carry on to the peaks of Pico Tesorero (2,570 m /8,432 ft) and Peña Vieja.

② Potes

🏛 **Cantabria** ℹ **C/Independencia 12; 942 73 07 87**

This small town on the Deva river, set amid snowcapped peaks, is the main centre of the eastern Picos de Europa. The narrow, winding streets lined with medieval stone houses are full of small shops, and on Mondays a colourful flea market takes place here.

The town's most characteristic monument is a 15th-century defensive tower, the Torre del Infantado. Also worth seeing is the late-Gothic 14th-century Iglesia de San Vicente, with a beautiful façade and Baroque altars brought here from the Dominican Convento de San Raimundo.

A good way to spend an afternoon in Potes is to hire a bicycle and ride for 9 km (5 miles) to the beautiful Romanesque Iglesia de Santa María Piasta.

THE BEST TRAILS

The best expeditions in the Picos de Europa start from Turieno, Cosgaya and Sotres. Free guided hikes are organized daily in summer from June to September, leaving from the boundary of the park. Hikers exploring higher areas of the mountains should make sure to bring appropriate equipment, boots and warm clothing, as the weather is prone to sudden and dramatic changes.

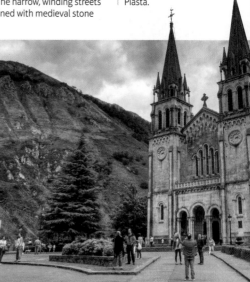

③
Covadonga

📍 Asturias

Set in the northern range of the Picos de Europa, Covadonga is a place of great significance for Asturias, and for the whole of Spain. It was here, in 718, that Pelayo, a leader of the Visigothic noblemen, won a battle to stop the further advance of the Moors in this part of Asturias. The town remains an important shrine, and crowds of pilgrims come to visit the cave where Pelayo is said to have lived, which is picturesquely set on a hillside. Inside the cave is a chapel containing the warrior's tomb. In 1886–1901, a Neo-Romanesque basilica was built on the spot where Pelayo scored his historic victory. The name of the town derives from *cova longa* (*cueva larga* in Spanish) – the long cave where the warriors prayed to the Virgin before the battle.

④
Cangas de Onís

📍 Asturias 🛈 Avenida de Covadonga 1; www.cangas deonis.com

The first capital of the Kingdom of Asturias, Cangas de Onís is one of the gateways to

↑ The Roman bridge across the River Sella in Cangas de Onís

the Picos de Europa National Park. Preserved here is the Ermita de Santa Cruz, which was built in 733 on the site of an earlier shrine, with a fascinating Bronze Age dolmen by the entrance. The ivy-clad bridge, with its tall arches, dates from the reign of Alfonso XI of Castile (1312–50). Watersports enthusiasts might wish to attempt the 3-hour canoe trip along the Río Sella from Cangas de Onís.

⑤
Arenas de Cabrales

📍 Asturias 🛈 Carretera General; 985 84 67 47

This village, situated 25 km (16 miles) east of Cangas de Onis, is famous as the place where *cabrales*, a pungent blue goat's cheese, is made. On the last Sunday in August, a lively Asturian cheese festival takes place here.

The village features many beautiful 17th- and 18th-century homesteads, of which the most arresting is the Casa Palacio de los Mestas.

On the right bank of the Ribelas river, which flows

← Admiring the Basílica de Santa María la Real de Covadonga

through the village, rises the small Gothic Iglesia de Santa María de Llas, affording fine views of the surrounding area.

In the vicinity of Arena de Cabrales there are three caves: Cueva El Bosque, Cueva de los Canes and Cueva de la Covaciella. Though quite difficult to get to, the caves are well worth visiting on account of the superb Palaeolithic cave art to be seen inside.

TOP 4 **PICOS FLORA AND FAUNA**

Chamois
Herds of these agile animals graze in the mountain meadows.

Spring Gentian
Flowering from March to August, gentians often grow on the limestone base of screes.

Pyramidal Orchid
With an 8-cm-(3-in-) long pink inflorescence, these orchids grow in the park's vast open meadows.

Griffon Vultures
One of Spain's largest birds, these scavengers nest in caves and on mountain ledges.

↑ Brightly coloured street leading to the Catedral de San Salvador

2

OVIEDO

D1 Marqués de Santa Cruz, 985 22 75 86; Plaza de la Constitución, 984 49 37 85

Founded in the 8th century under the Asturian ruler Fruela, Oviedo is the country's oldest Christian city. Today, this beautiful university city forms the cultural and commercial heart of the region. Many of the city's historic monuments were destroyed during the Civil War, but the delightful pedestrianized Old Town still has several medieval churches and squares.

①

Plaza Alfonso II El Casto

The nucleus of the medieval city, this stately square is named in honour of the Asturian king, Alfonso II. After defeating the Moors, Alfonso transferred the Asturian court to Oviedo in 792 and turned the town into an important pilgrimage centre. The square is bordered by a number of handsome old palaces, among them the Palacio de la Rúa, built by Alonso González, the treasurer to the Catholic Monarchs, Fernando and Isabel. One of few structures to survive a fire of Christmas Eve 1521, this elegant little 15th-century palace is thought to be the oldest secular building in the city.

②

Catedral de San Salvador

Plaza Alfonso II El Casto, s/n Times vary, check website catedraldeoviedo.com

This 16th-century cathedral is the best example in Asturias of Gothic style. In the 9th century, Alfonso II ordered the construction of the Cámara Santa, a holy chamber meant to house reliquaries recovered from Toledo after the Moorish invasion; the Romanesque part of this chapel is the result of remodelling carried out in 1109. Inside the cathedral are Alfonso II's tomb and a gilded altar of 1525 – one of the largest in Spain – by sculptor Giralte of Brussels.

EAT

Umami
Ultra-cool, family-owned restaurant serving up delicious Japanese dishes like fresh udon and sushi with theatrical flair.

Calle de Jacinto Benavente 6
restauranteumami.es

€€€

Sidrería El Gato Negro
Delicious fresh seafood and local meat dishes are served alongside the special house cider.

Plaza Trascorrales 17
sidreriaelgatonegro.com

€€€

Today the seat of a regional court, the Baroque Palacio de Camposagrado sports a Rococo façade embellished with fanciful masks and shields.

③
Iglesia de San Tirso

🏛 **Plaza Alfonso II El Casto, 4**

Also on the Plaza Alfonso II El Casto, to the left of the cathedral, stands the Iglesia de San Tirso, commissioned by King Alfonso II at the end of the 8th century. This aisled structure, on a basilican plan, was restored several times. It has consequently lost its original appearance, except for the triforium in the eastern wall, whose columns are adorned with plant motifs.

Of note is the Gothic chapel of St Anne, destroyed during a fire and later rebuilt by Juan Caeredo in the second half of the 16th century.

④
Palacio de Camposagrado

🏛 **Plaza de Porlier**
🚫 **To the public**

Commissioned by José Bernaldo de Quirós in the first half of the 18th century, the massive four-storey Palacio de Camposagrado was designed by two renowned architects: Francisco de la Riba Ladrón de Guevara and his pupil Pedro Antonio Menéndez de Ambás. Today the seat of a regional court, this Baroque palace sports a Rococo façade embellished with fanciful masks and shields.

🔍 HIDDEN GEM
Santa María del Naranco

Just 3 km (2 miles) from the centre of Oviedo, this 9th-century church, originally built as a palace for King Ramiro I, is a marvel of pre-Romanesque architecture (p110).

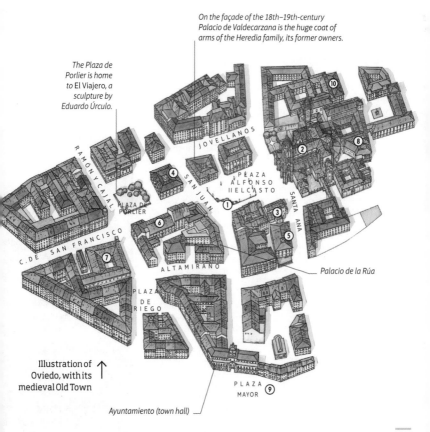

On the façade of the 18th–19th-century Palacio de Valdecarzana is the huge coat of arms of the Heredia family, its former owners.

The Plaza de Porlier is home to El Viajero, a sculpture by Eduardo Úrculo.

Palacio de la Rúa

Illustration of Oviedo, with its medieval Old Town

Ayuntamiento (town hall)

↑ *Campesinos de Gandía* by Hermen Anglada Camarasa at the Museo de Bellas Artes

⑤ Museo de Bellas Artes

🏛 Calle Santa Ana 1
🕐 Times vary, check website 🌐 museobbaa.com

In the city's old quarter, beside the cathedral, Oviedo's Museum of Fine Art occupies three buildings: the Palacio de Velarde (1767); the Baroque Casa Oviedo-Portal (1660) by the Cantabrian architect Melchior de Velasco; and a building from the 1940s.

Opened in 1980, the museum hosts the region's most exciting collections. The permanent exhibition comprises Spanish painting dating from the 15th to the 21st centuries, Asturian art, Italian and Flemish works from the 14th to the 18th centuries, and Spanish and Asturian sculpture from the 15th to the 21st centuries. In total, the museum's inventory numbers 15,000 items, including works by Goya, Murillo, Zurbarán, Picasso, Dalí and Miró.

⑥ Palacio Toreno

🏛 Plaza de Portlier 5 🕐 For exhibitions, check website 🌐 palaciocondetoreno.com

This palace was designed in 1663 for the Malleza Doriga family by the architect Gregorio de la Roza. Featuring an asymmetrical Baroque façade, the building accommodates the headquarters of RIDEA (Real Instituto de los Estudios Asturianos), the Royal Institute for Asturian Studies, which was established in 1946 to encourage research into Asturian culture. Within the building, which often hosts temporary exhibitions, is a patio with Tuscan columns.

⑦ The University

🏛 Calle de San Francisco 1

Oviedo's international university was founded in 1608 by the Inquisitor and Archbishop of Seville, Valdés-Salas. Officially opened on 21 September 1608, the institution had three faculties: Arts, Theology and Law.

The present rectorate building was designed by Gonzalo de Güemes Bracamonte and Juan de Rivero Rada. Especially impressive is the library, designed by Rodrigo Gil de Hontañón. Today, Oviedo University is the only public institution of higher education in Asturias, with departments spanning the sciences, engineering, and humanities, and facilities in Oviedo, Gijón and Mieres.

⑧ Museo Arqueológico Provincial

🏛 Calle San Vicente 5
🕐 9:30am-8pm Wed-Fri, 9:30am-2pm & 5-8pm Sat, 9:30am-3pm Sun
🌐 museoarqueologicode asturias.com

Since 1952, the Archaeological and Ethnographical Museum has been housed in the old Benedictine monastery of San Vicente, founded in 761. On display are Palaeolithic tools, Roman finds – including a mosaic from Vega del Ciego – pre-Romanesque treasures, such as an altar from the Iglesia de Santa María del Naranco, and Romanesque and Gothic exhibits. The permanent exhibitions are arranged thematically.

⑨ Plaza Mayor and Iglesia de San Isidoro

On this square, usually known as Plaza Constitución

→ The Baroque exterior of the Iglesia de San Isidoro

Did You Know?

Legend says that Oviedo was founded by two monks, Maximo and Fromestano, in 761.

(Constitution Square), stands the Ayuntamiento (town hall), which dates from the 16th–17th centuries. Almost completely destroyed during the Civil War, the town hall was rebuilt in 1939–40.

Looming over the square is the tower of the Jesuit Iglesia de San Isidoro, which adjoins a college that was run by the Jesuits until 1767, when Carlos III banished them from the city during the Suppression of the Jesuits. The church, featuring a Neo-Classical façade and Baroque ornamentation within, was consecrated in 1681. The building has only one tower; a second, identical tower was planned but never completed.

⑩
Monasterio de San Pelayo

🏠 Calle San Vicente 11
🕐 Church: for mass only: 8:30am, 7:30pm Mon–Fri; 8am, 7pm Sat; 8:30am, 11am, 7pm Sun; monastery: closed to public

San Pelayo is a functioning Benedictine monastery with a strict monastic rule, and is closed to visitors except for the church, which opens to the public for mass. Its construction was begun in the 10th century under the patronage of Teresa Ansúrez, the widow of Sancho de León, dubbed El Gordo (The Fat One). Initially, the church was to be dedicated to St John the Baptist, but this was changed in 987 when the reliquary of the martyr San Pelayo was brought to Oviedo. Imprisoned by the Moors, Pelayo refused to relinquish his Christian faith, for which he was brutally tortured: his hands and his feet were cut off, and he was beheaded

in 925. The remains of the Visigothic nobleman were recovered and taken to León (p134), from where they were transferred to Oviedo.

THE FIRST KINGS OF ASTURIAS

By the time Asturias was annexed by the Kingdom of León in 910, 13 rulers had sat on the Asturian throne. The first of these was the legendary Pelayo (718–35). The new state grew powerful under Alfonso II (791–842), who maintained close contact with his contemporary Charlemagne. Alfonso's successor, Ramiro I (842–50), was an avid art enthusiast, beginning construction of several churches in the vicinity of Oviedo that still exist to this day.

PRE-ROMANESQUE CHURCHES OF OVIEDO

Established in the 8th century, the Kingdom of Asturias cultivated Visigothic traditions, creating a highly original style known as Asturian. Long before the appearance of Romanesque, the Asturian architectural style was characterized by barrel vaults covering entire buildings, the use of buttressing and long arches, and low-relief sculptural decoration, inspired by Visigothic art. Preserved around Oviedo are several superb examples of this style: Santa María del Naranco; San Miguel de Lillo; and San Julián de los Prados.

SANTA MARÍA DEL NARANCO

Built in 848, Santa María del Naranco was used as a royal chamber known as the "aula regia", where royal councils of the court of King Ramiro I would be held. A two-storey structure, the building's lower part is divided into three sections. The aisleless church is illuminated by sunlight entering through the arcaded galleries (solaria) – a novel solution in European architecture of the time. Nearby, the Centro de Recepción e Interpretación Prerrománico has information about the churches in the area.

SAN MIGUEL DE LILLO

The Iglesia de San Miguel de Lillo (Church of the Archangel Michael) was commissioned in the 9th century by Ramiro I as a royal chapel. Following 18th-century remodelling, it now resembles a Byzantine building. The church is famous for its decorative motifs, based on geometric designs. It was made a UNESCO World Heritage Site in 1985.

SAN JULIÁN DE LOS PRADOS

Also known as Santullano, the Iglesia de San Julián de los Prados is the oldest pre-Romanesque shrine in Asturias, commissioned by Alfonso II in 812–42. The church features lavish murals with plant and geometrical motifs – its colours are still vibrant today.

At each end of the structure arcaded galleries allow light to stream inside.

Column shafts carved with a rope motif

Santa María del Naranco details

Triple-arched Windows

The arches of the arcades are slightly elongated rather than semicircular, which lends the building a certain slenderness.

Decorative Columns

Columns feature Romanesque spiral rope motifs *(soqueado)*. The capitals are embellished with plant motifs.

Byzantine Medallion

The interior of Santa María del Naranco features a Byzantine medallion. There are also medallions above the arcade columns.

The barrel vaulting used in the church did not appear elsewhere in Europe until the 11th century.

Richly sculpted capitals

↑ The Pre-Romanesque Santa María del Naranco, Oviedo

Santander, flanked by stunning sandy beaches ↑

❸

SANTANDER

⚑F1 **☖**Cantabria **✈**6 km (4 miles) S 🚌 🚍 🚍 **ℹ**Jardines de Pereda, s/n; www.turismodecantabria.com

Cantabria's capital enjoys a splendid location near the mouth of a deep bay, with the port on one side and mountains on the other. An important trading hub since medieval times, today the city is a centre of commerce and the arts, with a clutch of spectacular museums and galleries.

① Centro Botín

⚑Muelle de Albareda, s/n, Jardines de Pereda **⊙**Times vary, check website **🌐**centrobotin.org

Designed by prize-winning architect Renzo Piano, this museum is housed in a spectacularly eye-catching building that looks out onto the Bay of Santander. You'll need as much time to admire the building's own architecture and fine views of Santander from the rooftop terrace as you will to appreciate the extensive collections here. The centre hosts a rolling programme of modern works encompassing sculpture, installations, video, paintings and photography.

②
MAS

⚑C/Rubio 6 **⊘**For renovations, check website **🌐**museosantandermas.es

The Museo de Arte Moderno y Contemporáneo (MAS) was founded in 1907. Its collections focus on modern and contemporary art. As well as works by Cantabrian landscape artists, there is a portrait of Fernando VII by Goya, canvases by Miró and paintings by the 17th-century Portuguese artist Josefa D'Obidos. Since 1924 the museum has been housed in a building designed by Cantabrian architect Leonardo Rucabado, near Santander's main square.

---

③
Iglesia del Sagrado Corazón

⚑Calle de San José, 15

The city's Sacred Heart is a good example of Neo-Gothic

←

The futuristic exterior of the Centro Botín museum

style. This much-remodelled church, whose crypt (c 1200) was constructed on the remains of an earlier Roman building, was rebuilt after a fire in 1945. The Romanesque-Gothic aisled interior measures 31 m (102 ft) long and 18 m (59 ft) wide. Found here are the reliquaries of two martyrs – San Emeterio and San Celedonio – who were Roman legionnaires born in León. When the Romans began to persecute Christians, the brothers made a public declaration of their faith, for which they were sentenced to death by beheading; their severed heads were brought by fishing boat to Santander. The city is named after the first of these two martyrs (Portus Sancti Emeterii shortened to Sant'Emter, or Santander).

4
Museo de Prehistoria

🏠 Mercato del Este, C/ Hernán Cortés 4 🕐 Times vary, check website 🌐 museosdecantabria.es

After leaving the church, it is worth paying a visit to the Museo de Prehistoria, with its interesting collection of finds from Cantabrian caves that were inhabited in prehistoric times, such as Altamira and Puente Viesgo.

5
Playa el Sardinero

The beautiful 2-km- (1.2-mile-) long Playa el Sardinero, which shares its name with the city's northern suburbs, is one of the eight most unpolluted beaches in the world. It became popular in the mid-19th century, when the Madrid aristocracy began to visit. Bordering the beach are gardens, cafés and luxury hotels, including the imposing Hotel Real, as well as casinos. In July and August, the beach plays host to a theatre and music festival.

At the end of the bay, on the Magdalena Peninsula, is the **Palacio de la Magdalena**, a summer residence of Alfonso XIII. Built in 1911, the palace was designed by two Cantabrian architects – Javier González Riancho and Gonzálo Bringas – and is furnished in belle époque style.

Palacio de la Magdalena

🏠 Av de la Reina Victoria, s/n 🕐 For guided tours, check website 🌐 palaciomagdalena.com

EAT

La Vinoteca
Sample a tasting menu of modern Spanish-fusion dishes at this elegant restaurant.

🏠 Calle de Hernan Cortes 38 📞 942 07 57 41

€€€

DRINK

Little Bobby Speakeasy
Sip cool cocktails amid quirky decor, with classic films playing in the background.

🏠 Calle del Sol 20 🌐 littlebobby.es

Rvbicón
An easy-going jazz bar where you can enjoy a beer while listening to live music.

🏠 Calle del Sol 4 🌐 rubiconbar.es

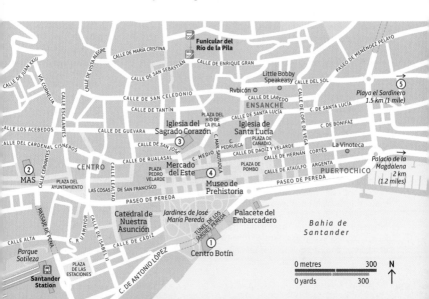

Exploring cobbled Calle Cantòn in the heart of Santillana del Mar →

④

SANTILLANA DEL MAR

🗺 **F2** 🚌 ℹ️ C/Jesús Otero 20; www.santillanadelmar turismo.com 🌐 Museo Diocesano and cloister: santillana museodiocesano.com

In his novel *Nausea*, Jean-Paul Sartre called Santillana del Mar (Santillana of the Sea) the "most beautiful town in Spain". Here an ensemble of opulent 15th- to 18th-century buildings survives largely intact, attesting to the town's aristocratic legacy.

Despite its name, Santillana del Mar is actually 3 km (nearly 2 miles) away from the sea. The town grew up around the collegiate church of Santa Juliana, an important pilgrimage centre. Today, this church houses the tomb of the local early medieval martyr St Juliana, said to have captured the devil – an event which is depicted in the murals on the walls of the church. Within, visitors can also admire the 17th-century painted reredos and a carved south door, and in the lovely cloisters, the vivid biblical scenes sculpted on the capitals.

Laid out along a north–south axis, the town's two main cobbled streets are lined by houses built by local noblemen. These have either fine wooden galleries or iron balconies, and coats of arms inlaid into their stone façades. One such mansion, on the enchanting Plaza Mayor, has been turned into a parador, offering a luxurious stay. To the east of the town centre is the Museo Diocesano, within a restored convent. It has a collection of medieval and Baroque painted carvings of religious figures, and Spanish and colonial silverware.

AGE OF THE NOBILITY

The nobility often placed extravagant mottoes and coats of arms on the façades of their residences. Many examples of this can be spotted in Santillana: the Casa de los Hombrones has a beautiful family cartouche encircled by two bearded figures; while the Casa de los Bustamante is adorned with the surprising inscription, "The Bustamante daughters are given as wives to kings".

The Torre de Don Borja, a Gothic defensive tower, is now the headquarters of the Fundación Santillana, where exhibitions and conferences are held.

In the church cloisters the Romanesque capitals are carved with images of animals and hunting scenes.

The Casa del Águila y la Parra, dating from the 16th and 17th centuries has a collection of Cantabrian art.

The Colegiata de Santa Juliana is an important Cantabrian pilgrimage centre and the most beautiful monument in Santillana.

On this cobblestoned street you'll find the 18th-century Casa de los Bustamante with its characteristic balconies.

Housed in the Convento de Regina Coeli (1592), the Museo Diocesano has a rich collection of painted figures of saints.

The pedestrianized centre of pretty Santillana del Mar ↑

11,000 BC

A rock fall sealed the entrance to the caves until their discovery in 1868.

The painted ceiling in the Museo de Altamira's replica cave chamber ↑

5

MUSEO DE ALTAMIRA

F2 **Cantabria** **Museum: 9:30am-6pm Tue-Sat (to 8pm May-Oct), 9:30am-3pm Sun** **Mon, 1 & 6 Jan, 1 May, 24-25 & 31 Dec** **museodealtamira.es**

In 1868, hunter Marcelino Sanz de Sautuola uncovered the entrance to the Altamira caves, but it was his young daughter María who first noticed the magnificent artworks here in 1879. Today visitors can admire the stunning prehistoric art at this UNESCO World Heritage Site, and learn more at the on-site museum.

The engravings and drawings at Altamira are among the oldest in Europe, with some works dating back to 36,000 BC. The depictions of herds of bison, horses and deer are painted with remarkable accuracy and expressiveness, evidently based on close observation. Close to the entrance, the Great Ceiling chamber has the greatest number of animal paintings. Most impressive is the huge deer, measuring 2.25 m (7 ft) in length.

Public entry to the caves is restricted, but the on-site museum holds an impressive replica of part of the original cave based on scientific study of methods and materials used by the occupants of Altamira in prehistoric times. There is also a programme of changing exhibitions.

VISITING THE MUSEUM

Apart from a 20-minute tour, visitors can also take part in workshops exploring the technology of Altamira's Upper Palaeolithic inhabitants. Children and adults can recreate the hand stamp art of ancient cave painters, use prehistoric techniques to make fire, or learn about the tracking techniques of Altamira's hunters and how to make and handle prehistoric weapons.

1 In the Altamira museum and research centre there are detailed replicas of hand-stencil cave paintings.

2 Palaeolithic hunting methods and prehistoric weapons are used in the hunting workshop.

3 The entrance to the Altamira caves and museum.

EXPERIENCE Asturias and Cantabria

⑥

GIJÓN

🗺 D1 ⚑ Asturias 🚆 🚌 ℹ Calle Rodriguez San Pedro (Puerto Deportivo); www.gijon.info

Asturias' largest city, this vibrant industrial port is flanked by long sandy beaches, and peppered with museums and historic ruins. Take a walk through the winding lanes of the Old Town, an ancient fishermen's quarter, for a taste of the city's Roman history.

①
Cimadevilla

Set on a narrow isthmus overlooking a popular beach, this neighbourhood is the oldest part of the city; fishermen began to settle here in Roman times. Today, the district has preserved its maritime character, offering visitors one of the most breathtaking views of the Cantabrian Sea.

A good place to start a tour of the neighbourhood is the Parque del Cerro de Santa Catalina, which features the 1990 sculpture *Elogio del Horizonte* – the symbol of the city – by the Basque artist Eduardo Chillida.

Nearby, narrow streets cluster around the Plaza Mayor, with its 19th-century

town hall, near to which stands the **Museo Casa Natal de Jovellanos**. This 16th-century house is the birthplace of Gaspar Melchor de Jovellanos – the city's most

famous resident – an eminent 18th-century author, reformer and diplomat. The house, which dates from the end of the 16th century, abuts the walls of the medieval citadel. To the right of the Plaza Mayor are the Baños Romanos, or Roman baths, built in the 1st century BC. The seafront leads to the long sandy beach, Playa San Lorenzo, which is popular with surfers.

Museo Casa Natal de Jovellanos
⚑ Plaza Jovellanos
☎ 985 18 51 52 ⏱ 9:30am-2pm & 5-7:30pm Tue-Fri, 10am-2pm & 5-7:30pm Sat-Sun

---

ASTURIAN BAGPIPES

Spanish bagpipe music combines elements of Celtic and Iberian cultures. In Spain there are six types of bagpipes, the best-known being the Galician *(gaita)* and the slightly larger Asturian. Though similar in appearance to the Scottish instrument, they differ in terms of the number of bourdon pipes, melodic range and fingering technique.

↑ Fishing boats in Gijón's busy Puerto Deportivo

② Palacio de Revillagigedo

🅐 Plaza del Marqués 2 📞 985 34 69 21 🕐 For temporary exhibitions

Built between 1704 and 1721 at the behest of Carlos Miguel Ramírez de Jove, today this Baroque palace holds a Centre for Modern Art, opened in 1991. Even if there isn't an exhibition on, it's worth seeking out for its imposing façade. Opposite the palace stands a statue of Pelayo, the Visigothic ruler who began the Reconquest (*p103*). Nearby is the Torre del Reloj, a modern tower built on the site of a 16th-century building – head to the top for stunning views of the city.

③
Museo del Pueblo de Asturias

🅐 Paseo del Doctor Fleming 877, La Güelga 🕐 Times vary, check website 🌐 museos.gijon.es

At this open-air museum, a wealth of exhibits, along with an archive and library, document the history of Asturias

and its peoples. Exhibits include the interior of a traditional Asturian cottage, two granaries, a period house from 1759 and a typical homestead from the central part of the Asturian region. A pavilion houses a permanent exhibition entitled "Asturians in the Kitchen. Everyday Life in Asturias, 1800–1965". Also part of the museum is the Museo de la Gaita (Bagpipe Museum), which contains a collection of instruments from Europe and North Africa.

Acuario

🅐 Playa de Poniente, s/n 🕐 Times vary, check website 🌐 acuario.gijon.e

Gijón's modern aquarium provides great family entertainment, with huge tanks teeming with all kinds of sea life. As well as sharks, rays and exotic fish from distant oceans, there is an exhibit re-creating the freshwater habitat of an Asturian river.

Must See

EAT

V. Crespo
An elegant place to try authentic Asturian cuisine; opt for the tasting menu.

🅐 Calle Periodista Adeflor 3 🌐 restaurante vcrespo.es

€€€

Ciudadela
The gourmet tapas and daily specials here are prepared with whatever is in season. Try creative variations of *pote Asturiana* (a hearty stew), or the steak with port wine.

🅐 C/Capua 7 📞 985 34 77 32 🚫 Sun dinner; Mon

€€€

0 metres 400 N
0 yards 400 ↑

Parque del Cerro de Santa Catalina

Comandancia Militar de Marina

CALLE HONESTO BATALON

CALLE CLAUDIO ALVARGONZÁLEZ

Puerto

① Cimadevila

AVE LA SALLE

Mar Cantábrico

Palacio de ② Revillagigedo

PLAZA MAYOR

Ayuntamiento

C. MEJQUIADES ALVAREZ

Acuario 500 m (550 yd) ④

C. RODRÍGUEZ SAN PEDRO

CALLE MARQUÉS DE SAN ESTEBAN

PL. DE ITALIA

CALLE DEL INSTITUTO

CALLE SAN BERNARDO

C. DE CABRALES

PASEO DEL MURO DE SAN LORENZO

Playa San Lorenzo

Museo del Pueblo de Asturias 1.5 km (1 mile)

PL. DEL CARMEN

C. MARIANO MORE

EL CARMEN

C. DE GARAYA

C. DE LA LIBERTAD

CALLE JOVELLANOS

Ciudadela

CENTRO

AVE DE RUFO GARCÍA RENDUELES

③

C. SANZ CRESPO

PL. DEL HUMEDAL

C. DE LOS MOROS

C. DE BEGOÑA

CALLE DE MENÉNDEZ VALDÉS

PLAZA DE SAN MIGUEL

C. DE MARQÉS DE CASA VALDÉS

CALLE PLAYA

AVE DE PORTUGAL

C. CANDÁS LLANES

MAGNUS BLIKSTAD

CALLE DE ARGÜELLES

PLAZA SEIS DE AGOSTO

CALLE C. VELASCO

San Lorenzo

CALLE URÍA

AVE DE LOS CAMPOS

AVE DE LA COSTA

Jardines de Begoña

PLAZA DE EUROPA

V. Crespo

CALLE DE CABRALES

CALLE DINDURRA

AVE DE LA COSTA

CALLE ADOSINDA

LAVIADA

AVE DE LA CONSTITUCIÓN

AVE DE SCHULTZ

Nuestra Señora de Begoña

EXPERIENCE MORE

The gorgeous Cudillero harbour, bathed in sunshine ↑

7

Castro de Coaña

🅰C1 🏛Asturias 📍5 km (3 miles) SW of Navia
📞985 97 84 01 🕐Wed–Sun

This is one of the most important centres of Celti-Iberian culture. *Castros* were the most common type of settlement at the end of the Bronze Age, consisting of circular dwellings surrounded by moats and palisades. The Castro de Coaña, with 80 dwellings, dates from the Iron Age; the first archaeological digs took place here in 1877. The on-site museum displays finds that have been unearthed, and guided tours are offered in July and August.

Nearby Navia is a typical Asturian fishing village. On 15 August is its festival of the cult of the Virgin, who, according to legend, saved a group of fishermen from drowning. The fiesta has its own local delicacy – *Venera de Navia*, a beautifully decorated almond cake. There are lovely beaches just to the east at Frexulfe near Puerto de Vega.

8

Castropol

🅰C1 🏛Asturias
ℹ Plaza del Ayuntamiento; www.castropol.es

This pretty fishing port, with its narrow streets and white-washed buildings, occupies the eastern bank of the Eo river, which marks the border between Asturias and Galicia. The town lies opposite Ribadeo in Galicia (*p80*). Its name derives from the nine well-preserved ancient *castros* located here.

For centuries, the town was an important commercial centre, where trade in grain, timber, iron, salt, wine and textiles flourished.

Castropol also played an important role as a town situated on the pilgrimage route to Santiago de Compostela (*p70*). The parish Iglesia de Santiago dates from the 17th century, having been built on the site of an earlier church. Until the 19th century, it served as a shelter for weary pilgrims.

Also noteworthy is the Capilla Santa María, built in 1461, with a Gothic alabaster figure of the Virgin and Child inside. It was apparently the only building in the town to have escaped a devastating fire in 1587. Of interest, too, are the palaces that once belonged to the port's wealthier inhabitants, such as the Palacio Vellador, the Palacio de los Marqueses de Santa Cruz and the Palacio Villarosita, which bear family coats of arms on their façades.

The town's green space is the lovely, manicured Parque de Vicente Loriente. Opened in 1911, it is named after a Cuban émigré who undertook several initiatives to aid the town's development.

9

Cudillero

🅰D1 🏛Asturias
ℹ Puerto del Oeste; www.cudillero.es

With its streets winding down an impossibly steep cliffside to end at a picture-perfect harbour, this fishing village attracts large numbers of visitors, thanks also to its outdoor cafés and excellent seafood restaurants. The houses, with their red roofs, seem to merge imperceptibly with the hillsides that cascade down towards the sea. The name Cudillero derives from the word *codillo* (elbow), referring to the shape of the village. A pleasant walk can be taken to the port and observation point, from where there is a panoramic view of the surrounding area. The landscape and gorgeous vistas certainly inspired director José Luis Garci, who shot here some of the scenes for *Volver a Empezar* (1982) – the first Spanish film to win an Oscar.

The port itself is graced with fine architecture. The oldest buildings are a 13th-century Romanesque chapel – the Capilla de Humilladero – and the Gothic Iglesia de San Pedro, from the 16th century.

CELTIBERIAN CULTURE

When the Celts reached the Iberian Peninsula during the first millennium BC, their cultures mixed and mingled with that of the native Iberian peoples, and a new local Celtiberian culture was established. The Bronze Age Celtiberians were a people particularly skilled at metalwork. They built distinctive settlements across Northern Spain and Portugal, of which the Castro de Coaña is one of the most important examples.

 10

Taramundi

C1 Asturias Solleiro 14; www.taramundi.net

Situated in the remote Los Oscos region, on the border with Galicia, is the small village of Taramundi. In the surrounding forests visitors can not only admire the beautiful natural environment but also acquaint themselves with the traditions of local craftsmanship. The tourist information office can provide information on six hiking routes through the area. Of particular interest is Grandas de Salime – 30 km (19 miles) to the southeast – where traditional handicrafts are displayed in the local **Museo Etnográfico**.

Taramundi is celebrated above all for its wrought-iron craftsmanship. Iron ore was first mined in the area by the Romans, and today there are many forges in and around the village, where craftsmen can be seen making traditional knives with decorated wooden handles. The skill of artistic smithery is still passed down through the generations.

Taramundi is also justly renowned for the high-quality liqueurs produced here.

Museo Etnográfico

 Avda del Ferreiro 16, Grandas de Salime 985 62 72 43 May-Sep: 11am-2:30pm & 4-8pm Tue-Sat, 11am-3pm Sun; Oct-Apr: 11am-2pm & 4-6:30pm Tue-Fri, 11am-2:30pm & 4-6:30pm Sat, 11am-3pm Sun

---

11

Luarca

D1 Asturias Plaza Alfonso X El Sabio, s/n; www.turismoluarca.com

This picturesque fishing port is considered one of the most attractive places on the northern coast. Specializing in tuna, Luarca arose at the mouth of the meandering Río Negro, across which many bridges have been built. Its traditional character is reflected in the charmingly old-fashioned *chigres*, or tavernas, where one can sample the excellent local cider. The port brims with bars and good-value restaurants serving up the catch of the day, unloaded every afternoon when the fishermen return with their boats. On a cliff overlooking the narrow beach are a chapel and an impressive lighthouse.

EAT

Ronda 14
Go to Ronda 14 in Avilés for tapas with a twist. The chefs combine Japanese and Peruvian cuisine to create unique dishes.

D1 Calle de Alfonso VII 20, Avilés ronda14.es

Restaurante Los Arándanos
A winding walk up to this restaurant rewards you with sweeping views of the surrounding hills, and regional specialities, like rich fabada bean stew.

C1 Caserio Almallos, Taramundi 615 25 72 53 Lunch only, phone ahead

---

Casa Vicente
Helpful and attentive staff will make you feel at home while you enjoy a lunch of fresh seafood or superb steak overlooking the river.

C1 Avenida Galicia, Castropol 985 63 50 51

The most beautiful building in Luarca is undoubtedly the town hall, which was commissioned in 1906 by an influential family who had returned after making a fortune in Spain's colonies. Some of the rooms have been converted into exclusive tourist accommodation. Luarca's most important fiesta is San Timoteo, which begins on the evening of 21 August with a fireworks display on the seafront.

⑫

Parque Natural de Somiedo

🅰D2 **ℹ️ Centro de Recepción, Pola de Somiedo; www.somiedorural.com**

One of the most untouched areas of wilderness left in western Europe, this large park straddles the Cantabrian mountains, covering 300 sq km (116 sq miles). A UNESCO Biosphere Reserve, Somiedo is one of the most representative mountain ecosystems on the Iberian Peninsula. Its beech and oak forests, and high meadows provide sanctuary for wolves, brown bears and capercaillies (a large European grouse). Somiedo's meadows are home to several species of wild flowers, which temper the harsh landscape.

The park's post-glacial Saliencia lakes are remarkable for their breathtaking settings and diverse geology of slate, quartzite and limestone. The most spectacular lake here is the Lago del Valle, the largest in Asturias, which lies 1,550 m (5,085 ft) above sea level.

Scattered throughout the landscape are distinctive traditional thatched stone cabins known as *teitos*. Herdsman live in these cabins in spring and summer while their animals graze in the lush mountain pastures.

↑ San Martín de Teverga, sheltered by the slopes of the Valle de Teverga

⑬

Valle de Teverga

🅰D2 **🄰 Asturias**
ℹ️ Calle Dr García Miranda; www.tevergaturismo.com

This area lies to the south of Oviedo (p106). Its main attractions are forests, wild scenery, meandering rivers and foaming waterfalls. Three caves – Cueva Huerta, Cueva de Vistulaz and Vegalonga – have prehistoric wall paintings. The **Parque de la Prehistoria** illustrates the lives and art of the earliest cave dwellers.

The regional capital is La Plaza, whose Iglesia de San Pedro was built in 1069–76. Just to the west of La Plaza is Villanueva, with its equally beautiful Romanesque Iglesia de Santa María. The local culinary delicacies are roast mutton and *masera* cheese.

Parque de la Prehistoria

⊛⊛ **🄰 San Salvador de Alesga** **🄾 Times vary, check website** **🅦 parquedelaprehistoria.es**

⑭

Salas and Valle del Narcea

🅰D1 **🄰 Asturias 🚌**
ℹ️ Plaza de la Campa, Salas; 985 83 09 88

Salas is the birthplace of the Marquis de Valdés-Salas, the founder of the university in Oviedo and one of the main instigators of the Inquisition. The main highlight is the beautiful Old Town, built around the imposing castle, once the residence of the archbishop. The Iglesia de San Martín was consecrated in 896 and rebuilt in the 10th century. Also noteworthy is the Iglesia de Santa María, which dates from 1549 and is situated on the main square.

South of Salas extends a beautiful, wild valley known as the Valle del Narcea. Green and secluded, it is an excellent place for walking, hiking and fishing. The villages here are known for fine ham and traditional crafts.

BROWN BEARS

The brown bear - Europe's largest land predator - is found in the mountain regions of Asturias and in nature reserves such as Somiedo. In the Middle Ages, the brown bear enjoyed great respect, as evidenced by the fact that images of the animal often appeared in coats of arms. Hunting and the destruction of its natural forest habitat caused a rapid decline in numbers. However, things have been improving steadily since the 1990s, and it is estimated that there are now 250 brown bears in Somiedo.

⓯

Avilés

🅐D1 🅐Asturias 🅸Calle Ruíz Gómez 21; 985 54 43 25

Though primarily an industrial town and a transport hub, Avilés rewards visitors with its delightful Old Town and various significant historical buildings. In the heart of the Old Town, the Plaza de España is surrounded by 14th- and 15th-century buildings, and home to the majority of the town's shops, bars and hotels. Here too is the vast Parque de Ferrera, maintained in the style of an English garden. Well worth visiting is the 12th-century Romanesque Iglesia de San Nicolás de Bari, occupying the site of an earlier shrine built as part of a Franciscan monastery.

The town's four well-preserved palaces are the 14th-century Palacio de Valdecarzana, the oldest secular building in Avilés; the Palacio del Marqués de Camposagrado, completed in 1663 but Renaissance in appearance; the Palacio del Marqués de Ferrera, from the start of the 18th century, frequented by visiting royalty; and the early 20th-century Palacio de Balsera, which houses a music conservatory.

A short walk from the Old Town is the modernist **Centro Niemeyer**, designed by influential Brazilian architect Oscar Niemeyer and opened in 2011. The architecturally striking centre hosts performances and exhibitions, and contains a viewing tower.

Avilés celebrates its Easter Fiesta del Bollo with a parade of floats and street parties. The festivities are named for the sweet buns given to children by their godparents on Easter Sunday.

Centro Niemeyer

 🅐Av del Zinc 🕙Times vary, check website 🆆niemayercenter.org

⓰

Bárzana and Bermiego

🅐D2 🅐Asturias 🅸Carretera General, Bárzana; 985 76 81 60 (summer only)

These are two of the most beautiful mountain villages in Asturias. It was here that the Visigothic aristocracy hid during the Moorish invasion. Today Bárzana and Bermiego are known for their excellent bread and colourful fiestas.

Bermiego features traditional red-roofed houses and characteristic *hórreos (p85)*. The village is surrounded by the Gamonal hills, and it's an easy hike to the summit of Gamonitero mountain, from which there are beautiful panoramic views. Bermiego's local landmarks are the church of Santa María and a yew tree beside it of impressive dimensions: 14 m (46 ft) high, and with a trunk some 13 m (43 ft) in diameter.

In attractive Bárzana the excellent **Museo Etnográfico de Quirós** presents life in the Asturian countryside in times past. On the first floor is a series of reconstructed farm buildings and cattle pens; on the second, a display of tools and craft products.

Museo Etnográfico de Quirós

 🅐Bárzana 🕙Times vary, check website for details 🆆quiros.es/museo-etnografico

---

STAY

Hotel La Rectoral de Taramundi

This lovely old stone building looks out onto forested hills.

🅐C1 🅐Cuesta de la Rectoral, Taramundi 🆆larectoral.com

€€€

Hotel Villa Rosario II

Palatial four-star luxury just a stone's throw from the beach.

🅐E1 🅐Calle Dionisio Ruisanchez 6, Ribadesella 🆆hotelvillarosario.com

€€€

←

Traditional stone paving and arcaded shops in Avilés

17

Valdediós

E1 Asturias Monasterio de Santa María; www.monasteriovaldedios.com

A highlight of this hamlet is the pre-Romanesque Iglesia de San Salvador, founded by Alfonso III in 893. The interior painted decoration is very well preserved, assuming in places geometric, Moorish forms. Nearby stands the Cistercian Monasterio de Santa María, which dates from 1200, with beautiful cloisters from 1522. The San Juan Order runs a hostel here to finance restoration works.

Around 5 km (3 miles) southeast of Valdediós is Nava, well known for its July cider festival. The local, four-room Museo de la Sidra houses an interesting exhibit on the cider-making process.

18

Villaviciosa

E1 Asturias Calle Agua 29; www.villaviciosa.es

The Ría de Villaviciosa, which cuts inland for 8 km (5 miles), is rich in plant and animal life. You can take a fishing boat or kayak trip along the *ría* (estuary), which is lined by nice beaches. At the end of the *ría* is Villaviciosa, a little resort town with well-preserved Romanesque buildings. The most famous is the Iglesia de Santa María de Oliva, built in the late 13th century. The stonemasons introduced early Gothic elements: the pointed arches in the main portal and rose windows. This mixing of architectural styles is very evident in Amandi, a small but picturesque district of the town. The Iglesia de San Juan of 1134, initially designed as a monastery church, is an example of late Romanesque style, its interior adorned with fine sculptural decoration.

Villaviciosa is also known as the cider capital of Asturias, and is surrounded by apple orchards, with many traditional *sidrerías* (cider bars) in town.

19

Ribadesella

E1 Asturias Paseo Princesa Letizia; www.ribadesella.es

The old port straddling the mouth of the Sella river dates from the reign of Alfonso X of Castile, who founded this enchanting seaside town. It has always been of strategic importance for the area.

Today, on one side of the river is the lively seaport full of tapas bars serving fresh fish, while on the other is the more modern part, with a beautiful broad beach.

On the edge of the town is the **Cueva de Tito Bustillo**, a series of interconnected caves with beautiful prehistoric paintings dating from the Palaeolithic era. They include superb black-and-red images of stags' and horses' heads. To protect the paintings, only 15 visitors are allowed on each guided tour.

Nearby is the charming town of Llanes, ever popular for its medieval quarter, busy fishing port and beautiful sandy beaches.

The Asturian coast is the most important Jurassic site in Spain. The interactive, family-oriented **Museo Jurásico** near Colunga, 20 km (12.5 miles) west of Ribadesella, contains around 20 replica dinosaurs. A great walking trail, which takes in some of the best fossils and dinosaur tracks in the region, begins on nearby Griega beach.

INSIDER TIP
Descent of the Sella

A mighty flotilla of colourful kayaks rushes through Ribadesella on the first Saturday in August, when there's a thrilling race downriver to the sea. Grab a spot on or by the bridge.

Cueva de Tito Bustillo
Ribadesella
Mid-Mar-Oct: 10am-5pm Wed-Sun. Children over 7 only centrotitobustillo.com

Museo Jurásico
Playa de la Griega, Colunga Times vary, check website museojurasicoasturias.com

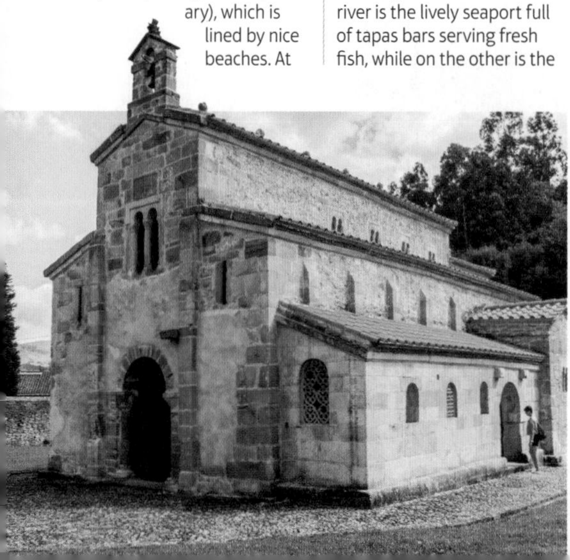

←
The pre-Romanesque church of San Salvador in Valdediós

Dancing at Nava festival, which celebrates the produce of Asturias ↑

ASTURIAN SPECIALITIES

Asturian food is hearty, based on flavourful meat, fresh fish, strong cheeses and fresh vegetables. Above all, Asturias is famous for its cider *(sidra)* – an alcoholic drink that is used in many dishes, too.

PLENTIFUL PRODUCE

Across Northern Spain, bay-studded coasts and mountain streams provide delicious fresh fish and seafood. Trout from mountain streams, red mullet, and mackerel are often served simply grilled or simmered in hearty *caldereta* (fish stew) along with shellfish like gooseneck barnacles and shrimp. While inland, fertile valleys bear delicious fruit and vegetables, such as the apples destined for Asturian cider. The region's lush pastures form the heart of Spanish dairy country: rich milk, cream and over 40 varieties of excellent cheese come from Asturias.

ASTURIAN CIDER

Cider has been produced in Asturias since medieval times. Usually drunk at *sidrerías* or *chigres* (cider houses), this fizzy alcoholic beverage is celebrated at festivals in Nava and Gijón, during which dancing and Asturian folk songs add to the festivities. Traditionally cider is poured into a glass from a bottle held high above the head to give it a fizzy top.

↑ Pouring cider in the traditional Asturian way at Gijón's cider festival

REGIONAL DELICACIES

Queso Asturiano
Asturian cheese, made from cow's, sheep's or goat's milk, has a pungent taste and aroma. Cabrales and Taramundi are the best known.

Asturian Honey
The village of Llanos de Somerón is famous for its delicious mixed-blossom honey, produced from the nectar of heather and chestnut flowers.

Sidra
Cider is stored in wooden casks at the optimum temperature of 9-10°C (48–50°F). Ideally, the maturation process should take five to six months.

Fabada Asturiana
A tasty regional comfort food, *fabada* is made from Asturian beans *(fabes)* and meats, including local chorizo, bacon and ham, which infuse the beans with savoury flavour.

⑳ Comillas

🗺 F2 📍 Cantabria
ℹ Plaza Joaquín del Piélago
I; www.comillas.es

This pretty resort is known for its unusual buildings designed by Catalan Modernista architects. Comillas' best-known monument is **El Capricho de Gaudí**, built in 1883–5, a part-Mudéjar-inspired fantasy palace. Antonio López y López, the first Marquis of Comillas, hired Joan Martorell to design the **Palacio de Sobrellano** (1881), a huge and intricate Neo-Gothic edifice. Visits are by guided tour only.

The Modernista Universidad Pontificia was designed by Joan Martorell to plans by Domènech i Montaner.

Some 11 km (7 miles) from Comillas is the tiny Cabezón de la Sal, known already in Roman times as a centre of the salt trade. Of note are the magnificent residences, especially the 18th-century Palacio de la Bodega, and the Baroque Iglesia de San Martín, dating from the beginning of the 17th century. The best time to visit Cabezón de la Sal is on the second Sunday in August – Regional Cantabria Day – when you can gain an insight into the colourful local traditions.

↑ Ceramics adding colour to Gaudí's Moorish El Capricho in Comillas

Palacio de Sobrellano

🕐 ♿ 📅 Times vary, check website 🌐 centros.cultura decantabria.com/sobrellano-palace

El Capricho de Gaudí

🕐 ♿ 📍 Barrio de Sobrellano 📅 Times vary, check website 🌐 elcaprichodegaudi.com

---

㉑ Alto Campoo

🗺 F2 📍 Cantabria
ℹ Estación de Montaña; www.altocampoo.com/la-estacion

High in the Cantabrian mountains, this small but excellent ski resort lies below the three alpine peaks of El Cuchillón, El Chivo and Pico de Tres Mares. The last of these, the "Peak of the Three Seas", is so called because the rivers rising near it flow into the Mediterranean, the Atlantic and the Bay of Biscay. From its 2,175-m (7,136-ft) summit, reached by chairlift, there is a breathtaking panorama of the Picos de Europa and other

---

> ### GAUDÍ IN CANTABRIA
>
> El Capricho de Gaudí is one of very few designs by Antoni Gaudí located outside Barcelona. The Catalonian architect was commissioned to create this fantasy palace by entrepreneur Eusebi Güell, who had admired Gaudí's work at a 1878 exhibition in Paris. Gaudí would create the caprice of architecture, El Capricho, for Güell's father-in-law, Antonio López y López, the Marquis of Comillas. Typifying Gaudí's eclectic style, the fairytale structure reveals his characteristic freedom of composition.

> **The "Peak of the Three Seas" is so called because the rivers rising near it flow into the Mediterranean, the Atlantic and the Bay of Biscay.**

mountain chains. The resort has downhill runs totalling 27 km (17 miles) in length and 22 pistes.

___

Valle de Cabuérniga

F2 · **Cantabria**
Ayuntamiento, Ruente; 942 70 91 04

This picturesque valley is home to many interesting villages. A good place to start is Bárcena Mayor, which is notable for its typical Cantabrian rural architecture. The inhabitants of the village cultivate old craft traditions – in particular carpentry. The village of Lamiña features a 10th-century hermitage (Ermita de San Fructoso), while Ucieda has a beautiful nature reserve with beech and oak forests.

___

San Vicente de la Barquera

F2 · **Cantabria**
Avda del Generalísimo 20; 942 71 07 97

The first mention of this beautiful maritime town dates from Roman times, when a major port existed here. In medieval times, Alfonso I of Asturias populated the expanding town under his colonization policy, and in subsequent centuries, it became an important stopover for pilgrims travelling to Santiago de Compostela (*p70*). Today, San Vicente has a rich artistic legacy, which includes the impressive Iglesia de Santa María de los Ángeles, built between the 13th and 16th centuries. The church holds the lovely tomb of the Inquisitor Antonio del Corro, who is shown reclining, immersed in the pages of a book.

The 15th-century monastery of El Santuario de la Barquera and El Convento de San Luis is worth a visit. Now a private property, it is open to visitors between April and July, and in mid-September–October.

To the north of San Vicente there are broad picturesque beaches, while inland (28 km/ 17 miles) south) is the magnificent cave of **El Soplao**. The cave chamber has brilliant white helictites (like stalactites, but with a curious twisted form), which are so dazzling that El Soplao has been nicknamed "the subterranean Sistine Chapel".

El Soplao

⊗ ⊗ · 28 km (17 miles) S of San Vicente · Times vary, check website · elsoplao.es

TOP 4 · REGIONAL FIESTAS

La Folía
On the second Sunday after Easter, boats are paraded through San Vicente de la Barquera, while girls sing traditional songs on the shore.

Nuestra Señora de Covadonga
Crowds converge on the shrine of Covadonga to pay homage to the patron saint of Asturias on 8 September.

Virgen del Carmen
Comillas pays homage to the Virgin with processions and parades on 16 July.

Battle of the Flowers
On the last Friday of August, floats adorned with flowers are paraded through Laredo.

The unusual and delicate helictites in the El Soplao cave ↑

EAT

El Marqués

Set on the riverbank, this eatery offers an à la carte menu along with a vast variety of tapas. Make sure to try the catch of the day – fresh seafood is its speciality.

 F2 Calle Manuel Pérez Mazo, Puente Viesgo 648 09 22 12

€€€

Mesón Marinero

The seafood could hardly be fresher here, overlooking Castro Urdiales' harbour. The varied menu includes luxurious choices for a special treat.

 G2 Calle de la Correría 19, Castro Urdiales mesonmarinero.com

€€€

Castro Urdiales

G2 Cantabria Avda de la Constitución 1; www. turismocastrourdiales.net

Visitors flock to this popular holiday resort for the beautiful beaches: Playa del Brazomar and Playa Ostende, which can be reached along an attractive trail that skirts the cliffs. There is also a lovely harbourside *paseo* (walkway). Rising on a promontory above the town is the imposing Iglesia de Santa María, a fascinating example of Cantabrian Gothic. It was built in the 13th century, after which numerous Gothic elements were added. Inside is a tall Gothic sculpture of Mary with the infant Jesus in her lap, and a moving canvas of *The Dying Christ* attributed to Francisco de Zurbarán.

Valle del Besaya

F2

As early as Roman times, a north–south road linking the

 GREAT VIEW
Swirling Seas

Castro Urdiales' medieval bridge offers pretty harbour vistas, but peer down for an even more mesmerizing view: a pool of seawater surrounds the bridge, hypnotically crashing against the rocks.

Cantabrian coast with central Spain ran through this long valley. Romanesque buildings can be found here, including small churches, which would have been covered initially with wooden roofs. Of special interest are the severe-looking Iglesia de Barcena de Pie de Concha and the Iglesia de Santa María de Yermo. The latter has an interesting portico comprising five archivolts; below it is a sculpture of a knight fighting a dragon.

Torrelavega, the capital of the Valle del Besaya, has several historic monuments, such as the Convento de las Adres, the Iglesia de la Virgen Grande and the Iglesia de la Nuestra Señora de Asunción.

Fishing boats clustered in Castro Urdiales harbour ↑

Around 50 km (30 miles) south of the valley, Retortillo is famous for its excellent therapeutic spa. At nearby Julióbriga are the remains of a town built by the Romans during the Cantabria wars fought against Ancient Cantabrians. The Domus de Lulobriga is a reconstruction of a Roman villa, which has been erected among the ruins of an original Roman dwelling.

↑ The village of Puente Viesgo, set amid verdant hills

26 Laredo

🅰 G2 🅰 Cantabria
🛈 Alameda Miramar, s/n; www.laredo.es

Laredo is a historic port and Cantabria's biggest beach resort. In its beautiful Old Town are remnants of medieval walls and gates. The narrow streets lead up to the 13th-century Gothic Iglesia de Santa María la Asunción, with a 15th-century Flemish reredos of the Virgin Mary of Bethlehem. Worth visiting, too, is the 16th-century Convento de San Francisco and its museum, designed in the Herrera style with a Renaissance cloister.

On the last Friday in August, Laredo hosts its Batalla de Flores, "Battle of the Flowers". Floats bearing gigantic figures elaborately decorated with flowers are paraded through the streets, after which the winner is chosen and the evening's partying can begin.

27 Soba and Ramales de la Victoria

🅰 G2 🛈 Calle Barón de Adzaneta 5, Ramales de la Victoria; 942 64 60 04

These two villages are set in the mountain valley of Asón, once used as a route linking the port of Laredo with central Spain. Soba offers excellent sightseeing trails with panoramic views. Ramales de la Victoria owes the second part of its name to the victorious battle fought here by the liberals during the first Carlist War (p55). While in Ramales, be sure to visit the mid-17th-century Iglesia de San Pedro and the Iglesia Gibaja, which was begun in the mid-16th century. Prehistoric caves can be seen nearby, such as the Cueva de Covanalas, 2 km (1.2 miles) south of Ramales, where depictions of human and animal figures can be viewed in two small galleries.

28 Puente Viesgo

🅰 F2 🅰 Cantabria
🛈 puenteviesgo.es

This charming spa village is best known for **El Monte Castillo**, a complex of caves dotted around the surrounding limstone hills. Late Palaeolithic cave dwellers used the complex as a sanctuary and left intriguing, expressive cave paintings. The Cueva "El Castillo", discovered in 1903, has walls covered in drawings of horses and bison, but the highlight is the series of hand prints, regarded as the earliest examples of cave art in the Franco-Cantabrian zone, preceding all other geometric and figural images. The prints were made by blowing mineral dyes – probably through a bone pipe – onto a hand pressed against the wall.

The Cueva "Las Monedas" contains beautiful stalactites and stalagmites, with unusual coloration due to the mixture of minerals and calcium. The paintings in this cave were made with coal and thus are black; they depict horses, reindeer, goats, bears and bison, as well as some signs, dating back 13,000 years.

El Monte Castillo
Ⓢ Ⓓ ⏰ Times vary, check website 🆆 cuevas.culturade cantabria.com

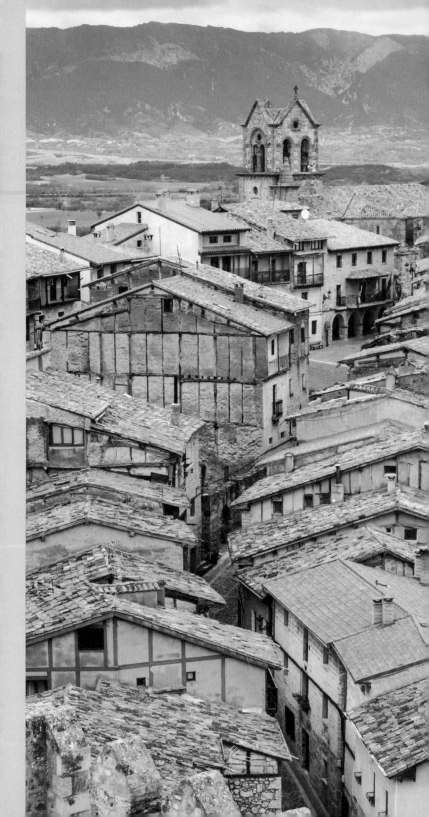

NORTHERN CASTILLA AND LEÓN

The territories of the two rival medieval kingdoms of Castile and León, occupying the northern half of the great plateau in the centre of Spain, now form the country's largest region, or *comunidad autónoma*.

Castile and León were first brought together under one crown in 1037 by Fernando I, and the powerful kingdom became one of the driving forces of the *reconquista*, seizing territory from the Moors. El Cid, the legendary Christian hero, was born near Burgos. The two kingdoms were divided again on the death of Alfonso VII in 1157 and were only consolidated into one kingdom in 1230. Alfonso IX of León had bequeathed his kingdom to his two eldest daughters, Sancha and Dulce, on his death, but his son, Fernando III of Castile, successfully contested the will and formed the united kingdom of Castilla y León.

This kingdom became the cradle of the nation. Through the marriage of Isabel I of Castile to Fernando II of Aragón in 1469, Catalonia became part of the domain and Isabel and Fernando's reign saw the beginnings of a united Christian Spain, with the conquest of Moorish Granada in 1492. In the 16th century, wealth poured into the area as a result of the wool trade and spoils seized from the New World. These newfound riches financed the building of great monuments to Castilla y León's eminence, including Burgos' exuberantly decorated Gothic cathedral, and León's cathedral, with its wonderful stained glass.

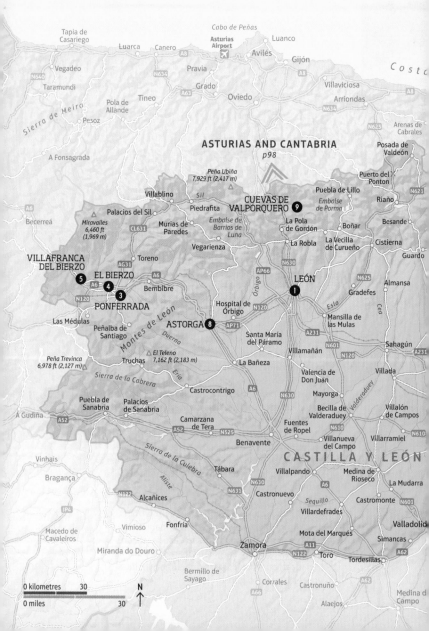

NORTHERN
CASTILLA
AND LEÓN

*Atlantic
Ocean*

Mar Cantabrico

Tapia de
Casariego

Luarca   Canero

Vegadeo

Taramundi   N634

Sierra de Meiro

Pola de
Allande

A Fonsagrada

Pesoz

Tineo

A61

Cabo de Peñas

Asturias
Airport

Avilés

Luanco

Gijón

Costa

A8

Villaviciosa

Pravia

Grado

Oviedo

Arriondas

N634

N625

Arenas de
Cabrales

ASTURIAS AND CANTABRIA
p98

Posada de
Valdeón

Puerto del
Ponton

N621

Peña Ubiña
7,929 ft (2,417 m)

Villablino

Palacios del Sil

Becerreá   Miravalles
6,460 ft
(1,969 m)

CL631

**VILLAFRANCA
DEL BIERZO**

A6

EL BIERZO

N120

4

3
PONFERRADA

Las Médulas

Peñalba de
Santiago

Peña Trevinca
6,978 ft (2,127 m)

Vinhais

Braganza

IP4

Macedo de
Cavaleiros

5

Sil

Piedrafita

Murias de
Paredes

Vegarienza

Toreno

AG31

Bembibre

A6

Montes de León

Sierra de la Cabrera

Puebla de
Sanabria

Palacios
de Sanabria

N122

Alcañices

Vimioso

Fonfría

Miranda do Douro

*Embalse de
Barrios de
Luna*

Órbigo

La Pola
de Gordón

La Robla

CUEVAS DE
VALPORQUERO

Puebla de Lillo

9

*Embalse
de Porma*

Riaño

Besande

La Vecilla
de Curueño

Boñar

Cistierna

Guardo

N630

AP66

LEÓN

1

N625

Almansa

Gradefes

Mansilla
las Mulas

A231

Esla

Hospital de
Órbigo

ASTORGA

8

AP71

El Teleno
7,162 ft (2,183 m)

Duerno

Truchas

Santa María
del Páramo

La Bañeza

Eria

Castrocontrigo

A6

N630

Camarzana
de Tera

A52

N525

Benavente

Sierra de la Culebra

Tábara

N630

N631

Castronuevo

Aliste

Zamora

N122

Toro

Bermillo de
Sayago

Corrales

Castronuño

Alaejos

Sahagún

A231

Villamañán

N601

Valencia de
Don Juan

Mayorga

Villanueva
del Campo

N601

N610

Becilla de
Valderaduey

Villalón
de Campos

Valderaduey

N610

Villarramiel

CASTILLA Y LEÓN

Villalpando

A6

Medina de
Rioseco

La Mudarra

Castromonte

N601

Villardefrades

Sequillo

Mota del Marqués

A11

Tordesillas

A62

Villada

Villalón

Cea

0 kilometres   30

0 miles   30

N
↑

Medina del
Campo

A66

Valladolid

Simancas

Portsmouth,
Plymouth

NORTHERN CASTILLA AND LEÓN

Must Sees
1. León
2. Burgos

Experience More
3. Ponferrada
4. El Bierzo

5. Villafranca del Bierzo
6. Aguilar de Campoo
7. Briviesca
8. Astorga
9. Cuevas de Valporquero
10. Frómista

The Renaissance Palacio de los Guzmanes, in León's old quarter

---

❶

LEÓN

🅰D3 ✈8 km (5 miles) W 🚂 🚌 ℹ️ Plaza de Regla, 2; www.leon.es

León was founded in AD 68 as a camp for the Romans' Seventh Legion. In 914, King Ordoño II transferred the Christian capital here from Oviedo. The town united with Castile in the 13th century, though Castile, with its capital in Burgos, began to overshadow León as the regional power. León remained strong, however, and its most stunning monuments, such as the impressive cathedral (p136), date from this period.

① Plaza Mayor

This square, in León's picturesque Old Town, is surrounded by old houses with delightful arcades. The focal point of the city's fiestas, the square comes alive in the last week of June, during the feast days of St John, with riverside fireworks, fairs and medieval festivities as well as modern forms of entertainment. During the Semana Santa (Easter Week) celebrations, the square hosts processions of monks dressed in special costumes who carry richly decorated *pasos* – platforms bearing figures of saints and scenes from the Passion of Christ.

② Palacio de los Guzmanes

🏠 Calle Ruiz de Salazar, 2 🚫 To the public

One of the most beautiful Renaissance residences, built in 1559–66, stands next to the Plaza de Santo Domingo. This three-storey building, currently the seat of the provincial authorities, is centred on an arcaded patio, with gargoyles on the roof, corner towers and numerous elaborate coats of arms on the façade.

---

③ Casa de Botines

🏠 Plaza San Marcelo, 5

Resembling a Gothic castle, this magnificent structure was designed by Antoni Gaudí in 1892. It was erected in record time – a mere 10 months. Gaudí agreed to take on the task as he was working simultaneously on the Palacio Episcopal in Astorga (p144), and could oversee both projects at once. The façade sports a figure of St George fighting the dragon, a replica of which later appeared in Gaudí's Sagrada Família in Barcelona. The building is currently used by a bank.

---

④

Basílica de San Isidoro

🏠 Plaza San Isidoro 4 🕐 Times vary, check website 🅦 museosanisidorodeleon.com

Adjoining the city walls, this basilica was built on the

remains of an earlier church to house the relics of San Isidoro of Seville. Its construction spanned the 10th to mid-18th centuries. The walls of the royal mausoleum – the final resting place of 23 monarchs, 10 princes, 9 counts and several nobles – are decorated with 12th-century murals. Among them is a cycle devoted to the life of Christ, including a powerful Last Supper, and one surviving sign of the zodiac. The museum contains paintings and frescoes from the royal mausoleum.

⑤
City Walls

The old quarter is encircled by imposing walls. The history of this Roman town is a stormy one; it was not always successful in repelling attacks by the Moors. In 996, for instance, León was plundered by the ruler of the Cordoban Caliphate, Al-Mansur. The walls were subsequently fortified.

⑥
MUSAC

🏠 **Avenida Reyes Leoneses 24** ⏰ **Times vary, check website** 🌐 **musac.es**

Behind this avant-garde building's colourful façade is a contemporary art gallery, in which collections focus on works from 1989 to the

↑ The bright exterior of MUSAC art museum

present day. The gallery hosts a dynamic programme of courses and workshops.

⑦
Museo de León

🏠 **Plaza de Santo Domingo 8** ⏰ **Times vary, check website** 🌐 **museodeleon.com**

This small museum near the Convento de San Marcos has in its collections a famous ivory crucifix, the Cristo de

STAY

Hostal de San Marcos

Built in the 16th century by King Ferdinand, this late-Renaissance building is one of the finest luxury *parador* hotels in Spain. It is due to reopen in early 2020 after major refurbishments.

🏠 **Plaza de San Marcos, 7** 🌐 **parador.es**

€€€

Carrizo, dating from the 11th century. The piece originates from the Cistercian Monasterio de Carrizo, which was founded in 1176. Also displayed here is another striking crucifix – the Cruz de Penalba, encrusted with precious gems – and an altar from the Iglesia de San Marcelo.

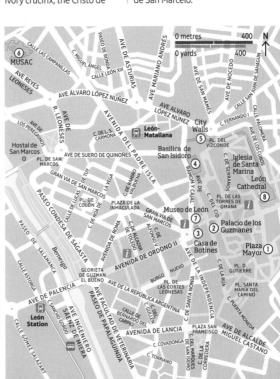

⑧ 🏛 🅼🅰

LEÓN CATHEDRAL

🏠 Plaza de Regla, León 🅿 🚌 🕐 Cathedral: Oct-Apr: 9:30am-1:30pm & 4-7pm
Mon-Sat, 9:30am-2pm Sun; May-Sep: times vary, check website for
details; Museum: times vary, check website for details 🌐 catedraldeleon.org

Santa María de León Cathedral is one of Spain's greatest religious
landmarks, expressing the devotion of the people who built it and
inspiring awe even today. The highlight of this Gothic cathedral is its
vibrant stained glass, which depicts local life over the centuries.

The present structure of golden sandstone,
built on the site of King Ordoño II's 10th-
century palace, was begun in the mid-13th
century and completed less than 100 years
later. The façade is covered with splendid
13th-century Gothic carvings. Among these,
above the Puerta de la Virgen Blanca, is one
depicting a scene from the Last Judgment.
The plan of the building is a Latin cross.

It combines a slender but very high nave,
measuring 90 m (295 ft) by 40 m (130 ft) at
its widest, with huge panels of stained glass
that flood the interior with light. To best
appreciate the dazzling colours of the stained
glass, visit on a sunny day. There is also a
museum in the cathedral, where Pedro de
Campaña's panel, *The Adoration of the Magi*,
is one of the many treasures on display.

LEÓN'S STAINED GLASS

León Cathedral's great
glory is its superb glass-
work. The 125 large
windows and 57 round
ones date from the 13th
to the 20th centuries
and cover a huge range
of subjects. *La Cacería*,
on the north wall,
depicts a hunting
scene, while the rose
window in the Capilla
del Nacimiento shows
pilgrims worshipping at
the tomb of St James in
Santiago de Compostela
in Galicia *(p66)*. Learn
more about the scenes
on a guided tour.

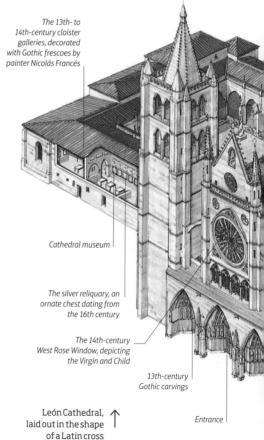

The 13th- to
14th-century cloister
galleries, decorated
with Gothic frescoes by
painter Nicolás Francés

Cathedral museum

The silver reliquary, an
ornate chest dating from
the 16th century

The 14th-century
West Rose Window, depicting
the Virgin and Child

13th-century
Gothic carvings

León Cathedral,
laid out in the shape ↑
of a Latin cross

Entrance

← The cathedral rising from the Plaza de Regla

→ The Renaissance retrochoir, with its alabaster sculptures

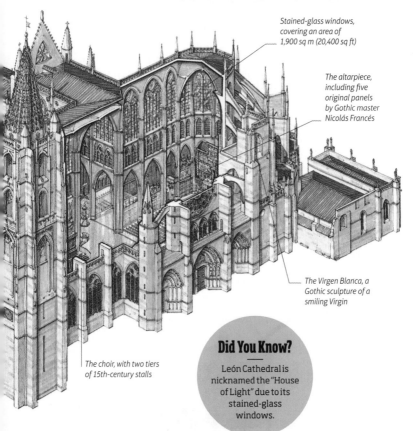

Stained-glass windows, covering an area of 1,900 sq m (20,400 sq ft)

The altarpiece, including five original panels by Gothic master Nicolás Francés

The Virgen Blanca, a Gothic sculpture of a smiling Virgin

The choir, with two tiers of 15th-century stalls

Did You Know?

León Cathedral is nicknamed the "House of Light" due to its stained-glass windows.

❷

BURGOS

▲F3 ⌂Burgos ▣🚌 🛈Plaza de Alonso Martínez 7; www. turismoburgos.org

Founded in AD 884, Burgos has played a significant role in Spanish history. It was the capital of the united kingdoms of Castile and León from 1073 until after the fall of Granada in 1492. The city grew rich from the wool trade during the 15th and 16th centuries, financing great art and architecture. Franco chose Burgos as his Civil War headquarters.

①

Iglesia de San Esteban

⌂Calle San Esteban 1 ⊙Jul-Sep: 10am-2pm & 4-7pm Tue-Sat, 10am-2pm Sun

This Gothic church replaced a Romanesque church that once stood on this site. It is no longer used for worship but houses the Museo del Retablo, a collection of 18 historic altarpieces that were taken from churches across the region, and brought here to be restored and displayed. Religious paintings, crucifixes and chalices make up a second collection.

②

Iglesia de Santa Águeda

⌂Calle Santa Águeda 12

Also known as the Iglesia de Santa Gadea, this church sits on the site where El Cid made King Alfonso VI swear that he had played no part in the murder of his elder brother, King Sancho II, in 1072. The incident is re-enacted by actors on summer evenings.

③

Real Monasterio de las Huelgas

⌂Calle de los Compases 📞947 20 16 30 ⊙10am-2pm & 4-6:30pm Tue-Sat, 10am-3pm Sun ⊠Some public hols

This 12th-century Cistercian convent was founded by Alfonso VIII. Inside is the Museo de Ricas Telas, displaying ancient fabrics from the convent's royal tombs.

EL CID

Rodrigo Díaz de Vivar was born in Vivar del Cid, north of Burgos, in 1043. He was banished from Castile after becoming embroiled in the fratricidal squabbles of the king's sons, Sancho II and Alfonso VI. He fought for the Moors, then changed side again to capture Valencia for the Christians in 1094, and ruled the city until his death. For his heroism he was named El Cid, from the Arabic *Sidi* (Lord). His tomb lies in Burgos Cathedral.

↑ The night-time skyline of Burgos, dominated by the city's cathedral

④

Iglesia de San Lorenzo

🏠 Calle San Lorenzo 8

Not far from the city's cathedral (p140), this church dedicated to St Lawrence is worth visiting for its superb Baroque ceiling.

⑤

Arco de Santa María

🏠 Plaza Rey San Fernando 9

The bridge of Santa María leads into the old quarter of Burgos through the restored Arco de Santa María, a gateway carved with statues of various local worthies.

⑥

Casa del Cordón

🏠 Plaza de la Libertad

The Casa del Cordón is a 15th-century palace that now houses a bank. It's recognizable by the Franciscan cord motif carved over the portal. A plaque declares that this is where the Catholic Monarchs welcomed Columbus in 1497, on his return from the second of his famous voyages to the Americas.

⑦

Museo de Burgos

🏠 Calle Miranda, 13 🕐 Jul-Sep: 10am-2pm & 5-8pm Tue-Sat, 10am-2pm Sun; Oct-Jun: 10am-2pm & 4-7pm Tue-Sat, 10am-2pm Sun 📅 1 & 6 Jan, 11 & 29 Jun, 1 Nov, 24, 25 & 31 Dec 🌐 museodeburgos.com

The Casa de Miranda, a Renaissace palace, houses the Museo de Burgos. The archaeological section displays finds from the Roman city of Clunia.

⑧

Museo de la Evolución Humana

🏠 Paseo Sierra de Atapuerca 🕐 10am-2:30pm & 4:30-8pm Tue-Fri, 10am-8pm Sat, Sun & public hols 🌐 museo evolucionhumana.com

This huge museum exhibits fossils dating from some 780,000 years ago. A combined entrance ticket includes transport and entrance to Yacimientos de Atapuerca, the site of one of Europe's earliest human settlements.

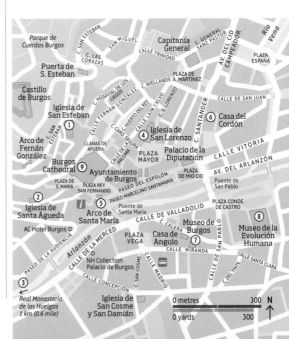

BURGOS CATHEDRAL

📍 Plaza de Santa María ⏰ 9:30am-7:30pm daily (Nov-Mar: 10am-7pm)
🌐 catedraldeburgos.info

The lacy, steel-grey spires of Santa Iglesia Catedral Basílica Metropolitana de Burgos soar above the city. Spain's third-largest cathedral, it is best known for being the final resting place of Burgos' most famous son – El Cid *(p138)*.

Burgos' cathedral was founded in 1221 by Bishop Don Mauricio under Fernando III. The ground plan – a Latin cross – measures 84 m (276 ft) by 59 m (194 ft). Its construction was carried out in stages over three centuries and involved many of the greatest architects and artists in Europe. The style of the cathedral is almost entirely Gothic, and shows influences from Germany, France and the Low Countries. The architects cleverly adapted the building to its sloping site, incorporating stairways inside and out.

Did You Know?

The cathedral doors represent forgiveness, the assumption and the immaculate conception.

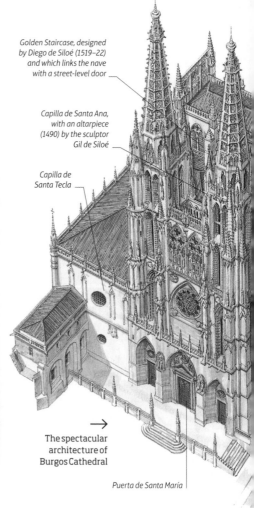

Golden Staircase, designed by Diego de Siloé (1519–22) and which links the nave with a street-level door

Capilla de Santa Ana, with an altarpiece (1490) by the sculptor Gil de Siloé

Capilla de Santa Tecla

→ The spectacular architecture of Burgos Cathedral

Puerta de Santa María

↑ The intricate, crocketed spires of the cathedral stretching into the sky at dusk

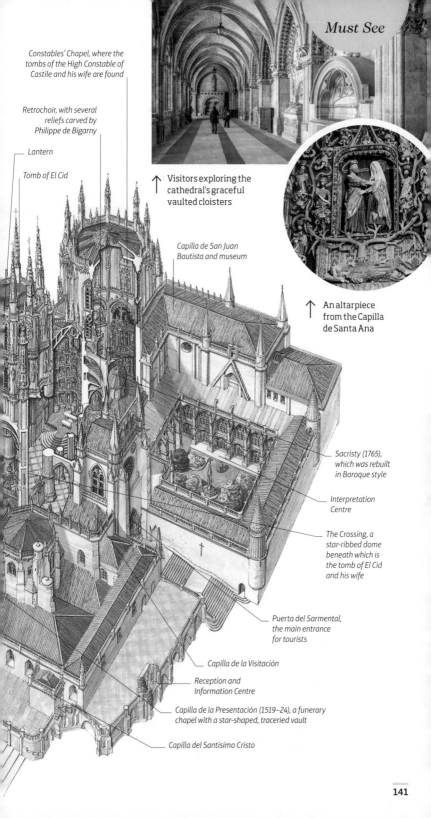

Constables' Chapel, where the tombs of the High Constable of Castile and his wife are found

Retrochoir, with several reliefs carved by Philippe de Bigarny

Lantern

Tomb of El Cid

↑ Visitors exploring the cathedral's graceful vaulted cloisters

Capilla de San Juan Bautista and museum

↑ An altarpiece from the Capilla de Santa Ana

Sacristy (1765), which was rebuilt in Baroque style

Interpretation Centre

The Crossing, a star-ribbed dome beneath which is the tomb of El Cid and his wife

Puerta del Sarmental, the main entrance for tourists

Capilla de la Visitación

Reception and Information Centre

Capilla de la Presentación (1519–24), a funerary chapel with a star-shaped, traceried vault

Capilla del Santisímo Cristo

EXPERIENCE MORE

❸
Ponferrada

C3 León ❼Calle Gil y Carrasco 4; www.ponferr ada.org/turismo/es

Set among hills, this town owes its name to a medieval bridge reinforced with iron *(pons ferrata)*, commissioned in 1042 by Bishop Osmundo of Astorgo to provide a crossing point over the Sil river for pilgrims; Ponferrado was, and still is, a major stop on the way to Santiago. Rising above a deep valley is the majestic Castillo de los Templarios (Castle of the Knights Templar), built from 1218 to 1380. This imposing fortress, equipped with towers and battlements, was built to protect the pilgrims travelling to Santiago. Clustered around the foot of the castle is the old quarter,

> ### HIDDEN GEM
> **Wireless Tech**
>
> Radio fans will enjoy Ponferrada's Museo de la Radio in Calle Gil y Carrasco. It displays more than 200 old sets belonging to Luis del Olmo, a celebrated Spanish broadcaster born in the town in 1937.

> **Rising above a deep valley is the majestic Castillo de los Templarios (Castle of the Knights Templar), built from 1218 to 1380.**

whose narrow streets with delightful arcades accommo- date most of Ponferrada's monuments. These include the 17th-century Baroque town hall on the Plaza Mayor, entered through the Puerta del Reloj (Clock Tower Gate), and the 10th-century Iglesia de Santo Tomás de las Ollas, a mix of Visigothic and Mozarabic architecture with later Romanesque and Baroque elements. The most impressive feature in the church is its oval chancel, with blind arcades and Moorish arches.

❹
El Bierzo

C2-D2 León ❼Ponferrada; www. turismodelbierzo.es

This northwestern region of León, cut off from the outside world by beautiful mountains,

Craggy, tree-clad hills → around ancient gold mines of Las Médulas

has breathtaking landscapes, pretty villages and pictur- esque lakes. This is an area with its own identity – the inhabitants speak a dialect of *galego*, and have a unique tradition of folklore and very hearty food.

Since Roman times, the area has also been mined for coal, iron and gold. The Romans used water to under- mine and weaken the hills of Las Médulas; the ore was then washed from the millions of tonnes of rockfall in a system of canals and sluice gates. It is estimated that the Romans extracted more than 500 tonnes of precious metal from the hills between the 1st and 4th centuries AD. Their tech- nique, described by Pliny the Elder as "the wrecking of the mountains", has left behind an extraordinary landscape of exposed ochre-coloured crags. The goldmines of Las Médulas are now a UNESCO World Heritage Site. You can best appreciate the area from a viewpoint at Orellán, reached via a rough, steep track.

←

The magnificent medieval Castle of the Knights Templar in Ponferrada

Also worth seeing is the Sierra de Ancares which lies north of the A6 highway, marking the borders with Galicia and Asturias. Part of this wild region of slate mountains forms a nature reserve – the eastern part of the Reserva Nacional de Os Ancares *(p78)*. The landscape of heathland, dotted with oak and birch copses, is home to wolves and capercaillies.

The area around El Bierzo has much to offer architecture enthusiasts. In the eastern part, along the old road to Santiago de Compostela, are typical pilgrim churches. Several isolated hill villages, such as Campo del Agua, contain pre-Roman stone *pallozas (p85)*.

---

⑤
Villafranca del Bierzo

🅰C3 🅰León 🚹C/Díez Ovelar 10; www.villa francadelbierzo.org

The tiled-roof houses, hilly surroundings and crystal-clear Burbia river lend this town a special charm. It was here, in the Romanesque Iglesia de Santiago (1186), that pilgrims who were too weak to make the final gruelling hike across

the hills of Galicia to Santiago de Compostela could obtain dispensation at the Puerta del Perdón (Door of Mercy).

Noteworthy too are the Iglesia de Santa María, housed since 1544 in a former Cluniac monastery, and the Iglesia de San Francisco on the Plaza Mayor, founded, according to legend, by St Francis of Assisi during his pilgrimage to Santiago. The churches are usually closed, but guided visits can be arranged through the town's tourist office.

Visitors can also sample the local speciality, cherries marinated in *aguardiente*, a strong spirit.

↑ Shepherd and flock in the quiet backstreets of Villafranca del Bierzo

EAT

Restaurante Coscolo
A favourite with locals, with an exceptional menu and friendly staff.

🅰D3 🅰Calle de Magdalena 1, Astorga 🔤restaurante coscolo.com

Las Termas
Simple home cooking is given a new lease of life at this homely eatery.

🅰D3 🅰Calle Santiago 1, Astorga 📞987 60 2212 🕐1–4pm

Hosteria de Los Palmeros
For those looking to indulge, this traditional Spanish restaurant is an elegant option.

🅰F3 🅰Plaza San Telmo, 4, Frómista 🔤hosteriadelos palmeros.com

---

La Casona
Inviting establishment which offers fine dining without the price tag.

🅰C3 🅰C/ Real 72, Fuentesnuevas, Ponferrada 🔤restaurantela casona.com

---

Sibuya Urban Sushi Bar
If you fancy a break from Spanish cuisine, try this chic sushi bar.

🅰C3 🅰Plaza Tierno Galvan 1, Ponferrada 🔤sibuyaurban sushibar.com

↑ A Gaudí masterpiece of turrets and spires, the Palacio Episcopal at Astorga

 6

Aguilar de Campoo

⬛F2 ⬛Palencia (Castilla y León) 🚆 🚌 ⓘPaseo Cascajera 10; www.aguilar decampoo.com

Aguilar de Campoo is a well-preserved medieval town. Rising above it is an 11th- to 12th-century castle, built on the ruins of a Celtic *castro*.

The houses and palaces in the town, including the Palacio de Manrique, are decorated with coats of arms; identical ones can be seen on the massive tower of the Colegiata de San Miguel.

 GREAT VIEW
Parador Paramour

Head up to the parador outside Cervera de Pisuerga, 25 km (15 miles) northwest of Aguilar de Campoo, for a drink. Although the building itself is unremarkable, the view over the Reserva Nacional de Fuentes Carrionas is spectacular *(www.parador.es)*.

This eclectic church is mainly Gothic, but with a preserved Romanesque portal and a Spanish Baroque tower.

Also worth seeing is the Romanesque Iglesia de Santa Cecilia, with its beautiful leaning tower. A few medieval bridges also survive in Aguilar.

7

Briviesca

⬛G3 ⬛Burgos (Castilla y León) 🚆 🚌 ⓘC/Santa María Encimera 1; www. turismo-briviesca.es

Briviesca was originally located in the nearby hills, but in the 14th century it was moved lower down to its present site.

The town's best-known monument is the 16th-century Convento de Santa Clara, with a Renaissance walnut reredos carved with scenes depicting the Tree of Jesse and the Way of the Cross. On the Plaza Mayor stands the Iglesia de San Martín, with a 16th-century Plateresque façade. Nearby is a 17th-century Ayuntamiento (town hall) with a clock tower and three coats of arms.

 8

Astorga

⬛D3 ⬛León 🚆 🚌 ⓘGlorieta Eduardo de Castro 5; www.turismo astorga.com

The Roman town of Asturica Augusta was a strategic stop on the Vía de la Plata (Silver Road) linking Andalucía and Galicia. Destroyed by the Moors in the 11th century, the town soon recovered its status as an important stage on the pilgrimage route to Santiago de Compostela.

Its character is influenced by the Maragatos, a people probably descended from enslaved Carthaginian and Punic people brought here by the Romans to work the mines. Astorga was an important trading centre for the Maragatos from the 8th century onwards, and until the building of railways in the 19th century, they were the main transporters of goods between Galician ports and Madrid. Among the goods they brought were chocolate and sugar, which is why this inland town is known for producing chocolates and (sweet biscuits).

Aside from its Gothic cathedral, begun in 1471, Astorga's most interesting monument is the fairytale Palacio Episcopal (1889–93) by Catalan architect Antoni Gaudí *(p126)*. The turreted grey granite block so horrified the diocese that no bishops ever lived in it. Inside is the Museo de los Caminos, devoted to the Santiago pilgrimage.

  9

Cuevas de Valporquero

⬛E2 ⬛León 🕐Oct–Apr: 10am–5pm Thu–Sun; May–Sep: 10am–6pm daily 🚫Mid-Dec–Feb 🌐cuevade valporquero.es

Beneath the village of Valporquero extends a

complex of spectacular limestone caves, formed in the Miocene period between 5 and 25 million years ago. Iron and sulphur oxides have tinted the stalactites and stalagmites with subtle shades of red, grey and black. Skilful lighting picks out the limestone concretions.

Less than half of the system, which stretches 3,100 m (10,200 ft) underground, is open to the public. Guided tours take parties through the series of galleries and chambers. They begin with the Pequeñas Maravillas (Small Wonders), which feature fantastic rock formations, such as Las Gemelas (Twins) and La Torre de Pisa (Tower of Pisa). The vast Gran Rotonda, covering an area of 5,600 sq m (60,200 sq ft) and reaching a height of 20 m (66 ft), is the most stunning.

As the interior is cold and the surfaces often slippery, it is advisable to wear warm clothes and sturdy shoes.

Frómista

⛰F3 🏛Palencia (Castilla y León) 🛈C/ Francesa 41; 979 81 01 28

Tiny Frómista features traditional houses built in adobe (sundried brick made from clay and straw).

The Iglesia de San Martín is the highlight of the town, partly due to a restoration in 1904, leaving the church, dating from 1066, entirely Romanesque in style. The presence of pagan and Roman motifs suggests it may have pre-Christian origins. Similar decoration can be seen on the capitals of the columns inside the church – note how the fable of the Fox and the Raven is presented.

Located at Gañinas, 20 km (12 miles) to the northwest (just south of Saldaña), is the **Villa Romana La Olmeda**. It contains a number of mosaics, including a notable hunting scene. Finds are displayed in the archaeological museum in the Iglesia de San Pedro in Saldaña.

TOP 3 LOCAL FIESTAS

Good Friday
A procession of coloured sculptures, depicting scenes from the Passion, takes place in Valladolid.

Fire Walking
On 23 June in San Pedro Manrique, men walk barefoot over burning embers; it is said only local people can do it without being burned.

El Colacho
On the Sunday after Corpus Christi, babies born during the previous year are laid on mattresses in the streets of Castrillo de Murcia. El Colacho - a man dressed as the Devil - then jumps over them to free them from illnesses.

Villa Romana La Olmeda
♿🚫 🏛Pedrosa de la Vega 📞979 11 99 97 🕐10:30am–6:30pm Tue–Sun 🚫1 & 6 Jan, 24, 25 & 31 Dec

←
Visiting the Villa Romana La Olmeda, and *(inset)* a detail of the intricate mosaic floor

THE BASQUE COUNTRY

The Basque people are thought to be one of the oldest peoples in Europe. Occupying a region that straddles the border of what is now France and Spain for millennia, they are most likely descended from early Iberian farming peoples. Their isolation in mountainous regions has prevented them from complete assimilation with the Roman descendants of France and Spain, even to this day. Their distinct culture is different to anything else found in Europe and their language, *euskara*, isn't related to any known dialect, alive or dead, in the world.

Attempts to suppress the Basque culture have long been resisted. When, in the 19th century, Spain started to become more centralized, the Basques felt threatened and began to fight to maintain their privileges. With the onset of industrialization and arrival of thousands of people in search of work, nationalist sentiment took hold. At the end of the century the Basque Country was granted autonomy, though this was later repealed by the Franco regime. In the 1960s, the armed separatist group ETA began an armed struggle against Franco's repression, fighting violently for complete Basque independence. When democracy returned to Spain in the 1970s, the Basque Country was again granted autonomy, which was accepted by most moderate Basque nationalists. However, ETA continued its armed campaign for complete independence until a definitive ceasefire was called in 2011, followed by their complete dissolution in 2018.

THE BASQUE COUNTRY

Must Sees
1. Bilbao
2. San Sebastián
3. Vitoria-Gasteiz
4. Santuario de Loyola

Experience More
5. Lekeitio
6. Gernika-Lumo
7. Ondarroa
8. Ría de Bilbao and Plentzia
9. Bermeo
10. Hondarribia
11. Deba
12. Hernani
13. Zarautz
14. Getaria
15. Azpeitia
16. Bergara
17. Tolosa
18. Laguardia
19. Torre Palacio de los Varona
20. Gaceo and Alaiza
21. Salvatierra
22. Oñati

↑ Charming medieval houses along the river in Bilbao's Casco Viejo (Old Town)

①

BILBAO

🅰A5 🔼Vizcaya 🚊🚇🚌🚉 *i* Plaza Circular 1; www.bilbaoturismo.net

An important port and the largest city in the Basque Country, Bilbao (Bilbo) rivals Madrid and Barcelona, with its unique culture, illustrious history and fabulous museums, housed in ground-breaking buildings. The city's development gathered pace in the mid-19th century, when iron ore was first extracted from deposits northwest of the city. But since the dawn of the 21st century, the old steelworks, shipyards and factories have been transformed into exciting public spaces.

①

Museo de Bellas Artes

🏛Plaza del Museo 2
🕙Times vary, check website 🌐museobilbao.com

Located in the leafy Doña Casilda Iturrizar park is the large Museo de Bellas Artes (Museum of Fine Art), one of Spain's best art museums. It displays art ranging from 12th-century Basque and Catalan pieces to modern works by international artists, including

Vasarely, Kokoschka, Bacon, Delaunay and Léger. There are also works by Basque artists.

Entry to the museum is free after 6pm. Guided tours are in Spanish or Basque only. The café's terrace is open in the summer months.

→ A visitor admiring the works in the city's Museo de Bellas Artes

②

Euskal Museoa Bilbao Museo Vasco

🏛Plaza Miguel de Unamuno 4 🕙10am-7pm Mon & Wed-Fri, 10am-1:30pm & 4-7pm Sat, 10-2pm Sun 🔒Public hols 🌐euskal-museoa.eus

Housed in a 17th-century building within the city's medieval heart, the Museo Vasco's permanent collection presents Basque art, folk artifacts and photographs of Basque life.

Not to be missed is the Idol of Mikeldi, an animal-like carving dating from the 3rd to 2nd century BC, which sits in the cloister.

③

Palacio de la Congresos y de la Música Euskalduna Jauregia

🏛Avenida Abandoibarra 4
🕙For concerts
🌐euskalduna.eus

This striking building sits at the site of the old shipyard. In tribute to the city's industrial past, it resembles a ship. The Palacio is home to the ABAO Bilbao Opera and the Bilbao Symphony Orchestra. Inside is an auditorium, congress halls and an exhibition hall. There are free guided tours in Spanish – and occasionally in the Basque language – on Saturdays. Tours in other languages can be arranged at any time for a fee.

Azkuna Zentroa

🏠 Plaza Arriquibar 4
🕐 Daily 🌐 azkuna zentroa.eus

In 2010, a century-old wine exchange warehouse that had stood empty for over 30 years was converted into this stunning cultural centre.

 GREAT VIEW
Fun-icular

Those keen to escape Bilbao's bustle should make for a funicular railway west of the city. The Funicular de Artxada ascends to the village of La Reineta, and offers a stunning panorama across the dockyards.

Originally known as the Alhóndiga Bilbao, its name was changed in 2015 to honour the city's mayor Iñaki Azkuna, who had died the previous year. The centre features design shops and restaurants, a library, a fabulous pool and a rooftop terrace, with a bar.

Itsasmuseum Bilbao

🏠 Ramón de la Sota Kaia 1
🕐 Summer: 10am-8pm Tue-Sun; winter: 10am-6pm Tue-Fri, 10am-8pm Sat, Sun & public hols 🌐 itsas museum.eus

Bilbao's maritime history is expertly displayed at this museum, located on the city's old docks. Exhibitions both inside and outside the museum recount the history of Bilbao Estuary, one of the city's most important lifelines. Visitors can download a free app to their smartphone in order to access additional information during their visit, including an audio guide.

EAT

Mercado de la Ribera
A stylish restaurant sits alongside *pintxos* bars.

🏠 Calle de la Ribebra, s/n
🌐 lariberabilbao.com

€€€

Bikandi Etxea
Expect traditional Basque dishes here.

🏠 Paseo Campo Volantin 4
🌐 bikandietxea. wixsite.com

€€€

Casa Rufo
This gem lies beneath a forgettable exterior - try the steak.

🏠 Calle Hurtado de Amezaga 5
🌐 casarufo.com

€€€

⑥ 🗺 Ⓜ 🍴 🖥 🛍

MUSEO GUGGENHEIM BILBAO

📍 Avenida Abandoibarra 2 Ⓜ Moyua 🚌 1, 10, 11, 13, 18, 27, 38, 48, 71 🕐 10am-8pm Tue-Sun (daily Jul & Aug); Art After Dark: 10pm-1am one Fri a month 🌐 guggenheim-bilbao.eus

The Museo Guggenheim Bilbao is the jewel in the city's cultural crown. The building itself is a star attraction: a mind-boggling array of silvery curves by the American architect Frank Gehry, alleged to resemble a ship or a flower. Inside, the collection is just as impressive.

The Guggenheim Bilbao's collection represents an intriguingly broad spectrum of modern and contemporary art, and includes works by Abstract Impressionists such as Willem de Kooning and Mark Rothko. As well as this stellar permanent collection, the museum regularly hosts intriguing temporary exhibitions, and often shows works from the permanent collections of its sister institutions – the Guggenheim museums in New York and Venice.

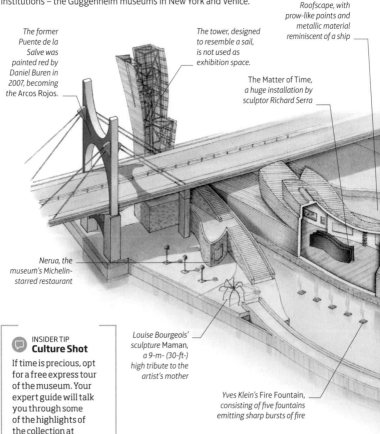

The former Puente de la Salve was painted red by Daniel Buren in 2007, becoming the Arcos Rojos.

The tower, designed to resemble a sail, is not used as exhibition space.

Roofscape, with prow-like points and metallic material reminiscent of a ship

The Matter of Time, a huge installation by sculptor Richard Serra

Nerua, the museum's Michelin-starred restaurant

Louise Bourgeois' sculpture Maman, a 9-m- (30-ft-) high tribute to the artist's mother

Yves Klein's Fire Fountain, consisting of five fountains emitting sharp bursts of fire

> 💬 INSIDER TIP
> **Culture Shot**
>
> If time is precious, opt for a free express tour of the museum. Your expert guide will talk you through some of the highlights of the collection at breakneck speed.

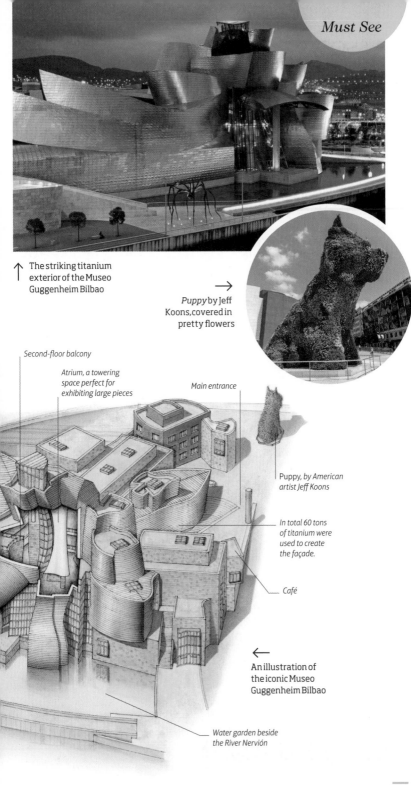

↑ The striking titanium exterior of the Museo Guggenheim Bilbao

→ *Puppy* by Jeff Koons, covered in pretty flowers

Second-floor balcony

Atrium, a towering space perfect for exhibiting large pieces

Main entrance

Puppy, *by American artist Jeff Koons*

In total 60 tons of titanium were used to create the façade.

Café

← An illustration of the iconic Museo Guggenheim Bilbao

Water garden beside the River Nervión

A SHORT WALK
BILBAO

Distance 2 km (1.2 miles) **Nearest train station** Estación de Abando **Time** 20 minutes

Bilbao's *casco viejo* – Old Town – emerged in the 14th century along the banks of the river. Stroll from the riverside into the heart of this old quarter, through a tangle of lively streets punctuated by historic monuments such as the Gothic Catedral de Santiago. The famous Siete Calles (Seven Streets), from Barrenkale Barrena to Somera, are the focal point, busy with street life, lined with tapas bars serving delicious food, and full of crowds of boisterous locals every weekend.

*Built on an octagonal plan, the Baroque **Iglesia de San Nicolás de Bari** is dedicated to the patron saint of sailors. Peek inside at the beautiful reredos.*

*Rich in ornamentation, the early 20th-century **Teatro Arriaga** sits on the grand Plaza de Arriaga (known as El Arenal).*

*As you meander through the Old Town, look out for the imaginative **coats of arms** heralding the houses' former inhabitants.*

CORR

BIDEBARRIETA

JARDINES VICTOR

PER

BAR

PELOTA

LA RIBERA

SANTA MARIA

START

LA RIBERA

RIA DE BILBAO

← Velvet and gold leaf in the luxurious auditorium of the Teatro Arriaga

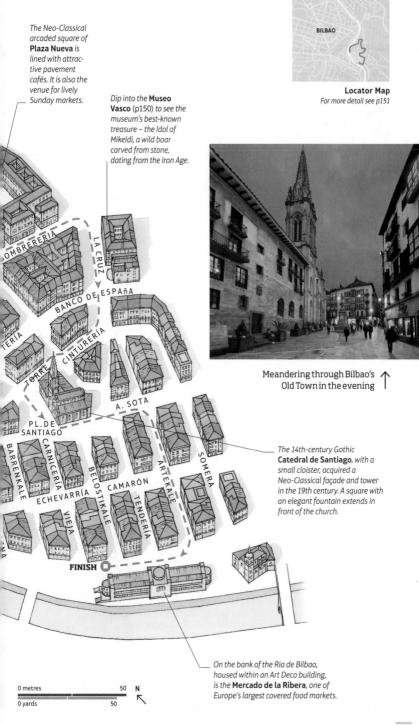

The Neo-Classical arcaded square of **Plaza Nueva** is lined with attractive pavement cafés. It is also the venue for lively Sunday markets.

Dip into the **Museo Vasco** (p150) to see the museum's best-known treasure – the Idol of Mikeldi, a wild boar carved from stone, dating from the Iron Age.

SOMBRERERIA

LA CRUZ

BANCO DE ESPAñA

TERIA

CINTURERIA

TORRE

A. SOTA

PL. DE SANTIAGO

BARRENKALE

CARNICERIA

ECHEVARRIA

BELOSTIKALE

CAMARÓN

VIEJA

TENDERIA

ARTEKALE

SOMERA

FINISH

Locator Map
For more detail see p151

BILBAO

Meandering through Bilbao's Old Town in the evening ↑

The 14th-century Gothic **Catedral de Santiago**, with a small cloister, acquired a Neo-Classical façade and tower in the 19th century. A square with an elegant fountain extends in front of the church.

On the bank of the Ria de Bilbao, housed within an Art Deco building, is the **Mercado de la Ribera**, one of Europe's largest covered food markets.

0 metres   50   N

0 yards   50

②

SAN SEBASTIÁN

 B5 ⚑ Guipúzcoa ✈ Hondarribia (22 km/14 miles) 🚌 🚏
ℹ Alameda del Boulevard 8; sansebastianturismo.com

Gloriously situated on a neat, shell-shaped bay, San Sebastián (Donostia) developed in the late 19th century into Spain's most elegant and fashionable seaside resort. It still has many luxury shops and one of Spain's grandest hotels, the María Cristina, but San Sebastián is now renowned for its great summer arts festivals and delicious Basque cuisine.

①
Plaza de la Constitución

Wedged between the bay and the Río Urumea is San Sebastián's fascinating Old Town (Parte Vieja). At its heart is the Plaza de la Constitución, a handsome, arcaded square. The square was once used as a bullring, and the numbers on the balconies date from this time, when organizers would sell a ticket for each numbered place. From this square you can explore the Old Town's alleys, which are packed with restaurants and tapas bars, and really come alive at night.

Overflowing stalls at the local fish market are a testament to this fishing city's past.

②
Monte Urgull

This mountain rises behind the Old Town. It's a bit of a hike to the summit, but is well worth the climb for the spectacular views. The summit is also home to a large statue of Christ and the ruined Castillo de Santa Cruz de la Mota, with old cannons.

③
Basilica de Santa María

 Calle 31 de Agosto 46
☎ 943 48 11 66 ⏰ 10:15am-1:15pm & 4:45-7:45pm daily

This 18th-century church's façade features an impressive vaulted niche. Built where a Roman church once stood, it's one of the oldest churches in the city. Don't miss the museum of religious artifacts.

→

Crowds gathering in front of the Basilica de Santa María

←

The pretty curve of San Sebastián, with the city lit up at night-time

④ 🛝 🎭 🍴

Aquarium

🏠 Plaza Carlos Blasco de Imaz 1 ⏰ Easter-Jun & Sep: 10am-8pm Mon-Fri, 10am-9pm Sat & Sun; Jul-Aug: 10am-9pm daily; Oct-Easter: 10am-7pm Mon-Fri, 10am-8pm Sat & Sun 🚫 1 & 20 Jan, 25 Dec 🌐 aquariumss.com

This remodelled aquarium has an interactive petting area and a 360-degree underwater tunnel, where visitors can view over 5,000 fish, including four species of shark. You can even have a sleepover beside the tanks.

The site also houses a Naval Museum, with exhibits on Basque naval history. On display are model ships, nautical maps and paintings.

Did You Know?

After the Siege of San Sebastián in 1813, British troops burned the city to the ground.

SAN SEBASTIÁN FILM FESTIVAL

This festival, founded in 1953, is one of the five leading European annual film festivals. It is held in late September, and draws more than 200,000 spectators. The special Donostia Prize is awarded as a tribute to the career of a star or director: past winners have included Meryl Streep and Ian McKellen. Visiting celebrities are rife, with the likes of Quentin Tarantino, Ethan Coen and Bertrand Tavernier among their ranks. Prizes also go to individual new films. An early winner was Hitchcock's *Vertigo*. Find out more at *www.sansebastian festival.com*.

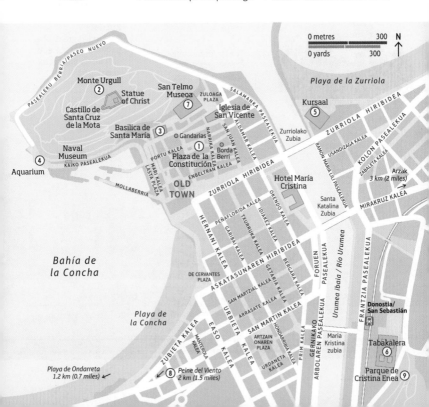

Kursaal

🏠 Avenida de Zurriola 1
🌐 kursaal.org

This cultural centre is housed in an iconic building, made up of cubes. Designed by Rafael Moneo, and opened in 1999, the current Kursaal was built on the site of the former Gran Kursaal, San Sebastián's old casino and event space that was demolished in 1972. The project was hugely expensive, but the two massive cubes have come to be viewed as icons of the city. They contain large auditoriums, home for most of the year to conferences and concerts, including frequent appearances by the Basque National Orchestra, and temporary art exhibitions in the Kubo-Kutxa Gallery. Kursaal is also used as a venue for the San Sebastián Film Festival (*p157*).

Tabakalera

🏠 Andre Zigarrogileak Plaza 1 🕐 9am–9pm Mon–Thu, 9am–10pm Fri, 10am–10pm Sat, 10am–9pm Sun & public hols 🌐 tabakalera.eu

Based in a former tobacco factory, San Sebastián's International Centre for Contemporary Culture is set across five floors connected by an exquisite old wooden staircase. The top floor has a roof terrace that offers an excellent view of the city. Entry to the building is free, and includes access to its temporary exhibitions, details of which can be found on the website. Free tours are also offered, although visitors need to register in advance.

Particularly popular with locals, the Tabakalera is an impressive cultural hub. It has its own media centre and cinema, plus a large library offering work stations with free WiFi. There is also a four-star hotel at the site: One Shot Tabakalera House.

The striking exterior of the Kursaal, and ↓ *(inset)* a workspace within the centre

San Telmo Museoa

🏠 Plaza Zuloaga 1 🕐 10am–8pm Tue–Sun 🚫 1 & 20 Jan, 25 Dec 🌐 santelmo museoa.eus

This is a large museum below Monte Urgull that is dedicated to the history of Basque culture. Housed in a 16th-century monastery, modern extensions have since been added, carefully designed to blend subtly with the original structure. In the cloister is a

> **TOP 3 BEACHES IN SAN SEBASTIÁN**
>
> **La Concha**
> This beautifully picturesque sandy beach is considered one of the best in Europe.
>
> **Ondaretta**
> Close to La Concha, this strand is often quieter and better for families.
>
> **Zurriola**
> This spot is great for a paddle in the sea, and absolutely perfect for keen surfers.

↑ *Peine del Viento*, or "Comb of the Wind", sculptures along the coastline

EAT

Arzak

Head to this three-Michelin-starred restaurant for fresh ingredients and Basque cooking. A tasting menu is available.

 Avenida Alcade José Elosegui 273 arzak.es

€€€

Borda Berri

Located in the Old Town, this rustic restaurant serves traditional Basque *pintxos* (snacks). It's popular with tourists and locals alike so you may need to queue for a table – but it's well worth the wait.

 Calle Fermin Calbeton 12 943 43 03 42

€€€

Gandarias

Nestled in the heart of the Old Town, this bar-restaurant offers a real taste of authentic Basque cuisine. There's a varied menu of *pintxos* and other dishes.

 Calle 31 de Agosto 23 restaurante gandarias.com

€€€

---

collection of Basque funerary columns dating from the 15th to 17th centuries. The museum, which has been in operation since 1900 and had been housed on two previous, smaller sites, was inaugurated here in 1932.

The museum also contains displays of furniture, tools and other artifacts, and paintings by local Basque artists: 19th-century works by Antonio Ortiz Echagüe, modern paintings by Ignacio Zuloaga, portraits by Vicente López and masterpieces by El Greco. The chapel holds 11 golden murals by the Catalan artist Josep Maria Sert, depicting Basque legends, culture and the region's seafaring life. The scenes almost seem to glow, making for an arresting sight.

Guided tours of both the permanent and temporary exhibits are available at a charge and must be booked in advance; normal entry to the museum is free every Tuesday.

⑧

Peine del Viento

 Ondarreta Beach

These three steel sculptures, called the "Comb of the Wind", are a collaboration between two San Sebastián natives – sculptor Eduardo Chillida and architect Luis Peña Ganchegui. Their setting is made all the more dramatic by the waves that crash against the rocks, sending water soaring into the sky around the visitors who have come to view them.

⑨

Parque de Cristina Enea

 Paseo Duque de Mandas May-Sep: 8am-9pm daily; Oct-Apr: 9am-7pm daily cristinaenea.eus

This urban park was designed by Pierre Ducasse following a commission from the Duke of Mandas who wanted to create the park for his wife, Cristina Brunetti de los Cobos. It's a calm, relaxing place – an ideal spot for a break from the city, where visitors can unwind and wander around. Here, you can walk beneath the shade of towering red sequoias and a magnificent Lebanese cedar. As well as the lush lawns and beds, there are ducks and even peacocks at the site.

A SHORT WALK
SAN SEBASTIÁN

Distance 1.5 km (1 mile) **Nearest bus stop**
Urgell **Time** 25 minutes

San Sebastián was the most fashionable
summer resort in Spain at the beginning
of the 20th century, and has an elegant
traditional promenade all along its
curving beach. Today the promenade
seems delicately old-fashioned.
To the western end of the beach, the
verdant hill of Monte Urgull makes for
pleasant strolling, affording panoramic
views of the bay and the tortoise-shaped
island of Santa Clara. Make your way
down into the cobbled lanes of the
charming Old Town, where street life
centres around unrivalled *pintxos*
(the local version of tapas).

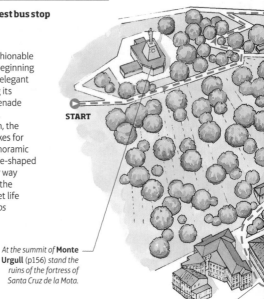

START

At the summit of **Monte
Urgull** (p156) *stand the
ruins of the fortress of
Santa Cruz de la Mota.*

Did You Know?

San Sebastián
(Donostia) locals
call themselves
"donostiarra".

Although the **Basica de
Santa María** (p156) *has earlier
origins, its current appearance is
18th century, combining elements
of Gothic, Churrigueresque and
Neo-Classicism.*

CAMPANARIO

↑ The Town Hall
presiding over the
Alderdi Eder gardens

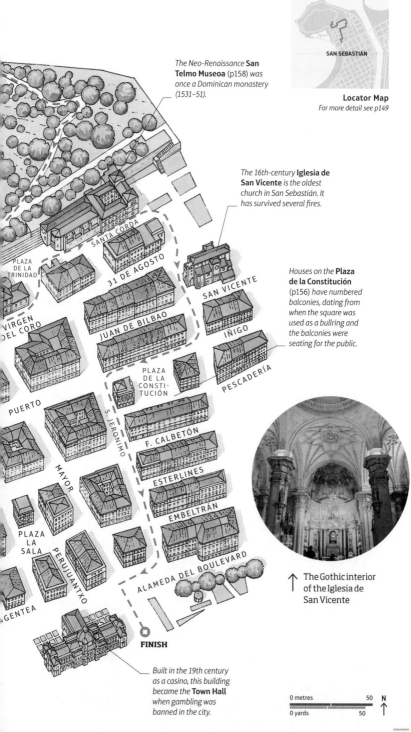

The Neo-Renaissance **San Telmo Museoa** (p158) was once a Dominican monastery (1531–51).

Locator Map
For more detail see p149

The 16th-century **Iglesia de San Vicente** is the oldest church in San Sebastián. It has survived several fires.

Houses on the **Plaza de la Constitución** (p156) have numbered balconies, dating from when the square was used as a bullring and the balconies were seating for the public.

PLAZA DE LA TRINIDAD

SANTA CORDA

31 DE AGOSTO

VIRGEN DEL CORO

JUAN DE BILBAO

SAN VICENTE

ÍÑIGO

PLAZA DE LA CONSTI-TUCIÓN

PESCADERÍA

PUERTO

S. JERONIMO

F. CALBETÓN

MAYOR

ESTERLINES

EMBELTRÁN

PLAZA LA SALA

PERUJUANTXO

ALAMEDA DEL BOULEVARD

GENTEA

FINISH

Built in the 19th century as a casino, this building became the **Town Hall** when gambling was banned in the city.

↑ The Gothic interior of the Iglesia de San Vicente

0 metres		50	N
0 yards		50	↑

VITORIA-GASTEIZ

🅰A5 ✈8 km (5 miles) N 🚇Plazuela de la Estación
🚌Plaza Euskaltzaindia, 1 🛈Plaza España 1;
www.vitoria-gasteiz.org/turismo

The inland city of Vitoria is the capital of the Basque Country and the seat of the Basque government. It was founded on a hill – the highest point in the province of Álava and the site of the ancient Basque town of Gasteiz. The city grew rich on the iron and wool trades, and today it is brimming with life. Visitors come to enjoy Vitoria's beautiful architecture and extensive parkland, and its excellent restaurants and tapas bars.

① Plaza de la Virgen Blanca

On this large square, named after the White Madonna, patron saint of Vitoria, stands a monument to a battle fought in 1813, when the Duke of Wellington defeated the French during the Peninsular War. Beethoven wrote a special concerto, *Wellington's Victory*, to commemorate this event. The monument, crowned with the figure of an angel, is the work of Gabriel Borrás. Old houses with glazed balconies surround the vibrant square, but the most important building is the Iglesia de San Miguel. This late Gothic aisled church, with Renaissance elements, was built between the 14th and 16th centuries. The high altar, by Gregorio Fernández, is Baroque (1624–32). The church is devoted to the cult of the White Madonna, and a 14th-century statue of her can be found in an outside niche.

② Catedral de Santa María (Catedral Vieja)

🅰Plaza Burulleria ⏰For tours only: 10:30am–2pm, 5–8pm, reserve online
🌐catedralvitoria.com

The 13th-century Gothic cathedral was once part of the city's fortifications. Preserved on the second buttress arch from the northern end is a stone decorated with a rose-like ornament, dating from Visigothic times. The interior is undergoing restoration.

THE AUTONOMOUS BASQUE GOVERNMENT

Since 1979, the Basque Country has enjoyed broad autonomy on the basis of the Statute of Gernika. It has its own parliament (located in the Lakua district of Vitoria-Gasteiz) and government, while the region's official languages are both Basque *(euskara)* and Spanish. The head of this government is called the *lehendakarí* (president), and is appointed by the Basque parliament every four years.

Museo de Bellas Artes

Paseo Fray Francisco 8
945 18 19 18 10am-
2pm & 4-6:30pm Tue-Sat,
11am-2pm Sun & hols

The Museum of Fine Arts is
housed in the eclectic Palacio
Augusti. The collection of
paintings and sculptures
includes Classical and Basque
art from 1850 to 1950.

Museo de la Armería de Álava

Paseo Fray Francisco 3
945 18 19 25 10am-
2pm & 4-6:30pm Tue-Fri,
10am-2pm Sat, 11am-2pm
Sun and public hols

Among the military exhibits
displayed here are uniforms
and weapons ranging from
prehistoric axes, through
Oriental and Arabic weaponry,
to 20th-century pistols.

Artium

C/Francia 24 Times
vary, check website
artium.org

Occupying a bold
white building in

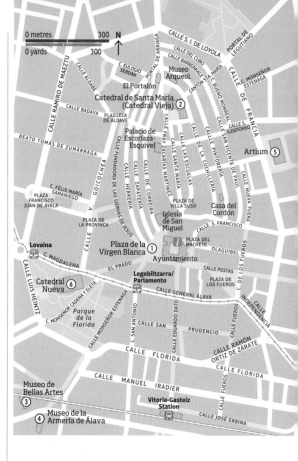

the centre of Vitoria's Old
Town, this Basque Museum of
Contemporary Art holds one
of Spain's largest collections
of modern and contemporary
art, displayed over three large
rooms. The focus of the permanent collection is on Spanish
artists like Dalí and Miró.

---

⑥

Catedral Nueva

Calle Magdalena 1
11am-2pm Mon-Sat
945 10 10 70

When a new diocese covering
all three Basque provinces

←

Plaza de la Virgen Blanca,
with its monument to a
Napoleonic battle of 1813

was established in the
19th century, it was agreed
that Vitoria needed a new
cathedral. The construction
of the Catedral Nueva de
María Inmaculada began in
1907 and finished in 1973.
The result – a huge, Neo-
Gothic shrine – has a nave,
four aisles and accommodates
15,000 people. Noteworthy
are the tall stained-glass
windows, the fine apse
and stunning gargoyles.

Did You Know?

Vitoria's mascot is *El
Caminante* - a statue
of a slender man
walking through the
Plaza del Arca.

4 ⊘ ⊘

SANTUARIO DE LOYOLA

🅰 B5 🏠 Loyola Auzoa, 16 🕐 Santa Casa: 10am–1pm & 3:30–7pm daily (to 1:30pm and 7:30pm Jun–Aug) 🌐 loyola.global/en

Set in the lush Urola Valley, this Basque landmark is a stunning sight to behold, with its grand basilica topped by a fine cupola. Constructed over centuries around the birthplace of St Ignatius, parts of this palatial fortress date back to the 14th century.

San Ignacio de Loyola, or St Ignatius Loyola (1491–1556), founder of the Jesuit order, was born in the stone manor known as Santa Casa (Holy House). The manor was incorporated in 1681–1738 into the Basílica de San Ignacio, a shrine designed by Carlo Fontana, and the rooms where the Loyola family had lived were converted into chapels. The most important of these is the Chapel of the Conversion, the room where Ignatius, as a young soldier, had a profound religious experience while recovering from a battle injury. The Baroque basilica, built from 1681 to 1738, is the shrine's highlight, with its Spanish Baroque dome and richly carved nave.

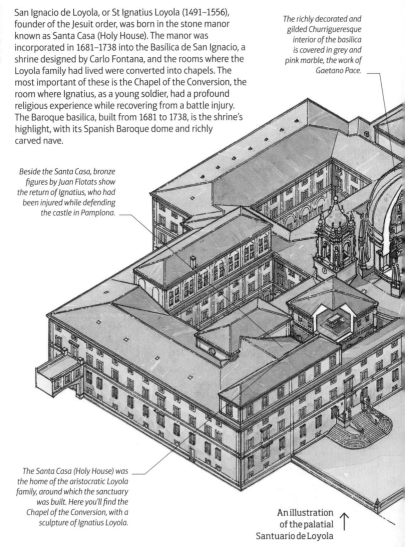

The richly decorated and gilded Churrigueresque interior of the basilica is covered in grey and pink marble, the work of Gaetano Pace.

Beside the Santa Casa, bronze figures by Juan Flotats show the return of Ignatius, who had been injured while defending the castle in Pamplona.

The Santa Casa (Holy House) was the home of the aristocratic Loyola family, around which the sanctuary was built. Here you'll find the Chapel of the Conversion, with a sculpture of Ignatius Loyola.

An illustration of the palatial Santuario de Loyola ↑

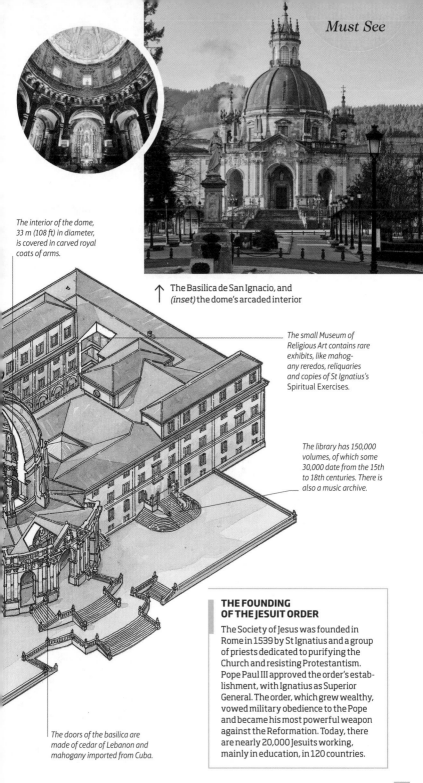

The interior of the dome, 33 m (108 ft) in diameter, is covered in carved royal coats of arms.

↑ The Basilica de San Ignacio, and *(inset)* the dome's arcaded interior

The small Museum of Religious Art contains rare exhibits, like mahogany reredos, reliquaries and copies of St Ignatius's Spiritual Exercises.

The library has 150,000 volumes, of which some 30,000 date from the 15th to 18th centuries. There is also a music archive.

The doors of the basilica are made of cedar of Lebanon and mahogany imported from Cuba.

THE FOUNDING OF THE JESUIT ORDER

The Society of Jesus was founded in Rome in 1539 by St Ignatius and a group of priests dedicated to purifying the Church and resisting Protestantism. Pope Paul III approved the order's establishment, with Ignatius as Superior General. The order, which grew wealthy, vowed military obedience to the Pope and became his most powerful weapon against the Reformation. Today, there are nearly 20,000 Jesuits working, mainly in education, in 120 countries.

Small fishing boats moored in the marina at Lekeitio ↑

EXPERIENCE MORE

 5

Lekeitio

🅰 A4 🅰 Vizcaya 🚌
ℹ lekeitio.org

Lekeitio is one of many fishing villages on the Basque coast, or "Costa Vasca", and its architecture is maritime in style. It also has several historic buildings, including the Gothic Basílica de la Asunción de Santa María. Inside is a 16th-century altar. Visible from the town's beautiful beach is the island of San Nicolás, which can be reached on foot at low tide.

For years, Lekeitio rivalled San Sebastián as the Basque Country's summer capital, with elegant 19th-century villas lining its pretty seafront. The surrounding area is good for walking.

6 (M)

Gernika-Lumo

🅰 A5 🅰 Vizcaya 🚇 🚌
ℹ Artekalea 8; www.gernika-lumo.net

This little town is of great symbolic significance to the Basques as an ancient seat of law-making and as the target of the world's first saturation bombing raid, carried out by Nazi aircraft at Franco's request in 1937.

The most important place in the town is the Neo-Classical Casa de Juntas, which houses the parliament of the province of Vizcaya. In the Parque de los Pueblos de Europa are sculptures by Henry Moore and Eduardo Chillida. Also of note are the Gothic Iglesia de Santa María,

the Museo de la Paz (Museum of Peace) and Museo Euskal Herria (Museum of the Basque Country).

7

Ondarroa

🅰 A5 🅰 Vizcaya 🚌
ℹ Erribera 9; www.ondarroa.eus

Ondarroa is a small but charming old port on the border with Guipúzcoa

---

THE TREE OF GERNIKA

For centuries, Basque leaders met in democratic assembly under an oak on a hillside in Gernika-Lumo. In the garden of the Casa de Juntas, inside a pavilion and closely guarded, is the petrified trunk of the *Gernikako Arbola*, symbolizing the ancient roots of the Basque people. It was over 300 years old when it dried out in 1860. Younger trees here have been grown from its acorns.

Did You Know?

Minke whales can sometimes be spotted along the Basque Coast.

province, with a lively harbour and a colourful fishing fleet. It has preserved its medieval town plan, with the names of the streets referring to geographical locations or to traditional Basque sports. The tourist office can organize guided walks.

Spanning the Artibai river is the Puente Viejo, a Roman bridge that was reconstructed in the 20th century. Other buildings typical of the area include the 15th-century Gothic Iglesia de Santa María, built on a clifftop, and the Torre de Likona, a border watchtower from the same period. It was here that the mother of St Ignatius Loyola, founder of the Jesuit order, was born.

The old town hall has a façade with Tuscan columns. On a nearby hilltop rises the Iglesia de Nuestra Señora de la Antigua, dating from the

12th century but rebuilt in the 17th century.

 8

Ría de Bilbao and Plentzia

▲G2

The Ría de Bilbao, created by the Nervión river, is known as the "main street of Vizcaya". It stretches 14 km (9 miles) northwest of Bilbao before entering the sea off the town of Portugalete, known for its "hanging bridge" (Puente Colgante) across the Nervión. Along the less industrial east bank of the *ría* is the attractive suburb of Getxo, with its beaches, marina and waterfront lined with 19th-century villas. At the *ría*'s northern end is Algorta, a former fishing port that has a beach, a pretty old harbour and streets winding up a steep cliff. Beyond there, the *ría* runs up to Plentzia – a small port town with an attractive old quarter.

 9

Bermeo

▲A4 🏛Vizcaya ℹParque Lamera, s/n; www.bermeo. eus

Bermeo is an important port on the Basque coast, with a busy fishing harbour and excellent seafood restaurants.

The town's oldest church is Santa Eufemia (13th–15th century), an aisleless Gothic structure that incorporates Byzantine elements. The nearby Gothic Torre Ercilla accommodates the **Museo del Pescador**, which has an exhibition on the Basques' long heritage of fishing and whaling across the Atlantic.

Several hermitages are located in Bermeo and the surrounding area. The most famous is the Ermita San Juan de Gaztelugatxe, situated on a rocky island a few kilometres from the town. Reached by climbing a flight of 231 steps across a bridge carved into the rocks, this craggy monolith affords breathtaking views of the Basque Coast.

To the west of Bermeo, Cabo Matxitxako is a remote headland with two lighthouses. The best beaches are to be found in Ibarrangelu, 24 km (15 miles) east of Bermeo; which also has the best surfing in Northern Spain. Elantxobe, in turn, is a picturesque fishing village that spreads up the precipitous slopes of the highest cliff on the Basque coastline – Monte Ogoño (280 m/918 ft above sea level).

Museo del Pescador

♿ 🏛Torre Ercilla
📞946 88 11 71 🕐10am–2pm & 4–7pm Tue–Sat, 10am–2pm Sun

↑ Steps leading to the San Juan de Gaztelugatxe hermitage, near Bermeo

NAVIGATORS OF THE BASQUE COAST

Juan Sebastián Elcano, born in Getaria, led the first expedition to circumnavigate the globe. Following the death of Magellan, Elcano assumed command on the famous round-the-world voyage. On 6 September 1522, after a voyage of 78,000 km (48,500 miles) lasting three years, Elcano returned to Seville on his ship, the *Victoria*.

Another Basque, Andrés de Urdaneta, led the second Spanish round-the-world voyage in the 1530s. In the 1560s Miguel López de Legazpi conquered the Philippines for Spain. Basque sailors later took part in the exploration of Mexico.

The lively fishermen's quarter of La Marina is famous for its tall, brightly painted houses and seafront cafés. Beaches stretch to the north. In the nearby port of Pasai-Donibane is the house where the French writer Victor Hugo once lived. Regattas are held in the bay here.

⓫

Deba

🅰B4 🏠Guipúzcoa 🚇
🚌 ℹ️ Ifar Kalea 4; www.
deba.eus

Deba was a fashionable resort in the 1900s, and so has a line of grand old villas beside its long, wide beach. With crashing surf, it still attracts scores of visitors on summer weekends. In the town are a few palaces from its 16th-century heyday. An important monument is the massive Gothic Iglesia de Santa María, with a beautiful cloister and colourfully decorated entrance.

Another well-known site is the shrine in the Itziar neighbourhood, dedicated to the Virgin Mary. Its interior has

❿

Hondarribia

🅰B4 🏠Guipúzcoa ✈️ 🚇 🚌
ℹ️ Arma Plaza 9; www.
bidasoaturismo.com

The historic quarter of this port town at the mouth of the Río Bidasoa (opposite France) is encircled by 15th-century walls with two gates. Within the quarter are old houses with carved eaves, balconies and coats of arms. The narrow cobbled streets cluster around the church of Santa María de la Asunción, a cross-vaulted Gothic structure dating from the early 15th century. The highlight here is a remarkable three-faced image of the Holy Trinity, found underneath the choir. In the 16th century, the Church condemned such images, and this is one of very few to have survived in Spain.

Hondarribia is one of the prettiest of all Basque towns.

↑ Tall, colourful houses in the La Marina harbour quarter of Hondarribia

↑ Couture on show at the Museo Cristobal Balenciaga, in the designer's home in Getaria

a Romanesque sculpture of Mary, patron saint of sailors. Outside is the bronze sculpture *La Maternidad*, by Jorge Oteiza.

A clifftop footpath with magnificent coastal views leads through fields and past huge old farms to Zumaia. This popular resort has broad, sandy beaches, a pleasant old quarter and attractive marina. In the **Espacio Cultural Ignacio Zuloaga**, home of a celebrated early 20th-century Basque painter, Zuloaga's colourful studies of Basque rural and maritime life are on show.

Espacio Cultural Ignacio Zuloaga

🕐 🏠Santiago Auzoa 3, Zumaia 🕐Apr-Sep: 4-7:30pm Fri (Fri & Sat Jul-Aug) 🌐espaciozuloaga.com

---

 Hernani

🅐B5 🏠Guipúzcoa 🚌 🚍
🚉Nafar 18; 943 33 70 28

This small medieval town is located around 8 km (5 miles) south of San Sebastián. Of note are the 19th-century town hall, supported on seven arches, and the Portalondo house, an example of medieval defensive architecture. Also of interest are the 16th-century church of St John the Baptist and the medieval Gudarien Enparantza, the main square. The town is surrounded by forests scattered with prehistoric remains, including megalithic monuments and burial mounds.

 Zarautz

🅐B5 🏠Guipúzcoa 🚉 🚍
🚉Nafarroa 3; www.turismozarautz.com

Like many old towns in the region, Zarautz was traditionally associated with whaling. Nowadays, it is known for the province's longest beach, which offers excellent conditions for surfing, and a lovely promenade. Nearby, vine-clad hillsides produce the region's famous *txakolí* wines. In the old quarter are houses with coats of arms, the Gothic Torre Luzea, the medieval Iglesia de Santa María La Real and the Renaissance Palacio de Narros. The local cuisine is considered to be very fine.

 Getaria

🅐B5 🏠Guipúzcoa 🚍
🚉Parque Aldamar 2; www.getariaturismo.eus

Getaria is a charming trawler port with lively cafés. It is also the centre of *txakolí* wine production and known for good food. Just off the coast lies the tiny island of Monte San Antón, known as *El Ratón de Getaria* (the Mouse of Getaria) because of its shape. The Museo Cristobal Balenciaga is a showcase for the fashion designer, who lived here.

Museo Cristobal Balenciaga

🕐🕐 🏠Parque Aldamar 6
📞943 00 88 40 🕐Mar-Oct: 10am-7pm Tue-Sun (daily to 8pm Jul-Aug); Nov-Feb: 10am-3pm Tue-Sun

15
Azpeitia

🅰B5 🅰Guipúzcoa 🚌
ℹ️ Loiola Tourist Office;
943 15 18 78

As many as 360 *caseríos* (Basque farmhouses) are preserved in the vicinity of Azpeitia. Many Basque families still live in these often half-timbered, chalet-style farmhouses, built by their forebears. The town itself features many beautiful buildings, some in the Mudéjar style; these include, for instance, the Casa Altuna, the magnificent Casa Anchieta and the 14th-century Magdalena hermitage. Also well represented is the Plateresque style, which is evident on the windows of the Casa Plateresca and on the portico of the church of San Sebastián de Soreasu, a Gothic structure whose tower was built by the Order of the Knights Templar.

↑ Santa Marina de Oxirondo in Bergara, and *(inset)* a sculpture of St Peter inside

One of the town's oldest buildings is the huge medieval Casa Torre de Enparan, now housing the municipal library. However, Azpeitia is most famous for its huge shrine to St Ignatius Loyola and other sites associated with the Basque founder of the Jesuit order *(p164)*.

16
Bergara

🅰A5 🅰Guipúzcoa 🚉🚌
ℹ️ Palacio Errekalde; www.
turismo.euskadi.eus

Bergara is one of the most characterful of Basque country towns, with an old centre full of distinguished colleges, churches and mansions built for aristocrats during the town's heyday in the prosperous 16th and 17th centuries. The first Carlist War ended here in 1839 *(p55)* – the treaty was signed in the 17th-century Casa Iritzar, which features wrought-iron balconies and a coat of arms at the corner of the building.

There are other fine buildings, such as the 16th-century Casa Arostegi, which holds exhibitions, and the Casa Jauregi (c 1500), which has reliefs depicting plant motifs and figures of royal couples.

The Basque Gothic style is represented by the aisled church of Santa Marina de Oxirondo, built on a square plan. Its tower is Baroque, as is the impressive reredos by Miguel de Irazusta and Luis Salvador Carmona. Also

↑ The Ría Oria flows through the heart of the town of Tolosa

BASQUE CULTURE

Long isolated in mountain valleys, the Basques preserved their unique language, myths and art for millennia. Their music and high-bounding dances are unlike those of any other culture. The *fueros*, or ancient Basque laws and rights, were suppressed under Franco, but since 1975 the Basques have had their own parliament and police force, having won great autonomy over their own affairs.

Baroque is the Iglesia de San Pedro de Ariznoa, with its squat tower; inside is a canvas with shepherds paying homage to the infant Jesus.

 17

Tolosa

B5 **Guipúzcoa** **Plaza Santa María 1; www.tolosaldea.net**

For centuries Tolosa, with its favourable location on the Ría Oria, was an important cultural, commercial and industrial centre. It was made the capital of Guipúzcoa province during the Carlist Wars, and in the 19th century, it was occupied by the French. The town's renowned carnival was held even during the Franco era, and its November choral music festival remains one of the best in the country.

Today, Tolosa is famous for its fantastic fresh produce, in the *alubias de Tolosa* – a red bean grown around the town and featured in hearty traditional Basque dishes. In summer you'll see the beans on sale in Tolosa's renowned Saturday farmers' market, which has been held in the Tinglado marketplace since medieval times.

In the Old Town's narrow streets and squares, there are many examples of Basque Gothic and Baroque architecture. The most impressive example of Basque Gothic is the imposing 17th-century aisled church of Santa María, set beside the Ría Oria. The church has cross-vaulting and a Baroque façade designed by architect Martín de Carrera. Under the choir is a late-Romanesque portico.

EAT & DRINK

Etxeberria Bar
A good selection of beers on tap, and tasty tapas for snacking.

B4 **Calle Mayor 27 Bajo, Hondarribia**
943 64 00 32

€€€

Orbela Taberna
This tavern entices with its *pintxos* menu and delicious cocktails.

B5 **Errementari Kalea 10, Tolosa**
943 01 67 80

€€€

Kaia-Kaipe
Sample the freshly grilled seafood and pick from a lengthy wine list.

B5 **C/General Arnao 4, Getaria**
kaia-kaipe.com

€€€

Laguardia

⚐ A6 ⚑ Álava ⛿ ⓘ Calle Mayor 52; www.laguardia-alava.com

This little wine town is the capital of La Rioja Alavesa, a part of southern Álava province where Rioja wines have been produced for centuries. It is a fertile, vine-clad plain, sheltered by high hills to the north. There are fine panoramic views from the road that climbs up to the Herrera pass. Laguardia is a medieval hill town, its encircling ramparts, towers and fortified gateways visible from afar. Along its steep, narrow cobbled streets there are many *bodegas* (wine cellars), offering wine tastings and tours throughout the year. It is usually necessary to make a booking in advance.

In Plaza Mayor, the main square, are the old 16th-century town hall and the newer 19th-century building that serves as the current town hall.

PICTURE PERFECT
Through the Keyhole

The intricate Gothic doorway to Laguardia's Santa María de los Reyes church, with its colourful sculpture that arcs above the double doors, makes for an impressive photograph.

The Gothic Iglesia de Santa María de los Reyes is well worth a visit, with its austere façade and a richly embellished inner portal that has retained its original colouring. Another church worth seeing is the Iglesia de San Juan Bautista, a 12th-century building built as a temple-fortress. The majority of the church was built in the Gothic style in the 13th and 14th centuries, and modifications in the 16th century reduced its fortresslike appearance. It now houses a museum of liturgical objects.

A walkable distance from Laguardia is the Poblado de la Hoya, a prehistoric excavation sight that explores the history of the Celtiberian peoples that once lived in the area.

Torre Palacio de los Varona

⚐ A5 ⚑ Villanañe, Álava ⚏ Valdegovía; 945 35 30 40 ⏰ Tours: 11:15am, 12:15pm & 1:15pm Sat & Sun

The small town of Villanañe is home to this fine example of medieval military architecture, the tower and mansion of the Varona family. Set on a hill, with commanding views of the surrounding countryside, this imposing structure is the most well-preserved 14th-century fortified building in the region. Its origins date back to the year 680, when the first tower was built on this site by the Visigoth admiral Ruy Pérez. Since the 15th century, the mansion has been home to the Varona family, and has evolved over the years with the needs of its occupants. Nonetheless, the interior contains a wealth of interesting historical detail, including period furniture. The upper rooms are decorated with strikingly colourful 17th- and 18th-century wallpaper, which replaced the tapestries that previously hung on the walls. Some of the floors are of wood, while others are tiled in traditional Manises porcelain decorated with scenes from the epic novel *Don Quixote*.

Gaceo and Alaiza

⚐ A5 ⓘ arabakolautada.eus

Not far from Vitoria, the villages of Gaceo and Alaiza conceal hidden treasure: medieval murals. In the Iglesia de San Martín de Tours in Gaceo, the 14th-century murals adorn the crypt and chancel, presenting the text of the catechism for the benefit of

Arcaded courtyards
of Oñati's Universidad
de Sancti Spiritus

> **The Universidad de Sancti Spiritus - designed by Picart and Gibaja - was the first Basque university, funded by Bishop Zuazola; it operated between 1551 and 1901.**

non-Latin-speaking believers. Murals also depict the Holy Trinity, the Last Judgment, scenes from the Way of the Cross and the life of Christ, and redeemed souls.

In Alaiza is the Iglesia de Santa María de la Asunción, featuring murals from the same period but less refined than those at Gaceo: the depiction is more schematic and the figures less complex.

Salvatierra

AB5 **♦**Álava **☐** **☐**
ℹ Mayor 8; 945 30 29 31

Set among green hills and beech woods is the small

Bodega Ysios near Laguardia, designed by Santiago Calatrava

town of Salvatierra. Rising above the surrounding area is the walled Old Town. Seek out the former hospital of San Lázaro y la Magdalena and the Gothic church of Santa María.

22
Oñati

AA5 **♦**Guipúzcoa
☐ **ℹ** San Juan Kale 14;
www.oñatiturismo.eus

A walk through old Oñati is a real treat for architecture enthusiasts. The **Universidad de Sancti Spiritus** – designed by Picart and Gibaja – was the first Basque university, funded by Bishop Zuazola; it operated between 1551 and 1901. The Plateresque façade is adorned with four pilasters and several figures referring to both mythological and religious tradition. A superb

courtyard can be found within. The Monasterio de Bidaurreta, in turn, is a mix of Gothic, Renaissance and Mudéjar. The interior contains aristocratic family tombs and two altars – one Baroque, the other Plateresque in style. Nearby, the Plaza de Santa Marina is surrounded by Baroque palaces.

From Oñati, a mountain road ascends for nearly 10 km (6 miles) southwards to the Santuario de Arantzazu, which lies in the valley at the foot of Alona Hill. It is believed that in 1469 a shepherd saw a vision of the Virgin here. This Modernist church, built to replace an earlier one, was designed in the 1950s by Javier Sáiz Oiza and Luis Laorga. It has a tall belfry, huge wooden altar and doors designed by the sculptor Eduardo Chillida. The Virgin of Arantzazu is the province's patron.

**Universidad de
Sancti Spiritus**
Ⓢ Ⓐ **☐** Univertsitate
Hiribidea **☎** 943 78 34 53
☐ Daily for guided tours
(phone in advance)

NAVARRA
AND LA RIOJA

Navarra was first ruled by the Vascones, ancestors of the Basque peoples who still live in the region, as well as in the bordering Basque Country. Emerging as an independent Christian kingdom in the 10th century, Navarra was vastly expanded in the early 11th century under the rule of Sancho III, to encompass lands stretching from Ribagorza in Aragón to Valladolid. Navarra's independence came to an end in the early 16th century, when it was annexed by Fernando II of Castile, though it retained its own laws and currency until the 1800s. The modern autonomous region came into being following Spain's transition to democracy in the 1970s and 80s. Today, northwest Navarra still retains its strong Basque heritage, with *euskara* an official language.

The first inhabitants of La Rioja were the dinosaurs, traces of which can be seen around the mountain village of Enciso. The territory – one of the smallest Spanish regions – was controlled in turn by the Romans, the Visigoths and the Muslims of al Andalus, before its reconquest by Christians in the 10th century. An important stage on the road to Santiago de Compostela, La Rioja claims superb architecture, such as in Santo Domingo de la Calzada or at the monastery of San Millán de Yuso. Today La Rioja is covered in vineyards, and is world renowned as a producer of the fine eponymous wine.

NAVARRA AND LA RIOJA

Must Sees

1. Pamplona (Iruña)
2. Logroño

Experience More

3. Las Cinco Villas del Valle de Bidasoa
4. Elizondo
5. Bosque de Irati
6. Valle de Salazar
7. Valle de Roncal
8. Sierra de Aralar
9. Roncesvalles
10. Puente la Reina
11. Monasterio de Leyre
12. Castillo de Javier
13. Sangüesa
14. Olite
15. Estella
16. Ujué
17. Monasterio de Irache
18. Monasterio de la Oliva
19. Tudela
20. Bárdenas Reales
21. Tafalla
22. Viana
23. Navarrete
24. Enciso
25. Calahorra
26. Nájera
27. Haro
28. Anguiano and Sierra de la Demanda
29. San Millán de la Cogolla
30. Santo Domingo de la Calzada

The elegant Plaza del Castillo in the heart of the Old Town

❶

PAMPLONA (IRUÑA)

⬛B5 🏛Navarra ✈8 km (5 miles) S 🚉Plaza de Estación 🚌C/Yanguas y Miranda 2 ℹ️C/San Saturnino 2; www. turismo.navarra.es

In 75 BC, the Roman general Pompey founded the town of Pompaelo on the site of the old Basque settlement of Iruña. Strategically located on the river at the foot of the Pyrenees, Pamplona was used as a fortified border town. Today, it is the financial, commercial and academic centre of Navarra, offering visitors fine cuisine and pleasant walks along the riverside or through the Old Town. Each July, the world-famous San Fermín festival, with its running of the bulls, totally transforms the city.

① Plaza del Castillo

This square owes its name to a castle raised here in the 14th century. Initially a marketplace and location for fiestas, it later became a venue for bullfights, when the balconies of the surrounding houses were used as seating areas. In 1931, a theatre along one of its sides was destroyed to make way for Avenida Carlos III, an avenue linking the square with the city's new districts. Nobel-prize-winning author Ernest Hemingway visited Pamplona on several occasions, and this square features as the centrepiece for his first novel, *The Sun Also Rises* (1926).

② Iglesia San Saturnino

🏛 Calle San Saturnino, s/n
🕐 Times vary, check website 🌐 iglesiasansaturnino. com/en

Also known as Iglesia de San Cernín, this Romanesque church (13th century) was built on the site where St Saturninus is said to have baptized some 40,000 pagan townspeople. One of its towers is a clock, topped by a cockerel – the Gallico de San Cernín, a symbol of the city. In the 18th century, its cloister was replaced by the Baroque Capilla della Virgen del Camino. Its beautiful reredos contains a 12th-century wooden robed figure of the Virgin, covered in silver tiles.

↑ The ornate gilded interior of the Iglesia San Saturnino

③
Ciudadela

🏛 Av. del Ejército, s/n

In 1571 Felipe II ordered the construction of Pamplona's citadel, to protect the city from the advances of the French army. Of the star-shaped five bastions, designed by the Italian engineer, Giacomo Paleary, only three survive. From the outside, the building looks rather decrepit – grass is yellowed by the sun, and its moats have long been empty – but once you pass through the main entrance, the impression is very different. Encircling the well-kept lawn are the citadel's former buildings, now converted into exhibition rooms. The oldest structure is the powder magazine (Polvorín), dating from 1694. .

GREAT VIEW
The City Walls

An arresting sight in themselves, Pamplona's fortress walls offer a glimpse of medieval history. A 5-km (3-mile) walk along the top of the structure affords spectacular views over the city.

④
Palacio de Navarra

🏛 Avenida Carlos III 2; 848 42 71 27 🕐 To large groups only (not individuals), by prior arrangement

This Neo-Classical palace, designed in 1840 by Juan de Nagusia, is the seat of the provincial government. Set in the tympanum above the palace entrance is the Navarra coat of arms flanked by two men – a highlander and an inhabitant of the river basin. Inside, the throne room is particularly luxurious, as is the office of the Navarrese president, where there is a portrait of Fernando VII by Goya, as well as many other paintings – mostly portraits – from the 19th and 20th centuries.

In front of the palace a symbolic statue of a woman upholding the historic laws (*fueros*) of Navarra stands atop a column. The palace's pleasant gardens are home to a giant sequoia tree.

Must See

STAY

Hotel Tres Reyes
This stylish hotel is located in the heart of Pamplona among the Taconera Park gardens.

🏛 Calle de la Taconera, s/n 🌐 hotel3reyes.com

€€€

Alma Pamplon
Here, high-end rooms and suites are complemented by a gourmet restaurant and spa. Some rooms are surprisingly affordable, with optional extras available.

🏛 Calle Beloso Bajo, 11 🌐 almahotels.com/pamplona

€€€

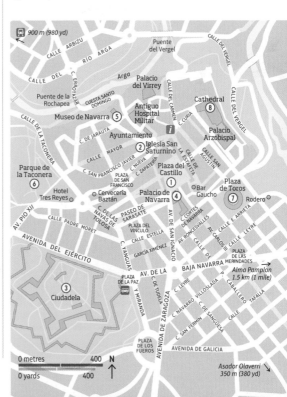

EAT & DRINK

Rodero

Michelin-star food presented with artistic flair. Go for the *menú degustación* (tasting menu) to sample a sumptuous variety of dishes with expert wine pairings.

🏠 Calle Emilio Arrieta 3
🌐 restaurante
rodero.com

€€€

Asador Olaverri

This swanky barbecue joint serves up anything that can be grilled. Steak is the speciality, accompanied by a fine vintage from the impressive wine cellar.

🏠 Calle Santa Marta 4
🌐 asadorolaverri.com

€€€

Bar Gaucho

This typically Basque bar combines a tempting drinks menu, perfect *pintxos* and a buzzy ambience to create one of Pamplona's most popular tapas bars.

🏠 Calle Espoz y Mina 7
📞 948 22 50 73

€€€

Cervecería Baztán

At this Irish bar with a Basque twist savour tasty tapas and craft ales.

🏠 Calle Nueva 125
📞 948 57 10 45

€€€

← Intricately carved 12th-century capital at the Museo de Navarra

⑤

Museo de Navarra

🏠 C/Santo Domingo 47; 848 42 64 92 🕐 9:30am–2pm & 5–7pm Tue–Sat, 11am–2pm Sun and hol 🗓 1 Jan, 6 & 7 Jul, 25 Dec

This museum of regional archaeology, history and art is located inside the former Hospital de Nuestra Señora de la Misericordia. Its highlights include Roman mosaics, Gothic and Baroque murals, Romanesque capitals from the cathedral cloister, and an 11th-century ivory casket that draws inspiration from Islamic decorative motifs. There is also a portrait by Goya and a collection of paintings by Basque artists.

Tours of the museum are available by prior arrangement, and entry is free on Saturday afternoons and on Sundays.

⑥

Parque de la Taconera

🏠 Calle Bosquecillo
🚌 Navas de Tolosa 🕐 24 hours, daily

The Taconera Gardens make for a peaceful escape from Pamplona's Old Town. Open to the public all year round, the gardens are a lovely spot for a picnic and a stroll, with colourful herbaceous borders, and architectural details such as the grand entrance, a Baroque triumphal arch. Wildlife in the park includes deer, rabbits, ducks, pheasants and peacocks.

---

⑦

Plaza de Toros

🏠 Calle de Alcalá 237

Pamplona's bullring, known as the Monumental, holds around 19,500 spectators and is surpassed in size only by the arenas in Madrid and Mexico City. Designed by

↑ Tree-shaded paths in Pamplona's lovely Parque de la Taconera

Francisco Urcola, the Monumental was officially opened in 1922. Several improvements were made in 2005, including the addition of a lift and vehicles for people with accessibility needs, making it one of the most modern bullrings in

Pamplona Cathedral's tranquil cloisters, and *(inset)* one of its impressive clock towers ↑

Spain. The July bull run, part of the week-long Fiesta San Fermín for which Pamplona is famous, ends here.

RUNNING OF THE BULLS

The *encierro* (running of the bulls) is a traditional Spanish event where a number of bulls are released into the streets, and people, often dressed all in white with red scarves around their waists and necks, try to outrun them. By far the most famous run is in Pamplona, which takes place during the San Fermín festival. Animal rights groups regularly protest against the event, as the bulls are often hurt or killed during or following the run.

Cathedral

⌂ C/Dormitalería 1; 948 21 25 94 ⏰ 10:30am-7pm Mon-Sat (to 6pm in winter)

The cathedral of Santa María la Real was built during the 13th–16th centuries, and later remodelled several times. The aisled Gothic shrine has a Rococo sacristy, chapels and a Neo-Classical façade by Ventura Rodríguez. One of the two towers holds a great 12-tonne bell, named María to honour the patron saint to which the cathedral is dedicated. Inside the cathedral, some of the lovely painted decoration on the walls and pillars has been restored. The cloister, with its beautifully carved 14th-century gateways – Puerta Preciosa and Puerta de Amparo – is a masterpiece of European Gothic style. The southern entrance to the cloister is the Puerta de la Preciosa, where the cathedral priests gather to sing an antiphon (hymn) to La Preciosa (Precious Virgin) before the night service.

The Museo Diocesano is housed in the cathedral's 14th-century kitchen and refectory. Here there are displays of Gothic altars, statues from all over Navarra, and a French 13th-century reliquary of the Holy Sepulchre.

The medieval stone
Puente de Piedra
crossing the River Ebro

2

LOGROÑO

**🅰A6 📍La Rioja ✈13.5 km (8 miles) E 🚌 ℹ️C/ Portales 50;
www.lariojaturismo.com**

Logroño lies on the banks of the Ebro river, spanned
by the Puente de Piedra, a 19th-century stone bridge
designed by Fermín Manso de Zúniga. Originally a
Roman settlement, the city owes its enduring existence to its riverside location and its importance as a
religious centre. Myriad grand churches and spectacular religious monuments pepper the city – testament
to its prominence as an important stopping point on
the Camino de Santiago pilgrimage route *(p70)*.

①

Catedral de Santa María de la Redonda

**🏛C/Portales, 14
🕐8am-1pm & 6-9:45pm
Mon-Sat, 9am-2pm &
6:30-9:45pm Sun
🌐laredonda.org**

The city's great showpiece is
its Gothic Catedral de Santa
María de la Redonda. Set in
the pleasant old quarter on
the River Ebro, the cathedral
has huge twin bell towers and
rich Baroque ornamentation.
Inside are the Capilla de
Nuestra Señora de la Paz,
containing a Plateresque
reredos and the tomb of

the cathedral's founder, Diego
Ponce de León.

②

Iglesia de Santiago el Real

**🏛C/Barriocepo, 8
🕐8:15am-1:15pm & 6:30-
7pm daily 🌐santiago
elreal.org**

This vast 16th-century church
once housed the archives of
the city council. Inside is an
image of the patron saint, Our
Lady of Hope, and above the
south portal, an equestrian
statue of St James. Beside the
church is the Fuente de

Santiago, a fountain where
pilgrims stopped to cool off.

③

Murallas de Revellín

🏛C/Once de Junio, 6

Only a small section of the
Murallas de Revellín – the

DRINK

As the capital of Rioja,
Logroño is an ideal place
from which to visit
wineries producing
the region's fine
eponymous wine.
Here are two of
our favourite
Logroño *bodegas*.

**Bodegas Franco-
Españolas**
🏛Calle Cabo Noval 2
🌐francoespanolas.com

**Bodega Marqués
de Murrieta**
🏛N-232a Km 402
🌐marquesdemurrieta.
com/bodegas-rioja

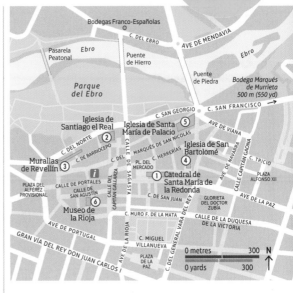

INSIDER TIP
Tapas Tour of Calle del Laurel

For a taste of local life take a wander along Calle del Laurel, a lively hub of bars and cafés offering mouthwatering tapas and bags of atmosphere *(www. callelaurel.org)*. Every spot has its own speciality: dip into Bar Soriano for mushrooms and grilled *gambas*, or head to Torrecilla for a steak sandwich with a rich honey dressing.

12th-century city walls – survives. The fortifications encompass the Puerta Revellín, and are adorned with the coat of arms of Carlos V.

④
Iglesia de San Bartolomé

C/San Bartolomé, 2
941 25 22 54 11:30am-12pm & 12:30-1:15pm daily

Near the cathedral stands the 13th-century Iglesia de San Bartolomé, which might have formed part of the city's fortifications. Its impressive Gothic portal is adorned with

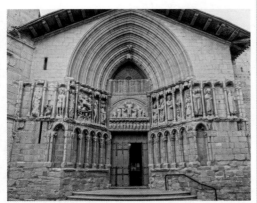

↑ The carved Gothic portal of the Iglesia de San Bartolomé

sculpted figures of Christ, the Virgin, the apostles and saints. The 16th-century tower shows Mudéjar influence.

⑤
Iglesia de Santa María de Palacio

C/ Marqués de San Nicolás, 36 9am-1:30pm & 6:30-8:30pm daily

Founded in the 11th century, the church of Santa María

de Palacio has taken on an irregular form over the centuries. Its most striking element is a beautiful 13th-century octagonal tower, resembling a massive pyramid, which locals have dubbed the *aguja* (needle). Inside are gilded Italian reredos, originally crafted for the cathedral, and an altarpiece by Arnao of Brussels. The Neo-Classical main portal is adorned with a figure of the Virgin and of angels playing instruments.

⑥
Museo de la Rioja

Plaza de San Agustín, s/n
10am-2pm & 4-9pm Tue-Sat, 10am-2pm Sun & public hols 25 Dec, 1 Jan
museodelarioja.es

Housed in an 18th-century Baroque palace, this museum of Rioja's history seamlessly transports visitors from the prehistoric through to the modern day with its informative, well-organized exhibits. Of particular note are the prehistoric artifacts, such as Palaeolithic tools and weapons, Roman coins, and pottery.

EXPERIENCE MORE

3

Las Cinco Villas del Valle de Bidasoa

 B5 Navarra
 Oieregui; www.turismo navarra.es

In the Bidasoa river valley are five attractive towns that owe their unique character not only to the beautiful forest scenery, but also to the proximity of the border with France and the iron industry that thrived here.

The most northerly is Bera (Vera), the largest of the five towns, which has a mix of agriculture and industry. Trade with France has played an important role in this town's history. The celebrated Basque writer Pío Baroja lived here. The highest point in the town is Larrún hill, from where there are magnificent views of the forested surroundings.

The road south passes through Lesaka, where the houses have wooden balconies under deep eaves, and continues to pass hills dotted with white farmsteads to reach Igantzi (Yanci), the smallest of the towns in the area. The nearby hills conceal several old *caseríos* (farmhouses) as well as a spring with therapeutic powers.

Arantza is the most secluded and remote of the towns. Since the 12th century, pigeons have been caught in huge nets strung across a pass above the nearby village of Etxalar. From the summit of La Rhune, on the French border above the valley, there are great views of the Pyrenees.

4

Elizondo

 B5 Navarra
 Museo Jorge Oteiza; 948 58 15 17

In the middle of a beautiful valley, straddling the banks of the Baztán river, lies the district capital of Elizondo. In Basque, the name of the town means "beside the church". Traditionally, the inhabitants of Elizondo farmed livestock, but today, despite the infertile soil, agriculture is the mainstay of the economy.

The local architecture features Gothic houses and nobles' residences decorated with coats of arms, testifying to Elizondo's long and splendid past. The town's best-known buildings are the Palacio de Arizcunenea, an 18th-century Baroque palace with a façade characteristically set back from the street, and the arcaded town hall. The eclectic Iglesia de Santiago, dedicated to the patron saint of Elizondo, was built at the beginning of the 20th century. The towers are imitation Baroque; inside is a Neo-Gothic organ.

On the northern border of Navarra is Zugarramurdi, a town infused with the

INSIDER TIP
Hellwater Path

From Elizondo, a 20-minute drive takes you to Etxalar, the start of the Sendero Infernuko Erreka. This hour-long hike winds alongside a creek through forest to reach an old restored watermill over an impressive waterfall.

Zugarramurdi caves, a witches' meeting-place near Elizondo ↑

sweet fragrance of herbs; surrounding it are pastures with grazing cows and hills dotted with large *caseríos*. Amid the scenery stand ancient houses with coats of arms and the 18th-century Iglesia de la Asunción, partially destroyed during the Napoleonic Wars. More famous, however, are the Cuevas de Zugarramurdi, just outside town, said to have been a meeting place for witches in the 16th century.

Cuevas de Zugarramurdi
⊛ ⏰ Winter: 11am–6pm Tue–Sun (to 7pm Sat & Sun); summer: 11am–8pm daily (booking advised) 📅 18–30 Aug 🌐 turismozugarramurdi.com

---

5
Bosque de Irati

🅰 C5 🅝 Navarra
🛈 Ochagavía; www.irati.org

In the dampest part of Navarra, spread across the Salazar and Aezkoa valleys,

↑ Beech foliage taking on glowing autumn colour in the Bosque de Irati

is this large forest, covering an area of 17,000 ha (42,000 acres). The trees are chiefly beech and fir, and there are many species of wild animal, including red deer, fallow deer, wild boar and capercaillie.

Hidden deep in the forest is Lago Irabia; there are also refreshing natural springs and the fast-flowing Irati river.

At the confluence of the Urbeltza and Urtxuria rivers stands the Ermita de la Virgen de las Nieves (Madonna of the Snows), while between the villages of Lumbier, Sangüesa and Liédena lie the ruins of a Roman settlement. Rising high above the treetops are the imposing peaks of Pico de Orhi.

In the district of Aezkoa are the ruins of a small 18th-century weapons factory – one of the best examples of Spanish industrial architecture of the period.

The Bosque de Irati leaves an unforgettable impression on visitors, especially in autumn, when the beech leaves turn beautiful colours. In 2017, it was declared part of the collective World Heritage Sites of beech forests.

> **THE WITCHES OF ZUGARRAMURDI**
>
> In 1609, the Inquisition accused 40 women from Zugarramurdi of witchcraft. Twelve of the women were burned at the stake. The women were charged for holding witches sabbaths (communions) in the Akelarre meadow at the entrance to the Cuevas de Zugarramurdi. The Basque word *akelarre*, originally meaning "he-goat" has come to stand for any kind of witches' gathering. Traditionally the witches' legend is commemorated in Navarra by a summer festival during which roast lamb is eaten.

6
Valle de Salazar

🅰 C5 🅝 Navarra
🛈 Ochagavía; 948 89 06 41

In the eastern part of the Navarrese Pyrenees extends the Salazar river valley. Thanks to its proximity to the sea, it is damper than other valleys in the region and is covered in beech woods.

Perched along the banks of the river are typical mountain villages featuring stone and timber houses with thatched roofs. The prettiest and most characteristic of these is Ochagavía. Preserved here are six stone bridges as well as the shrine of Santa María de Muskilda, where a lively fiesta in honour of the Virgin takes place in September each year.

The inhabitants of the Valle de Salazar earn their living principally from sheep farming and forestry. The idyllic countryside provides ample opportunities for relaxing walks and there is good terrain here for active sports, including skiing and mountain biking.

↑ Ancient beech forests near Belagoa in the lovely Valle de Roncal

⑦ Valle de Roncal

 C5 🏔 Navarra
🚌 From Pamplona 🛈 Paseo Julian Gayarre, s/n, Roncal; www.vallederoncal.es

Situated on the northeastern border of Navarra, the Valle de Roncal is the highest and most mountainous part of the province. Navarra's loftiest peak – Mesa de los Tres Reyes, or Table of the Three Kings – is situated here. Winters in the Roncal Valley are long and snowy; summers are mild. The village of Burgui to the south affords panoramic views of the valley, its contours carved by the Esca river. A medieval bridge can be seen here. Roncal (Erronkari), a village with cobbled streets and stone houses, is the geographical heart of the valley.

There are ski runs in the small, post-glacial Valle de Belagoa. The district can be toured in a variety of ways: on horseback, by bike, in a four-wheel drive or on foot.

Isaba (Izaba), the largest town in the valley, is a ski resort and a popular base for skiers and mountaineers. Situated at the confluence of three rivers, Isaba features fine houses with steep roofs and coats of arms on their façades. The 16th-century church of San Cipriano contains a painted Plateresque reredos and a Baroque organ.

The Valle de Roncal's spectacularly clear night skies have gained it recognition as a stargazing destination by the Starlight Foundation, an initiative of Spain's Astrophysics Institute of the Canary Islands dedicated to defending the quality of the night sky.

TOP 3 REGIONAL DELICACIES

Trucha a la Navarra
Trout stuffed with *jamón serrano* (thinly sliced cured ham), then braised in olive oil.

Cordero al Chilindrón
This traditional lamb stew features on almost every menu in Navarra.

Queso de Roncal
A sheep's milk cheese with a distinctive, slightly smoky flavour.

 GREAT VIEW
Mirador de San Miguel

A winding uphill drive through the Sierra de Aralar takes you to the Santuario San Miguel de Aralar. This delightful chapel on the summit is a vantage point for magnificent vistas.

⑧ Sierra de Aralar

 B5 🏔 Navarra
🛈 Plazaola 21, Lekumberri; 948 50 72 04

The Aralar mountain chain runs along the border between Navarra and the Basque province of Guipúzcoa. This ancient massif, covered in beech, oak and bracken, is criss-crossed by rivers; its highest peak is Irumugarrieta, at 1,427 m (4,682 ft) above sea level. Some of the mountainsides are so steep that, in order to cut the grass, farmers have to tie themselves to ropes attached to trees. This area is Basque-speaking.

Several megaliths still stand in the area, including the Albi dolmen. A short distance away are circular shepherds' huts known as *arkuek*.

High in the mountains is the Romanesque shrine of San Miguel, with three aisles and apses. The Archangel Michael was traditionally venerated in the area; it was believed he shared some traits with Hermes and was a messenger between heaven and earth. Inside the shrine is a silver-coated figure of him with a crucifix on his head. There is also a superb 12th-century enamelled reredos in the Romanesque-Byzantine style; its centrepiece is an image of the Virgin and Child surrounded by 18 medallions depicting mythological and religious scenes.

Lekumberri (Lekunberri) is a base for excursions into the valley and mountains. Here are some excellent *caseríos* (Basque farmhouses) bearing coats of arms as well as the aisleless Gothic church of San Juan Bautista, dating from the 13th century. Local crafts can be purchased in the town.

---

⑨

Roncesvalles

🅰C5 🏛Navarra
ℹ Antiguo Molino (Old Mill); www.roncesvalles.es

Set high on a pass through the Pyrenees – one of the oldest crossings in the mountains – is the village of Roncesvalles (Orreaga in Basque). This old settlement was built to serve travellers and pilgrims walking the Camino de Santiago *(p70)*.

The most important building in the village is the Colegiata Real, founded by Sancho VII the Strong, who chose it as his burial place. Inside the church is Sancho's white tomb, lit by a stained-glass window depicting his great victory at the Battle of Las Navas de Tolosa in 1212. Below a high canopy is a silver-plated Virgin and Child (Virgen de Roncesvalles). The church dates from the 13th century and is one of the best examples of Navarrese Gothic, although during the 17th century it was given a more Baroque appearance.

The 18th-century pilgrims' hospital – the only one to have survived to the present day – now accommodates a hostel for today's wayfarers.

In a slightly out-of-the-way location is the 12th-century Capilla del Espiritu Santo, considered to be the oldest building in the village. According to legend, it was here, after the battle of 778, that Charlemagne ordered Roland and the other fallen knights to be buried.

One of the village's more modern buildings is the presbytery, or Casa Prioral, which has an annexe containing a library and a museum displaying sculpture, painting, incunabula (early printed texts) and precious jewellery.

> ## ROLAND IN RONCEVALLES
>
> The 12th-century French epic poem, *The Song of Roland*, describes how the rearguard of Charlemagne's army – in which Roland led the Frankish knights – was slaughtered by the Moors. The truth is somewhat different, however: the victors were not Moors but warlike Basque highlanders from Navarra, who wanted to manifest their independence. Preserved in Roncesvalles is the stone upon which Roland tried to break his sword. A boulder marks the spot where Charlemagne is said to have found the fallen knight who, according to legend, was buried in the Capilla del Espiritu Santo in Roncesvalles.

↑ Navarrese Gothic vaulting over the nave of the Colegiata Real at Roncesvalles

10 Puente la Reina

B6 **Navarra** **Calle Mayor 105; 948 34 13 01**

Puente la Reina takes its name from the seven-span, humpbacked bridge built here for pilgrims in the 11th century. At its centre once stood a figure of the Virgen del Txori, which was transferred to the church of San Pedro in the 19th century.

On the eastern side of town rises the 13th-century, Romanesque-Gothic Iglesia del Crucifijo, a church ostensibly built by the Knights Templar. A walkway above the beautifully sculpted entrance connects the church with the pilgrims' hostel. Inside is a 14th-century Y-shaped crucifix carved from a single tree trunk.

Isolated in fields some 5 km (3 miles) east of Puente la Reina is the tiny 12th-century Romanesque Ermita de Santa María de Eunate. The hermitage's octagonal plan is clearly visible on the Mozarabic-inspired vaulting. It is fringed by a remarkable cloister with many arches, which may have given the church its name – in Basque *ehun atea* means "one hundred doors". West of Puente la Reina is the showpiece hill village of Cirauqui. It is quite charming, if rather over-restored. Chic little balconied houses line tortuously twisting alleys linked by steps. The Iglesia de San Román, built in the 13th century on top of the hill, has a sculpted west door.

Puente la Reina, a crossing point for pilgrims *(inset)* over the Arga river

> It is fringed by a remarkable cloister with many arches, which may have given the church its name - in Basque *ehun atea* means "one hundred doors".

11 Monasterio de Leyre

C5 **Yesa, Navarra** **From Yesa** **Daily (Wed-Sun only 7 Jan to 28 Feb)** **monasteriodeleyre.com**

The monastery of San Salvador de Leyre sits high above a reservoir, alone amid breathtaking scenery, backed by limestone cliffs. The abbey, mentioned in documents dating from the 9th century, was in its heyday in the 11th century, when it was rebuilt by Sancho III the Great. Sancho III and his successors made it the royal pantheon of Navarra.

In keeping with Cistercian rule, the church is austere in appearance. The tower, built on a square base, has triforia (galleries) in each of its walls. Nearby is the entrance to the unusual crypt – underneath its arches rises a forest of squat, completely unadorned columns. The kings of

Castillo de Javier, birthplace of St Xavier, Navarra's patron saint ↑

Navarra are buried here. The weather-worn façade of the west portal is decorated with carvings of strange beasts, birds and human figures intertwined with plant motifs. The monks' Gregorian chant during services is wonderful to hear. Part of the monastery now accommodates a hotel.

Castillo de Javier

⚑C6 ⊕Javier, Navarra 🚌From Pamplona 📞948 88 40 24 🕐10am–6:30pm daily

In the 10th and 11th centuries, prior to the construction of this castle, a watchtower stood here, to which new buildings were gradually added. In the 16th century, Cardinal Cisneros ordered the castle to be redesigned as a fortress, demolishing its battlements and towers. In recent times the complex has been restored, including its castle towers and drawbridge. It now houses a Jesuit college.

St Francis Xavier, a missionary and co-founder of the Jesuit order (and the patron saint of Navarra sportsmen), was born in the castle in 1506. Preserved here are his bedroom and a chapel with a Gothic walnut crucifix. According to legend, at difficult

moments in the saint's life, and on the anniversary of his death, droplets of blood have appeared on the crucifix.

The chapel walls are decorated with a macabre mural of grinning skeletons, a depiction of The Dance of Death. Every year from 4 to 12 March, the inhabitants of Navarra make a penitent pilgrimage to the castle chapel.

Sangüesa

⚑C6 ⊕Navarra 🚌 ℹC/Mayor 2; www.sanguesa.es

Set on the Camino de Santiago, Sangüesa was one of the main trading centres in the region. The town has two churches of note. The Iglesia de Santa María la Real, whose construction began in the 12th century, has a splendid Romanesque portal. Preserved in the sacristy is a 15th-century processional monstrance, measuring 1.35 m (4.4 ft) in height. The Romanesque-Gothic Iglesia de Santiago el Mayor has a battlemented tower. Inside, it is decorated with motifs of the pilgrimage route – scallop shells (vieiras), walking sticks and gourds. A polychrome stone figure of St James was discovered under the church.

EAT

Santxotena
Locally sourced, home-made Spanish food on the riverside, served up by very friendly and welcoming staff.

⚑B5 ⊕Calle Pedro de Axular, Elizondo 🌐santxotena.es

Mediavilla
A charming, homely restaurant, with set menus if you want to sample a good range of the Basque fare on offer.

⚑C6 ⊕Calle Alfonso El Batallador 15, Sangüesa 📞948 87 02 12

Restaurante Ciudad de Sangüesa
A decent three-course meal here will set you back less than €15, without compromising on quality.

⚑C6 ⊕Calle Santiago 4, Sangüesa 📞948 43 04 97

EXPERIENCE Navarra and La Rioja

14
Olite

B6 **Navarra**
**Plaza Teobaldos 4;
www.olite.es**

Olite, once a royal residence
of the kings of Navarra, still
has fragments of Roman
and medieval walls. In the
15th century, Carlos III set
about constructing here a
monumental, eclectic **Palacio
Real de Olite**, regarded as a
gem of Navarrese Gothic style.
The palace was meticulously
rebuilt in the 19th century
after a devastating fire. Next
to the complex is a network
of medieval underground
passageways – remnants of
Carlos III's plan to link his
residence with the palace in
Tafalla. The Gothic Iglesia de
Santa María La Real features
a richly carved portal and a
superb Renaissance reredos.
The highlights of the 12th-
century Iglesia de San Pedro
Apóstol are the Romanesque
cloister and a squat Gothic
tower topped by a huge spire.
   Olite puts on a medieval
festival in the second half of
August, leading up to the
26th, the saint's day of Olite's
patron, the Virgen del Coléra;
it commemorates the town's

Part of the Palacio de Los
Reyes de Navarra, in Estella,
now housing a museum

deliverance from a cholera
epidemic in 1885. This is
swiftly followed by the town's
lively Fiesta Patronales, in
mid-September.

Palacio Real de Olite
🕙🕙 **☏ 948 74 12 73** (phone
in advance to book tours)
◐ Oct-Mar: 10am-6pm Mon-
Fri, 10am-7pm Sat & Sun;
Apr-Jun & Sep: 10am-7pm
Mon-Fri, 10am-8pm Sat, Sun
& hols; **Jul & Aug:** 10am-8pm
daily **⊘1 & 6 Jan**

15
Estella

B5 **Navarra**
**Plaza San Martín
Enparantza 4; www.
estellaturismo.com**

King Sancho Ramírez, who
founded Estella in the 11th
century, ensured that the pilgrimage route to Santiago
passed through the town.
Today, Estella is famous for its
historic churches, palaces and
monasteries, for which it has
been dubbed the Toledo of
the North. Close to the Ega
river stands the Palacio de los
Reyes de Navarra, the only
surviving example of secular
Romanesque architecture in
the province. Near it, crowning
a steep hill, is the Iglesia de
San Pedro de la Rúa, with an
original 13th-century portal
and 12th-century cloister. The
north portal of the Iglesia de
San Miguel (12th- to 14th-
century) is adorned with a
bas-relief depicting St Michael
slaying a dragon. Preserved
on Calle Mayor are several

←

The fantastical building
complex making up the
Palacio Real, Olite

houses with coats of arms, including a 17th-century Baroque palace.

Ujué

🅰B6 🏠Navarra ℹPlaza Municipal; www.ujue.info

To the east of Olite is Ujué, one of the better-preserved hill villages in the lower Pyrenees, commanding a high spur at the end of a winding road. With quaint façades, cobbled alleys and steep steps, the town is concentrated around the imposing fortified Iglesia de Santa María, and has the atmosphere of a medieval stronghold. The impressive and austere church is in Gothic style, featuring a Romanesque chancel and an exterior lookout gallery. On the Sunday after 25 April,

> **On the Sunday after 25 April, pilgrims in black capes visit the Virgin of Ujué, whose image is displayed in the church.**

pilgrims in black capes visit the Virgin of Ujué, whose image is displayed in the church. The heart of Carlos II is also kept here. The ruined fortifications around the church offer fantastic views of the Pyrenees.

Monasterio de Irache

🅰B5 🏠Ayegui, Navarra 🚌 📞948 55 44 64 🕙10am-1:30pm & 4-7pm Wed-Sun (to 6pm in winter)

The word *iratze* means "fern" in Basque, and there were probably many ferns growing in the vicinity when the Benedictine monks began construction of their monastery in the 11th century. The pilgrims' hostel here was the first to be built in the region. Since the monastery has always been inhabited, the entire complex has been preserved in excellent condition. It comprises a 12th-century church, a cloister in the Plateresque style, a tower and a Spanish Baroque building that served as a university from 1569 to 1824. The aisleless church features three semicircular apses. The

famous Bodegas Irache next to the monastery has a wonderful drinking fountain with taps for both water and red wine, offering thirsty pilgrims a free glass of the beverage of their choice. A polite notice asks travellers not to fill up their plastic bottles from the wine tap.

The Irache vineyards were granted to the monastery in 1072 by King Sancho IV of Navarre. Today, its wines are internationally renowned, and some 3 million bottles are stored on-site here. In the **Museo del Vino**, more than 400 items relating to winemaking, together with bottles from historic vintages, are on display. There's also a shop and tasting area. Tours of the *bodega* start at noon.

Museo del Vino,
🏠Bodegas Irache 🕙10am-2pm & 3-7pm Mon-Sat
🌐irache.com

DRINK

The regions of La Rioja and Navarra claim some of the country's most famous wineries. Here are our favourites.

Bodegas Ochoa

🅰B6 🏠 35 C/ Miranda de Arga, Olite 🌐 bodegas ochoa.com

Bodegas Muga

🅰A6 🏠 Avda Vizcaya, Haro 🌐 bodegas muga.com

Viña Tondonia

🅰A6 🏠 Av Vizcaya, 3, Haro 🌐 lopezde heredia.com

Vivanco

🅰A6 🏠 Carretera Nacional, Briones 🌐 vivancocultura devino.es

Monasterio de la Oliva

🅰B6 🏠 Carcastillo, Navarra 🚌🚃 from Tafalla 📞 948 72 50 06 🕐 9:30am–noon & 3:30–6pm Mon–Sat, 9:30–11:30am & 4–6pm Sun

You'll experience a serene atmosphere at this Cistercian monastery, whose design is characterized by asceticism and simplicity. It was founded in 1143 by the king of Navarra, García Ramírez. Its aisled church has five chapels, the largest closed by a semicircular apse. Nearby is the complex's oldest building – the Capilla de San Jesucristo.

19

Tudela

🅰B6 🏠 Navarra 🚌🚃 ℹ Plaza Fueros 5; www.tudela.es

In medieval times, Tudela was subject to both Christian and Moorish influence, as is aptly demonstrated by the Romanesque-Gothic Colegiata de Santa María Magdalena. The church was built on the ruins of a mosque, and one of its Mudéjar chapels may originally have been a synagogue. Decorative elements from the former mosque are found in the Romanesque cloister. Next to the cathedral rises the 16th-century Palacio Decanal. Bullfights once took place on the busy Plaza de los Fueros, the city's main square. The Judería Vétula is the old Jewish quarter, with tall, narrow brick houses with broad eaves.

20

Bárdenas Reales

🅰B6 🏠 Navarra ℹ bardenas-reales.es

This breathtaking natural park of weathered cliffs and crags stretches between the Ebro and Aragón rivers. Bárdenas Reales is an uninhabited area almost devoid of vegetation. To the north rises a plateau, El Plano de Bárdenas; in the middle is the Bárdena

The Bárdenas Reales, perfect dirt-biking terrain ↑

This breathtaking natural park of weathered cliffs and crags stretches between the Ebro and Aragón rivers.

Blanca, named for its white gypsum cliffs, and to the south is the Bárdena Negra, composed of reddish clay and limestone. Centuries of erosion have given rise to plateaus, plains, rock-needles and river ravines.

In nearby Valtierra, local caves have been converted into a guesthouse, a good base for exploring Bárdenas.

Tafalla

🅰B6 🄝Navarra 🚌
ℹ Olite; 948 74 17 03

Legend has it that Tafalla was founded by Tubal, Noah's grandson. What is known for sure is that it performed an important defensive role by

guarding the Pamplona road. It was first mentioned in a 10th-century Arabic chronicle.

The old quarter, with its cobbled streets, retains a medieval feel. The originally Gothic Iglesia de Santa María, rebuilt in the 16th to 18th centuries, is a monumental structure of rather spartan appearance. The Iglesia de San Pedro – originally Romanesque – was also remodelled; its Baroque tower is crowned by an octagonal lantern.

Artajona, situated 11 km (7 miles) northwest of Tafalla, is unique in Navarra for its completely preserved medieval walls. The main element of the fortifications is the massive Gothic Iglesia de San Saturnino, which has loopholes in its walls and a tower that served as a prison, a belfry and an observation point.

Viana

🅰B6 🄝Navarra ℹPlaza de los Fueros 1; 948 44 63 02

In the Middle Ages, Viana was an important strategic town, fortified to defend Navarra from Castilian invasions. Its massive town walls with four gates date from that period, as do the castle and churches of Santa María and San Pedro. Viana thrived between the 16th and 18th centuries, when

↑ Viana's Iglesia de Santa María, the burial place of Cesare Borgia

aristocrats built Renaissance and Baroque palaces, decorated with coats of arms, wrought-iron balconies and wooden eaves.

Preserved to this day is the Gothic Iglesia de Santa María, with a 16th-century Plateresque façade. Its small windows testify to the building's original defensive purpose. Fine 18th-century paintings by Luis Paret y Alcázar hang in the chapel of San Juan del Ramo.

Near Viana, above the Embalse de las Canas reservoir, is a bird sanctuary.

CESARE BORGIA

The son of the corrupt Pope Alexander VI, Cesare Borgia (1475–1507) was an Italian noble, whose life would inspire Machiavelli's great treatise, *The Prince*.

Appointed Bishop of Pamplona at 17 and then cardinal at 22, he left the Church to become his father's chief henchman, and married the sister of Juan III of Navarra. The sudden death of his father in 1503 ended Borgia's influence at the papal court. He fled from Italy to Aragón, only to be imprisoned, but escaped to Navarra. Borgia died in a siege in 1507, in Viana.

↑ Encounter at a dinosaur footprint site near Enciso

②③

Navarrete

🄰 A6 **🄰 La Rioja** **🚌**
**🄸 Cuesta El Caño;
941 44 10 62**

The town of Navarrete, situated on what was once the border between Navarra and Castile, has been home to many noble families over the centuries. Today, thanks to a programme of renovation, many ancient houses have recovered some of their former splendour, and bear stone coats of arms of their former aristocratic inhabitants. Fine examples can be seen on Calle Mayor. Running behind this street is Cal Nueva, the former approach road to the underground *bodegas*.

The aisled Iglesia de la Asunción, with a Renaissance façade and two porticoes, was begun in the 16th century; inside is an impressive Baroque reredos.

Not far from Navarrete is a cemetery whose entrance gate is the portico of a former pilgrims' hostel. This Romanesque structure, with elements of early Gothic, is composed of five arches, including pointed ones, decorated with scenes from the lives of pilgrims and of St George fighting the dragon.

**DINOSAURS
FROM LA RIOJA**

In the Mesozoic period, La Rioja was a vast river delta – a marshy land-scape covered in rich vegetation. Dinosaurs, both carnivorous and herbivorous, left their footprints in the mud. Over the millennia, due to geological changes, the mud turned into rock, and many of the footprints have been preserved; they can be seen on trails that lead through the area.

②④

Enciso

🄰 B6 **🄰 La Rioja** **🚌**

This tiny village of white houses with red roofs was once a centre of sheep farm-ing and textile production, but its best days have long since passed. Nowadays only one factory produces the woollen rugs for which the village was once renowned. Enciso and the other villages in the area are now largely depopulated.

Two important churches survive here: the 16th-century Santa María de la Estrella, with a square tower and a beautiful 15th-century figure of the Virgin; and the aisleless San Pedro, featuring a 12th-century battlemented tower. A few hermitages and the ruins of a castle are also in the area.

Each year the region attracts a plethora of tourists eager to see the *huellas de dinosaurios* (dinosaur footprints) spread across several sites here. They date from the Mesozoic period, around 100 million years ago. Visitors can follow the marked dinosaur trail from **El Barranco Perdido** ("The Lost Canyon"), a small family adventure park with a pool that includes a museum of palaeontology with interactive exhibits.

El Barranco Perdido
Ⓐ Ⓑ **🄰 Enciso, La Rioja**
🄲 End Mar-mid-Jun & Sep-mid-Oct: 11am-6:30pm Sat, Sun & public hols; mid-Jun-mid-Jul: 11am-7pm Tue-Sun; mid-Jul-end Aug: 11am-8pm daily
🆆 barrancoperdido.com

EAT

Mesón Julián
First-rate, authentic Navarrese cuisine without any pretence. The attentive staff are happy to help with recommendations.

 B6 🏠 Calle de la Merced 9, Tudela 🌐 mesonjulian.com

€€€

Alameda
Savour flame-cooked steaks at this fantastic local *asador* (a traditional Spanish grill house).

 A6 🏠 Plaza Felix Azpilicueta 1, Fuen-mayor 🌐 restaurante alameda.com

€€€

25 Calahorra

🅰 B6 🏠 La Rioja 🚌 🚉
ℹ️ Plaza del Raso 16;
www.lariojaturismo.com

Calahorra's history stretches back almost 2,000 years. Originally known by its Roman name of Calagurris, it was one of the Iberian Peninsula's most important cities. On the banks of the Cidacos river, at the spot where its patron saints, the legionnaires Emeterio and Celedonio, are thought to have been martyred, rises a 15th-century cathedral with a Neo-Classical façade. The cathedral's chapel of San Pedro has a lovely Plateresque reredos (altarpiece).

The Iglesia de San Andrés, whose construction began in the 16th century, features a remarkable tympanum, with attractive relief carvings. On the door at the main entrance is a carving that symbolizes the victory of Christianity over paganism, the latter represented by the sun, the moon and a synagogue. The austere tower is built of stone and brick. Inside the church is a splendid Rococo altar.

The Monasterio de San José was built in the 16th century. At the high altar are murals depicting scenes from the life of St Theresa. To the side of the altar is a *Flagellation of Christ*, by Spanish Baroque sculptor, Gregorio Hernández.

---

26 Nájera

🅰 A6 🏠 La Rioja 🚌 ℹ️ Plaza de San Miguel 10; www. najera.es

At the beginning of the 11th century, when Sancho III of Navarra managed for a time to unite the lands of the Iberian Peninsula, Nájera was the capital of this vast empire. A pre-Roman town, Nájera had earlier played host to diverse cultures and communities, from ancient Basque tribes to the Moors. Cut by the Najerilla river, the town has many historic monuments. The most important is the **Monasterio de Santa María la Real**, established in the 11th century on the spot where, according to legend, a statue of the Virgin was found in a cave. The present buildings date from 1422 to 1453, with later elements added up until the 16th century. From the outside, the Gothic church is almost fortress-like in appearance, but its interior is richly decorated, adorned with sculptures including a lovely Romanesque depiction of the Virgin and Child beside the high altar. The beautiful late-Gothic choir is one of the finest examples of this style in Spain. At the back of this is a Renaissance royal pantheon holding the tombs of 12 former rulers of the Kingdom of Nájera-Pamplona. The Knights' Cloister (Claustro de los Caballeros) combines several different architectural styles including ornate filigree Gothic and Plateresque elements, and the Tapa del Sepulcro de Blanca de Navarra, a 12th-century Romanesque tomb lid.

Monasterio de Santa María la Real
♿ 🏠 Plaza de Santa María 🕐 Times vary, check website 🌐 santamarialareal.net

↑ The cathedral at Calahorra, on a hill where the Cidacos river flows into the Ebro

27
Haro

 A6 La Rioja
Plaza de la Paz; www.
haroturismo.org

Set among lush vineyards on the Ebro river, Haro is the capital of the Rioja Alta region. The town's main monument is a Baroque basilica devoted to its patron saint, Nuestra Señora de la Vega – there is a Gothic figure of her on the high altar. The Iglesia de Santo Tomás is also of note; it features star vaulting and a Baroque tower. The portal was designed as an altar and depicts scenes from the Way of the Cross.

But Haro's real highlight is its wine. The clay soil and the climate – the town is sheltered by a sierra to the north – create perfect vine-growing conditions. Sample the area's famous grapes at one of the many *bodegas*. Several of them offer tours and tastings (book in advance). You can also savour a glass – or two – at one of the charming cafés in the Old Town, which offer local wines and tapas at

→

Bronze statue depicting the stages of the wine-making process, Haro

> But Haro's real highlight is its wine. The clay soil and the climate - the town is sheltered by a sierra to the north - create perfect vine-growing conditions.

low prices in a convivial atmosphere. Haro is so enamoured by its grapes that it celebrates an annual Batalla de Vino (battle of wine) fiesta at the end of June, when revellers dressed in white squirt one another with bottles of wine.

___

28
Sierra de la Demanda

A6 La Rioja Rioja tourism; 941 29 12 60

The Sierra de la Demanda is an ancient mountain range that extends west from La Rioja into the province of Burgos. The forested hillsides (inhabited by wild animals) contain many post-glacial formations – moraines, cirques and lagoons; San Lorenzo (2,272 m/7,454 ft above sea level) is the highest peak. The mountain chain also conceals archaeological treasures such as medieval hermitages and necropolises: in Cuyacabras, there are 166 anthropomorphic tombs and the remnants of a church.

Preserved in the mountains are villages with typical highland homesteads and important historic monuments. To the north of the range, in the village of Anguiano an impressive medieval stone bridge, the Puente de la Madre de Dios, spans the Najerilla river valley. In the heart of the mountains, 30 km (18 miles) south of Anguiano, the village of Manislla de la Sierra

centres around a reservoir, and has a lovely 16th-century stone bridge. Nearby, the beautiful village of Canales de la Sierra is made up of centuries-old stone houses, including grand 16th-century buildings and the 12th-century Santa Catalina hermitage. Further south, 25 km (15 miles) from Canales de la Sierra, the villages of Vizcaínos and Jaramillos de la Frontera are home to magnificent Romanesque churches.

___

29
San Millán de la Cogolla

 A6 La Rioja From Logroño Paseo de San Julián 4, Nájera; www. najeraturismo.es

This village grew up around two monasteries. On a hillside above the village is the **Monasterio de San Millán de Suso** ("Suso" meaning upper). It was built in the 10th century on the site of a community of monks who lived in caves, founded by St Emilian (San Millán), a shepherd hermit, in 547. The church, hollowed out of pink sandstone, has Romanesque and Mozarabic features. It contains the tomb of St Emilian and the graves of seven infants of Lara who, according to legend, were kidnapped and beheaded by the Moors.

The **Monasterio de San Millán de Yuso** ("Yuso" meaning lower) sits in the Cárdenas Valley. It was built between the 16th and 18th centuries on the site of an 11th-century monastery. The part-Renaissance church has Baroque golden doors and a Rococo sacristy, where 17th-century paintings are hung.

Monasterio de San
Millán de Yuso in San
Millán de la Cogolla →

The treasury has a collection of ivory plaques, once part of two 11th-century jewelled reliquaries, then plundered by French troops in 1813.

Medieval manuscripts are also displayed in the treasury. Among them is a facsimile of one of the earliest-known texts in Basque and early Castilian. It is a commentary by a 10th-century Suso monk on a work by San Cesáreo de Arles, the *Glosas Emilianenses*.

Monasterios de San Millán de Suso and San Millán de Yuso

🎥 🕐 ⏰ By guided tour only, times vary, check website
🌐 monasteriodeyuso.org

30

Santo Domingo de la Calzada

🅰 A6 🏠 La Rioja 🚌 ℹ️ Calle Mayor 33; www.larioja turismo.com

This town on the Camino de Santiago pilgrim route is named after an 11th century hermit, Domingo. In the Middle Ages, Domingo established a hospital here and built a bridge over the Oja river to aid pilgrims on their journey to Santiago. In time, a town formed here.

Miracles performed by Domingo, who became a saint, are recorded in carvings on his tomb in the town's part-Romanesque, part-Gothic cathedral, and in paintings on the wall of the choir. Relics of Santo Domingo are held in the crypt beneath the building. The cathedral is worth visiting too for its splendid Medieval decoration. Rich ornamentation depicting the Tree of Jesse (the ancestry of Christ) adorns the pilasters by the entrance to the cathedral chancel. The former high altar, currently placed in one of the aisles, was created in 1541, the last work of the prominent Spanish Mannerist sculptor and architect, Damià Forment. The choir, decorated with figures of saints and inscriptions on the stalls, is a masterpiece of the Plateresque style.

THE CHICKENS OF SANTO DOMINGO

A live cockerel and hen are kept in the cathedral of Santo Domingo de la Calzada as a tribute to the saint's miraculous life-giving powers. Centuries ago, it is said, a German pilgrim refused the advances of a local girl, who denounced him as a thief. He was hanged as a consequence, but later his parents found him alive on the gallows. They rushed to a judge, who said, dismissively, "Nonsense, he's no more alive than this roast chicken on my plate." Whereupon, the chicken stood up on the plate and crowed.

A DRIVING TOUR
LA RIOJA
WINE REGION

Length 85 km (53 miles) **Stopping-off points** Haro; Elciego; Logroño **Terrain** Well-maintained main roads

La Rioja has been producing wine since the Middle Ages. Vines thrive on the region's sunny hillsides, in fertile soils irrigated by the Ebro river and its tributaries. There are over 450 wineries in the region, which can be visited on a leisurely driving tour. This route is dotted with *bodegas* offering tours and wine tastings, along with plenty of hotels and *casa rurales*.

Set off from **Briñas**, *a tiny village home to the Hospedería del Señorío de Briñas, an 18th-century palace, now a hotel.*

In **Haro** (p196) *you'll find the Viña Tondonia (p192), with its futuristic pavilion designed by Zaha Hadid.*

Ollauri *is known for its red wines, celebrated here with autumn wine fairs.*

The fortified town of **Briones** *is home to the Finca Allende winery and the Museo de la Cultura del Vino.*

San Asensio *hosts a wine battle on 25 July – the Batalla del Clarete, named after the local wine.*

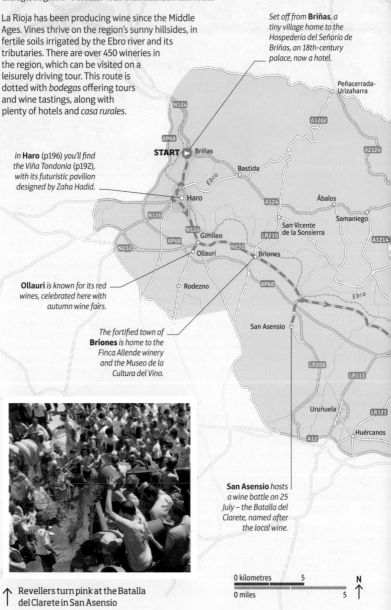

↑ Revellers turn pink at the Batalla del Clarete in San Asensio

0 kilometres 5
0 miles 5

N ↑

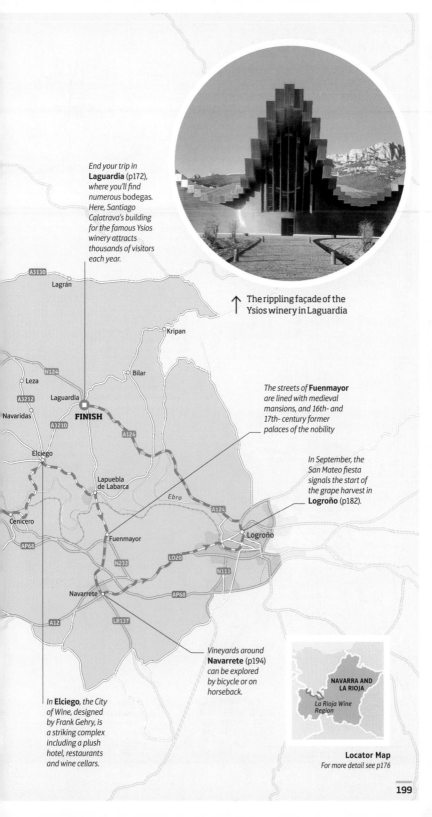

End your trip in **Laguardia** (p172), where you'll find numerous bodegas. Here, Santiago Calatrava's building for the famous Ysios winery attracts thousands of visitors each year.

↑ The rippling façade of the Ysios winery in Laguardia

The streets of **Fuenmayor** are lined with medieval mansions, and 16th- and 17th- century former palaces of the nobility

In September, the San Mateo fiesta signals the start of the grape harvest in **Logroño** (p182).

Vineyards around **Navarrete** (p194) can be explored by bicycle or on horseback.

In **Elciego**, the City of Wine, designed by Frank Gehry, is a striking complex including a plush hotel, restaurants and wine cellars.

NAVARRA AND LA RIOJA

La Rioja Wine Region

Locator Map
For more detail see p176

A DRIVING TOUR
THE NAVARRESE PYRENEES

Length 140 km (87 miles) **Stopping-off points** Elizondo; Oieregi; Ochagavía **Terrain** Winding mountain roads, particularly challenging on the way to Erro and Roncal

Locator Map
For more detail see p176

Encompassing idyllic valleys and forbidding mountain peaks, this tour grants travellers a taste of the astonishing diversity of the Navarrese Pyrenees. This varied landscape sets the scene for active pursuits like biking, rafting and paragliding, but also promises gentler terrain for pleasant walks, rest and relaxation. On this trip, you'll journey through unique Basque villages and wild national parks, passing alpine meadows grazed by sheep, and ancient megaliths that testify to the region's long history.

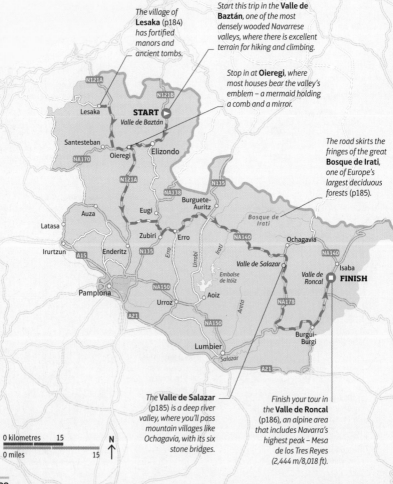

The village of **Lesaka** (p184) has fortified manors and ancient tombs.

Start this trip in the **Valle de Baztán**, one of the most densely wooded Navarrese valleys, where there is excellent terrain for hiking and climbing.

Stop in at **Oieregi**, where most houses bear the valley's emblem – a mermaid holding a comb and a mirror.

The road skirts the fringes of the great **Bosque de Irati**, one of Europe's largest deciduous forests (p185).

The **Valle de Salazar** (p185) is a deep river valley, where you'll pass mountain villages like Ochagavía, with its six stone bridges.

Finish your tour in the **Valle de Roncal** (p186), an alpine area that includes Navarra's highest peak – Mesa de los Tres Reyes (2,444 m/8,018 ft).

0 kilometres 15
0 miles 15
N ↑

↑ Dramatic Arbayún
canyon in the
Valle de Salazar

CENTRAL AND EASTERN PYRENEES

Stretching 440 km (273 miles) from the Bay of Biscay on the Atlantic Coast to the Cap de Creus on the Mediterranean, the Pyrenean mountain chain forms a natural border between France and Spain. In the 8th century, Charlemagne used these inaccessible lands as a buffer state, known as the Marca Hispanica, which separated the Moors of al Andalus in the south from his own Frankish kingdom in the north. As a consequence, the Pyrenean valleys were the birthplace of some of Spain's first Christian kingdoms. Later, after their rulers had moved south, the people who remained lived for centuries in isolation from the rest of Spain. Also thought to have been founded by Charlemagne is Andorra, now a tiny principality headed by two leaders, the Bishop of Urgell and the President of France.

Today the Pyrenees are a paradise for winter sports enthusiasts, scattered with excellent ski resorts. The foothills are crossed by the Aragonese variation of the Camino de Santiago, paths which take in ancient towns of Huesca and Jaca, and the architectural gem of the Monasterio de San Juan de la Peña.

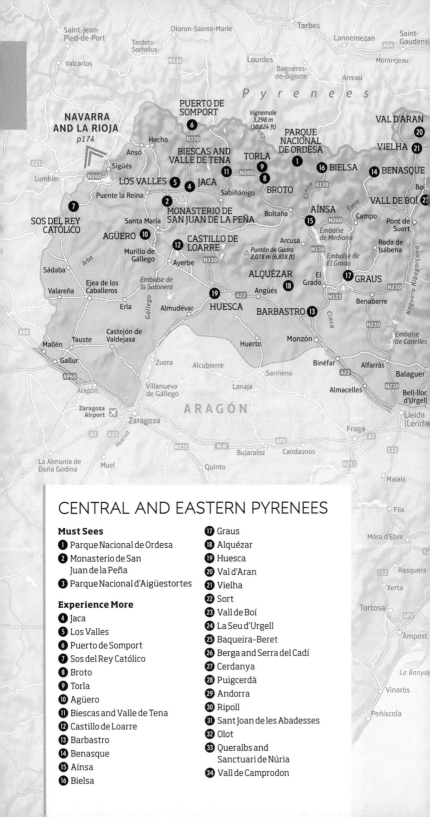

CENTRAL AND EASTERN PYRENEES

INSIDER TIP
Tips for Walkers

Several well-marked trails follow the valleys (see website for details). Walking boots are a must and the mountain routes may require climbing gear. Pyrenean weather changes rapidly – beware of ice and snow early and late in the season.

→

The Río Arazas rushing through the Valle de Ordesa

❶

PARQUE NACIONAL DE ORDESA

🗺 D5 🏠 Aragón 🚆 Change at Sabiñánigo for Torla 🚌 Sabiñánigo
🛈 Avenida Ordesa, s/n, Torla-Ordesa; www.ordesa.net

Within its borders the Parque Nacional de Ordesa y Monte Perdido combines the most dramatic elements of Spain's Pyrenean scenery. Made inaccessible by snow in the winter, Ordesa blooms into a paradise for walkers and nature lovers alike once the sun starts shining.

With its core of cobbled streets and slate-roofed houses around the church, the town of Torla-Ordesa is a popular base for visitors to Ordesa. From here you can walk through the Valle de Ordesa, where the Río Arazas cuts through the forest. This valley is one of four glacial canyons – the Añisclo, Pineta and Escuaín make up the quartet – that carve the great upland limestone massifs into spectacular cliffs and chasms.

The 70-m (230-ft) Cola de Caballo ("Horse's Tail") waterfall makes a scenic stopping point near the northern end of the long hike around the Circo Soaso. The falls provide just a taste of the scenery found along the route. Another route takes in the Cañon de Añisclo. A wide path leads along this beautiful, steep-sided gorge, following the wooded course of the turbulent Río Vellos through dramatic limestone scenery.

← A hiker traversing one of the mountainous trails through the park

The town of Torla-Ordesa, at the gateway to the Ordesa and Mount Perdido National Park

TOP 3 PICTURESQUE ORDESA SPOTS

Parador de Bielsa
At the foot of Monte Perdido, this parador looks out over dramatic rock faces streaked by waterfalls.

Mirador de Cacilarruego
This viewpoint on the Senda de los Cazadores trail rewards hikers with stunning vistas of the Ordesa Valley.

Cañón de Añisclo
This beautiful steep-sided gorge, the deepest in the park, follows the course of the Río Vellos through spectacular limestone scenery.

FLORA AND FAUNA OF THE PARQUE NACIONAL DE ORDESA

With some of the most dramatic mountain scenery in Spain, Ordesa is home to many unique species of flora and fauna. Trout streams rush along the valley floor and wooded slopes harbour otters, marmots and capercaillies (large grouse). Gentians and orchids shelter in crevices and edelweiss brave the most hostile crags. Higher up into the mountains, Pyrenean chamois skitter across near-sheer rock faces, and in the skies over Ordesa's rocky pinnacles, great eagles and bearded vultures swoop, dive and float on thermal air currents.

TERRAIN

The park can only be explored fully after the snow melts in spring, and even then much of it has to be visited on foot. In the mountains, breathtakingly steep rockfaces are cut through by waterfalls. Rocky massifs border gentle hills clad in dwarf mountain pine, and higher up, an alpine forest belt of fir and beech trees extends up to 2,400 m (7,900 ft) above sea level. At lower elevation, lush

vegetation provides pasture for grazing cattle and horses, and the meadows host myriad alpine flora and fauna.

FLORA

As well as lush pine and fir forests and birch, beech and wild cherry trees, there is an abundance of rare and special plants in the park. Esparceta (sainfoin), an important honey-yielding and fodder plant, is commonly found in the alpine meadows of the park *(left)*. This long-lived perennial, reaching a height of 60 cm (24 in), produces clusters of pretty pink or carmine flowers. Edelweiss, a symbol of the mountains, is a small flowering plant that grows in grassy alpine areas, usually on inaccessible rocky ledges. It prefers altitudes of 2,000 to 2,900 m (6,560 to 9,515 ft) above sea level. The mountain ash, with its bright berries, is a member of the olive family and is found up to 1,000 m (3,280 ft) above sea level.

↑ Pretty edelweiss growing high in the Pyrenean mountains

← Cattle grazing the lush alpine pastures of the Parque Nacional de Ordesa

PYRENEAN WILDLIFE

1 Otter

These curious, playful creatures can be spotted gambolling in the valleys and hunting in the cold-water streams and pools for trout. Social mammals, otters tend to travel in family groups, and are most active at dawn and dusk.

2 Bearded Vulture

With a wingspan of 2.5 m (8 ft), these rare birds soar above the mountains of Ordesa. Known in Spanish as *quebranta-huesos* (bone breakers), bearded vultures are scavangers, carrying carrion bones high into the air, and dropping them onto rocks below to extract the fatty bone marrow.

3 Asp Viper

In the Pyrenees this venomous snake tends to inhabit grasslands and mountain pastures, and has been found living as high up as 2,000 m (6,560 ft) above sea level. Asp vipers feed on small rodents and reptiles, and can be spotted sunbathing on roads or paths on clear days.

4 Eurasian Eagle Owl

Several species of owl in the park include the low-flying barn owl, the charming long-eared owl and, the largest, the Eurasian eagle owl. These great, barrel-shaped birds hunt by night, feeding on rodents, and even rabbits or caper-caillie. They are fiercely territorial.

5 Weasel

A relative of the stoat and otter, the weasel leads a solitary existence, active mostly during daytime and at dusk. It is a good runner and climber, feeding on fledglings, eggs and mice.

2 🕰

MONASTERIO DE SAN JUAN DE LA PEÑA

🔺C6 🏠Huesca 🕐Times vary, check website
🌐monasteriosanjuan.com

Perched improbably under a rocky overhang in the Aragonese Pyrenees, this medieval monastery is shrouded in complex and fascinating history, and one of the region's most popular sights.

The history of this site dates back to the Moorish invasion, when hermit-monks, fleeing the Moors, settled here. According to legend the monastery was an early guardian of the Holy Grail; the chalice used at the Last Supper was hidden in here to prevent its capture by the Moors. In the 11th century the monastery joined the Benedictine order, and became the first to use the Latin Mass in Spain. After a fire in the 1600s, the building was abandoned in favour of a newer one further up the hillside. This was later sacked by Napoleon's troops. The structure has since been restored and now houses an interpretation centre and a hotel. The central part of the monastery is split across two floors: the lower level is a 10th-century rock-hewn crypt, while the upper floor holds an 11th-century church hollowed out of the cliff face.

The 18th-century Royal Pantheon, whose walls are decorated with historical stucco reliefs, contains the stacked tombs of the early Aragonese kings: Ramiro I, Sancho Ramírez and Pedro I.

Museum

The Lower Mozarabic Church was built in 920 on the site of an earlier rock-hewn shrine dedicated to St John the Baptist.

Romanesque church

←
The medieval monastery, half-concealed by the mountain

CLOISTER CAPITALS

In the monastery cloisters are twenty 12th-century Romanesque capitals, carved with scenes from the Old and New Testaments by an anonymous artist, referred to as the "Master of San Juan de la Peña". The capitals constitute a pictorial Bible, set out in chronological order, beginning with the Creation and finishing with the Ascension of Christ.

↑ The striking 12th-century cloisters, carved with biblical scenes

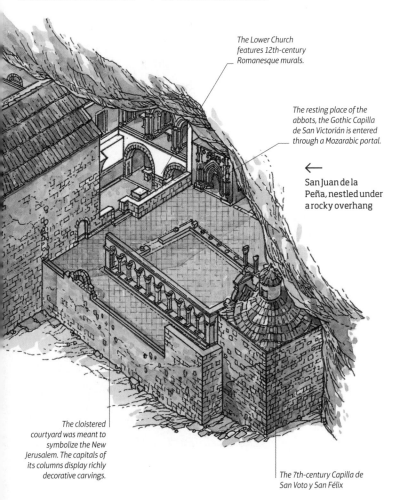

The Lower Church features 12th-century Romanesque murals.

The resting place of the abbots, the Gothic Capilla de San Victorián is entered through a Mozarabic portal.

← San Juan de la Peña, nestled under a rocky overhang

The cloistered courtyard was meant to symbolize the New Jerusalem. The capitals of its columns display richly decorative carvings.

The 7th-century Capilla de San Voto y San Félix

3

PARC NACIONAL D'AIGÜESTORTES

A E6 **C** Lleida **R** La Pobla de Segur **B** Pont de Suert, La Pobla de Segur
i Carrer de les Graieres 2, Boí: 973 69 61 89; Carrer Sant Maurici 5, Espot:
973 62 40 36 **W** parcsnaturals.gencat.cat/en/aiguestortes

The pristine mountain scenery of Catalonia's only national park is among the most dramatic in the Pyrenees. Marked by a dazzling string of post-glacial lakes, waterfalls and towering peaks, rugged Aigüestortes is home to chamois, beavers, otters and eagles.

Established in 1955, the park covers an area of 102 sq km (40 sq miles). The main access towns are Espot, to the east, and Boí, to the west. Dotted around the park are waterfalls and the sparkling, clear waters of around 150 lakes. The finest scenery is around Sant Maurici lake, which lies beneath the twin shards of the Serra dels Encantats (Mountains of the Enchanted). From here, there is a variety of walks, particularly along the lakes leading north to the towering peaks of the Agulles d'Amitges mountains. To the south is the vista of Estany Negre, the highest and deepest tarn in the park.

Early summer in the lower valleys is marked by a blossoming mass of bright pink and red rhododendrons, while later in the year wild lilies bloom in the forests.

TOP 4 PICTURESQUE SPOTS

Santa María de Taüll
A vibrantly coloured 12th-century mural in the church apse depicts Christ in Majesty.

Durro
This village has superb Romanesque churches, including the Església de la Natividad.

Esterri d'Àneu
You can admire the Romanesque bridge of this pretty village amid vivid rhododendrons.

Estany de Sant Maurici
The largest of the park's 100 lakes is surrounded by lofty peaks. Walking trails begin here.

Looking out over the Estany de Sant Maurici, the starting point for many mountain walking trails *(inset)* ↑

INSIDER TIP
Getting There

During the summer, buses run twice daily between Espot, Boí, Erill la Vall and Taüll, ideal for walkers wanting a lift between trails, or heading back to base after a long day's hiking *(www.alsa.es).*

① Romanesque Santa María church in Taüll sits on the southern edge of the park.

② A stunning mura adorns Santa María's central apse.

③ High up in the mountains of Aigüestortes are cosy wooden cabins and refuges for walkers.

EXPERIENCE MORE

4

Jaca

C6 ⚑Huesca 🚹Plaza
de San Pedro 11–13;
www.jaca.es

This picturesque town,
situated in the heart of the
Pyrenees, is Roman in origin
(2nd century AD). In 795, at
the Battle of Las Tiendas,
the town repulsed the Moors,
thanks to the bravery of local
women who fought to drive
back the Moorish armies. In
1054, Jaca became the first
capital of the Kingdom of
Aragón. This event precipit-
ated the construction of
Spain's first Romanesque
cathedral here, modelled on
French designs. The exterior
is mostly Romanesque, but
inside one can trace the
gradual evolution of church
architecture, from Gothic in

> **INSIDER TIP**
> **Animal Magic**
>
> The broad moat of
> Jaca's 16th-century
> citadel has long been
> drained, and today a
> herd of red deer graze
> the lawns that now
> form its floor.

the star vaulting of the aisles,
through Renaissance in the
chapel of St Michael, to
Baroque in the transept
pilasters and some of the
altars. The central apse has
paintings by Manuel de Bayeu,
the brother-in-law of
Francisco de Goya.

In the cloisters, the **Museo
Diocesano** has a fine collection
of Romanesque and Gothic
frescoes from local churches,
including the Iglesia de los
Santos Julián y Basilisa. The
frescoes from the apse of the
Ermita de San Juan Bautista in
Ruesta date from the first half

of the 12th century – a striking
image of the head of Christ
Pantocrator was uncovered
beneath a layer of paint.

Philip II built Jaca's Ciudadela
(citadel) in 1591, ornamenting
it with corner turrets. It is
one of only two surviving
pentagonal citadels in Europe.
Just west of the town centre
lies the Puente de San Miguel,
a famous medieval bridge on
the pilgrimage route.

Museo Diocesano

⊘⊗ ⚑Plaza de la Catedral
☎974 35 63 78 ◷10am–
1:30pm & 4–7pm Tue–Sat (to
8pm Sat, and mid-Jun–mid-
Sep), 10am–1:30pm Sun

5

Los Valles

C5 ⚑Huesca 🚌From
Jaca to Hecho 🚹Museo de
Arte Contemporáneo al
Aire Libre, Pallar d'Agustin,
Hecho; 974 37 55 05

The delightful valleys of Ansó
and Hecho, formed by the
Veral and Aragón Subordán
rivers respectively, were once
isolated due to poor road links,

The 11th-century
Jaca Cathedral, one
↓ of Spain's oldest, and
(inset) its fine interior

enabling their villages to retain traditional customs and a local dialect called Cheso. Now the area's crafts and costumes have made it popular with tourists. The Pyrenean foothills and forests above the valleys are good for walking, fishing and cross-country skiing. Ansó lies in the prettiest valley, which becomes a shadowy gorge where the Río Veral squeezes between vertical crags. Many of its buildings have stone façades and steep, tiled roofs. The 16th-century church has a museum of local costume. Pieces of modern sculpture lie scattered beside the tourist information office, from an open-air festival once held here.

↑ Beautiful 13th-century frescoes in the crypt of the Iglesia de San Esteban, Sos del Rey Católico

Puerto de Somport

C5 Huesca
i Plaza Ayuntamiento 1, Canfranc; www.can franc.es

On the French border, at the head of a long valley that runs down to Jaca, the Puerto de Somport is one of the most historic mountain passes in the Pyrenees. Used by the Romans, and for centuries by pilgrims, it takes its name from the Latin *Summus Portus*.

The pass, on which stands a small chapel with a figure of St James, marks the start of the Aragonese pilgrimage route to Santiago de Compostela, which is older than the more famous route through Navarra. The Aragonese route leads through Canfranc, Villanúa, Jaca, San Juan de la Peña and Santa Cruz de Serós, joining the Navarrese route in Yesa. Nowadays, the austere scenery is speckled with

holiday apartments built for skiing. Astún is the best-organized and most modern resort, while Candanchú is one of Spain's largest winter sports centres.

Sos del Rey Católico

C6 Zaragoza **i** Plaza de la Hispanidad 1; 948 88 85 24

Sos del Rey Católico is one of the Cinco Villas – a group of five picturesque towns granted privileges by Philip V for their loyalty during the War of the Spanish Succession. The town owes its name to King Fernando of Aragón, the "Catholic King", who was born here in 1452. The Palacio de Sada, his reputed birthplace, was built on the ruins of an old castle and features an 18th-century chapel. Also worth a visit, at the top of the town, is the 11th-century Iglesia de San Esteban, with beautiful carved capitals, a Romanesque font and 13th-century frescoes in two of the crypt apses.

The pass, on which stands a small chapel with a figure of St James, marks the start of the Aragonese pilgrimage route to Santiago de Compostela.

8
Broto

D6 Huesca From Sabiñánigo or Aínsa Avenida Ordesa 1; www.turismodearagon.com

Situated in the Ordesa valley, Broto is a good base for excursions to the western side of the Parque Nacional de Ordesa y Monte Perdido (p206). The tiny village derives its name from a Basque word meaning "place covered in blackberry bushes". Broto's inhabitants earn their living from cattle farming and tourism, and they maintain local traditions, such as performing traditional dances like the *rapatan*, a shepherds' dance, and *os palateaos*, a war dance.

Rising above the small town is the 16th-century Iglesia de San Pedro el Apóstol, from which there are breathtaking views of the valley.

A short walk from Broto leads to two other equally fine views: the 50-m (164-ft) Sorrosal waterfall and the Ermita de Nuestra Señora de Murillo, some 1,470 m (4,823 ft) above sea level.

9
Torla

D6 Huesca Plaza Aragón; 974 48 63 78 (Jul–Sep only)

This little town, at the gateway to the Parque Nacional de Ordesa y Monte Perdido (p206) and huddled beneath the forbidding slopes of Mondarruego, is the main tourist centre in this part of the Pyrenees. From here, local guides can be hired to take experienced walkers up to the surrounding peaks; the

→
The massive Mallos de Agüero, rising above the village

most popular of these is Monte Perdido, the "Lost Mountain", its summit 3,355 m (11,007 ft) above sea level.

Torla is a picturesque town with slate-roofed houses and a church dating from the beginning of the 16th century. Each year in February a carnival is held here, during which all the evil of the past year – personified by a man dressed up as a black beast – is destroyed by a brave hunter. In order to humiliate and overpower it, the beast is dragged through the streets of the town in a colourful procession accompanied by a lively singing crowd.

10
Agüero

C6 Huesca San Jaime 1; www.aytoaguero.es

The picturesque setting of this attractive little village, clustered against a dramatic crag of eroded pudding rock known as the Mallos de Agüero, amply rewards a brief detour from the Huesca to Pamplona

 PICTURE PERFECT
Mallos de Agüero

The huge crags behind Agüero lend themselves to any number of arresting images, whether silhouetted against a blue sky or forming a backdrop for the village below.

road. However, rising above the village, and reached by a stony track, is the most important reason to visit Agüero: the stunning Iglesia de Santiago, whose construction began c 1200. The capitals of the columns in this unusual triple-naved building are carved with fantastical creatures, as well as scenes from the life of Jesus and Mary. The most beautiful carvings are on the entrance portal, depicting scenes of the Epiphany and Salome dancing ecstatically. The lively, large-eyed figures appear to be the work of the Master of San Juan de la Peña, also known as the Master of Agüero (p211).

⑪

Biescas and Valle de Tena

D6 **Huesca** **Plaza del Ayuntamiento; www.valledetena.com**

The picturesque Valle de Tena is ideal for walkers and hikers; several well-marked trails lead from here to the surrounding peaks, some of which are over 3,000 m (9,842 ft) above sea level. The places most often visited include the Casita de las Brujas (Witches' Hut), the Ermita de Santa Elena and the Parque de Arratiecho.

Near the entrance to the valley – famous for traditional cheese-making techniques and regional delicacies, such as breadcrumbs with grapes – is the small town of Biescas, which spans the Gállego river. The river divides the town into its two districts of El Salvador and San Pedro, to whom the local churches are dedicated.

The Gállego is one of the most spectacular of the fast-flowing Pyrenean rivers, and Sallent de Gállego is a centre for whitewater rafting, kayaking, rock climbing, fishing and other adventure sports. The beautiful Panticosa gorge is home to the ski resorts of Formigal and Panticosa.

---

⑫

Castillo de Loarre

C6 **Huesca** **Mar–Oct: 10am–7pm daily (until 8pm mid-Jun–mid-Sep); Nov–Feb: 11am–5:30pm Tue–Sun** **1 Jan, 25 Dec** **castillodeloarre.es**

The ramparts of this fortress rise majestically above the road approaching from Ayerbe. On a clear day, the hilltop setting is stupendous, with views of the surrounding orchards and reservoirs of the Ebro plain. Inside the curtain walls lies a complex founded in the 11th century on the site of a Roman castle. It was later remodelled under Sancho I (Sancho Ramírez) of Aragón, who established a religious community here, placing the complex under the rule of the Order of Augustine. Within the castle walls is a Romanesque church containing the remains of St Demetrius.

Barbastro

D6 **Huesca**
Plaza Guisar 1; www.turismosomontano.es

This small town has strikingly beautiful architecture, including the 16th-century Gothic cathedral and two smaller churches – San Francisco and San Julian, from the same period. Clearly visible on a hilltop is the shrine of Santa María del Pueyo. Originally a Moorish fortress stood here, which was later captured by Pedro II. The Virgin Mary is said to have appeared between the branches of an almond tree, and the site has been a place of pilgrimage ever since.

Barbastro is also the centre of the up-and-coming Somontano wine region. The name means "beneath the

Did You Know?

Many of Barbastro's houses have their own small orchard, in the style of a traditional Moorish city.

mountains", and grapes have been cultivated here since at least the 2nd century. The countryside is dominated by vineyards and *bodegas*; Barbastro's tourist office can furnish you with details of the local "Ruta del Vino" – a scenic driving itinerary that takes in several *bodegas* offering tours and tastings.

Benasque

D6 **Huesca**
C/San Pedro 5; www.benasque.com

This village, tucked away in the northeastern corner of Aragón, lies at the head of the Esera valley. Its history stretches back to Roman times; from the 11th century, it belonged to the dukedom of Ribagorza. Its most interesting monuments are the 13th-century Iglesia de Santa María Mayor and the Renaissance Palacio de los Condes de Ribagorza.

Above the village rises the wild Maladeta massif (the name means "cursed mountains"), offering ski runs and mountaineering routes. Behind it are the two tallest peaks of the Pyrenees: Aneto

PICTURE PERFECT
Top of the Tower

For €1, you can climb the tower of Aínsa's Iglesia de Santa María. It's the perfect vantage point for a photograph of the looming Peña Montañes mountain, dramatically framed by a stone window.

(3,404 m/ 11,168 ft above sea level) and Posets (3,371 m/11,060 ft).

The neighbouring resort of Cerler has become a popular base for skiing and other winter sports. At Castejón de Sos, 15 km (9 miles) south of Benasque, the road passes through Congosto de Ventamillo, a scenic rocky gorge.

Aínsa

D6 **Huesca** **Avda Ordesa 5; 974 50 07 67**

The history of Aínsa began in 742, when people fleeing the Moors took refuge in the Pyrenees. Having established a small settlement, they decided to repel the Moorish invaders by force. During one

Aínsa, one of the most beautiful villages in the Spanish Pyrenees

such clash, a shining cross reputedly appeared on the battlefield, to which the victory was attributed. The victory is commemorated every other September during the Fiesta de la Morisma. In the years 1035–38, Aínsa was the short-lived capital of the Kingdom of Sobrarbe.

Aínsa's 12th-century Plaza Mayor, a broad cobbled square, is surrounded by arcaded houses of brown stone. Also on the plaza stands the belfry of the Romanesque Iglesia de Santa María, consecrated in 1181. Behind the church, steep narrow streets lead up to the restored castle with a preserved citadel, dating from the times of the Reconquest.

Bielsa

🅐D6 🄰Huesca 🄸Plaza Mayor (Ayuntamiento); www.bielsa.com

Just 12 km (7.5 miles) from the border with France, the village of Bielsa is a popular base for hikers and mountaineers. It is the main gateway to the eastern side of the Parque Nacional de Ordesa y Monte Perdido, and especially the

Valle de Pineta, one of the park's most beautiful parts. Information about trails is provided at Bielsa's tourist office.

Bielsa was destroyed during the Spanish Civil War, so the architecture of the mountain village is relatively new. The principal attraction here is the **Museo Etnológico de Bielsa**, where you can learn about the history of the region and the local carnival. The latter is based on a ritual performed in pagan times, in which the participants would say a symbolic farewell to winter and greet the arrival of spring. The participants of this fiesta, known as *Trangas*, have huge rams' horns on their heads, blackened faces and big teeth carved out of raw potato. They are said to represent fertility.

Museo Etnológico de Bielsa

🌐 🄰Plaza Mayor; 974 50 10 00 🄲Jul-Sep, Easter & Christmas: 12:30-1:30pm & 6-7pm Tue-Sun; other times by appt only

Graus

🅐D6 🄰Huesca 🄸Plaza Mayor 15; www.turismo graus.com

In 1063, it was here that the famous El Cid (p138) took part in the Battle of Graus, during which the king of Aragón, Ramiro I was killed. One of the northernmost enclaves of Moorish Spain, the town was reclaimed in 1083 during the Reconquest.

Today much of Graus's history is preserved in the architecture of its Old Town. In the heart of the old quarter lies the unusual Plaza de España, surrounded by brick arcades and frescoed half-timbered houses; one of these was home to the infamous Tomás de Torquemada, who in 1483 became Spain's first Inquisitor General. The town's lovely Basílica de la Virgen de

↑ Celebrating St Michael's day with costumed dancing in Graus

la Peña dates from 1538, and features a beautiful Renaissance portal.

About 20 km (12 miles) to the northeast, lies the hill village of Roda de Isábena, site of the smallest cathedral in Spain, built in 1056–67.

DRINK

Pastelería Fabrés
A great cup of coffee and a little something sweet are on the menu here in the centre of Benasque.

🅐D6 🄰Calle las Plazas 22, Benasque
📞974 55 17 82

Pub L'Abrevadero Aínsa
A wide selection of good craft beers and moreish cocktails. You can sit inside in the atmospheric bar or outside on the characterful cobbled street.

🅐D6 🄰Calle Mayor 3, Aínsa
🆆abrevadero.com

EAT

Restaurante Callizo
Gourmet food matched with theatrical presentation.

D6 Plaza Mayor, Aínsa
Ⓦrestaurantecallizo.es

€€€

La Tasca de Ana
Enjoy delicious fresh tapas in this frenetic local bar, one of the best in Aragón.

Ⓥ C6 Calle de Ramiro 3, Jaca Ⓒ 974 36 36 21

€€€

REFU Birreria Vielha
Unpretentious gastro-brewery with great craft beers and street-food-style tapas.

Ⓐ E5 Carrèr Major 18A, Vielha
Ⓦrefubirreria.com

€€€

Las Torres
Taste Michelin-starred dishes such as Iberian ham sushi in an impressive dining room.

Ⓐ D6 Calle de María Auxiliadora 3, Huesca
Ⓦlastorres-restaurante.com

€€€

---

18 Ⓜ

Alquézar

Ⓐ D6 Huesca
🛈 C/Arrabal, s/n;
www.alquezar.org

Some 48 km (30 miles) northeast of Huesca, in a spectacular setting, the village of Alquézar was established by the Moors; its name derives from the Arabic al-qasr, meaning "the fortress". Indeed, a castle was

↑ Well-preserved medieval streets and architecture in Alquézar

built here by Jalaf ibn-Rasid in the 9th century. In 1067, the valiant Sancho Ramírez captured the fortress and turned it into a Christian stronghold, the ruins of which can be seen above the village. Slightly later, in 1085, the king founded the Iglesia de Santa María la Mayor on the rocks above the Vero river canyon. The current, stately, collegiate church was built in 1525–32. From this original structure, lovely Romanesque cloisters with carved capitals remain, along with the free-standing Capilla del Santo Cristo.

19

Huesca

Ⓐ D6 Huesca
🛈 Pl Luis López Allué;
www.huescaturismo.com

Founded under the Roman empire in the 1st century BC, the independent city of "Osca" as it was known to the Romans had one of the first colleges in Spain. Captured from the Moors in 1096 by Pedro I, Huesca became the capital of Aragón until 1118, when the title passed to Zaragoza. Today, it is the second-largest city in the region.

Be sure to visit the Palacio Real and the Romanesque Iglesia de San Pedro el Viejo, originally a Benedictine monastery; it also served as a royal pantheon, where Alfonso I, Ramiro II and other Aragonese rulers are buried.

North of the church, in the heart of the city, stands the beautiful Gothic cathedral (1274–1515). Its west front is surmounted by an unusual Mudéjar-style wooden gallery, while the slender-ribbed star vaulting in the nave is studded with golden bosses. The alabaster reredos (1520–33) is considered to be the finest work of the Valencian sculptor Damià Forment; its series of Passion scenes is highlighted by illumination.

Opposite the cathedral is the Renaissance town hall (1577 and 1610); inside it hangs La Campana de Huesca, a gory 19th-century painting by José Casado del Alisal that depicts the beheading of a group of troublesome nobles in the 12th century by order of King Ramiro II. The massacre occurred in the Sala de la Campana, later belonging to the 17th-century university, and now part of the **Museo Arqueológico Provincial**. This museum has excellent archaeological finds and art that includes Gothic frescoes and early Aragonese painting.

Museo Arqueológico Provincial

🏛 Plaza de la Universidad 1
📞 974 22 05 86 🕐 10am–2pm & 5–8pm Tue–Sat, 10am–2pm Sun and hols 🚫 1 & 6 Jan, 24, 25 & 31 Dec

---

⑳

Val d'Aran

🅰 E5 🅰 Lleida 🚌 🅸 Carrer Sarriulèra 10, Vielha; www. visitvaldaran.com

This Valley of Valleys – *aran* means valley – is a beautiful 600-sq-km (230-sq-mile) haven of forests and flower-filled meadows on the north side of the Pyrenees, separated from the rest of Spain by towering peaks. The valley was formed by the Riu Garona, which rises in the area and flows out to France as the Garonne. With only two access routes from Spain – the Vielha tunnel or the road from Esterri d'Aneu over the spectacular Port de la Bonaigua pass – the valley has a more natural connection with France, and locals speak *Aranés*, a variant of Gascon Provençal.

The fact that the Val d'Aran faces north means that it has a climate similar to that of the Atlantic coast. Rare wild flowers and butterflies flourish in the perfect conditions created by the damp breezes and shady slopes.

Tiny villages have grown up beside the Riu Garona, often around Romanesque churches, notably at Bossòst, Salardú, Escunhau and Artíes.

The valley is ideal for outdoor activities such as skiing and walking. Well-marked trails lead up to the surrounding peaks and glaciers.

㉑

Vielha

🅰 E5 🅰 Lleida 🅸 Carrer de Sarriulera 10; 973 64 01 10

Surrounded by alpine peaks, Vielha has experienced some dramatic moments in history. Napoleon's forces entered it in 1810, occupying the entire Val d'Aran, which was returned to the Spanish crown five years later. Today, Vielha is the capital of the valley and has a modern ski resort that attracts visitors due to its picturesque setting and Romanesque Església de Sant Miguel. Inside the church is a superb wooden 12th-century crucifix – the *Mig Aran Christ*. It once formed part of a larger carving, since lost, which represented the Descent from the Cross. The **Musèu dera Val d'Aran**, is worth visiting for its fascinating exhibits devoted to Aranese history and folklore.

Musèu dera Val d'Aran

♿ 🅰 Carrer Major
🕐 Summer: 10am–1pm & 5–8pm daily; winter: 10am–1pm & 5–8pm Tue–Sat, 10am–1pm Sun 🚫 Public hols
🌐 visitmuseum.gencat.cat/en/museu-dera-val-d-aran

BUTTERFLIES OF THE VAL D'ARAN

A massive variety of butterflies and moths is found high in the mountains and valleys of the Pyrenees. In particular, the isolated Val d'Aran is the home of up to 100 species of butterfly, many rare in Europe and some unique to the area, including swallow-tails, apollos, the iridescent violet copper and the chequered skipper *(right)*. The best time of year to see the butterflies is between May and July.

← Val d'Aran nestled on the hillside, surrounded by snowcapped peaks

22

Sort

 E6 **Lleida** **Camí de la Cabanera, s/n; www.sort.cat**

A pretty mountain town, Sort has a charming old quarter, home to the remains of a castle and the Gothic church of Sant Feliu. It is a popular destination for sports enthusiasts – local activities include kayaking, whitewater rafting, hiking and skiing in nearby Port-Ainé. Sort is Catalan for "luck", and the town is said to boast more winning lottery tickets than anywhere else in Spain.

23

Vall de Boí

 E6 **Lleida** **Passeig de San Feliu 43, Barruera; www.vallboi.cat**

This small valley is dotted with tiny villages, many of

CATALAN ROMANESQUE CHURCHES

Simple and beautifully proportioned, the Romanesque style flourished across western Europe from the 10th to the 13th centuries. The high valleys of the Catalan Pyrenees are especially rich in Romanesque buildings, with a distinctive style seen in the great monasteries of Ripoll and Sant Joan de les Abadesses, and the village churches of the Vall de Boí or Cerdanya. The churches display tall belfries, massive round apses and an extraordinary wealth of fresco painting, influenced by Byzantine art.

which are concentrated around magnificent Catalan Romanesque churches. Dating from the 11th and 12th centuries, these churches are distinguished by tall belfries, such as the Església de Santa Eulàlia at Erill-la-Vall, with six floors. The two churches at Taüll, Sant Climent and Santa María, have superb frescoes. The originals are now in the Museu Nacional d'Art de Catalunya in Barcelona and replicas now stand in their place. Other churches worth visiting include those at Coll, Barruera and Durro.

At the head of the valley is the hamlet of Caldes de Boí,

which is popular for its thermal springs, and the nearby ski station, Boí-Taüll, the highest ski resort in the Pyrenees. It is also a good base for exploring the Parc Nacional d'Aigüestortes (p212), the entrance to which is only 5 km (3 miles) from here.

24

La Seu d'Urgell

 E6 **Lleida** **C/Major 8; www.turismeseu.com**

This ancient Pyrenean town was made a bishopric by the Visigoths in the 6th century. Feuds between the bishops of Urgell and the Counts of Foix over land ownership led to the emergence of Andorra in the13th century. The town's 12th-century cathedral, Santa María d'Urgell has an admired Romanesque statue of Santa Maria. Ramón Llambard worked on the construction of the church until 1175, but it remains unfinished to this day.

The Carrer de Canonges, the town's main thorough-fare, is lined with handsome old houses, including the Ca l'Armenter, a property of the influential de los Luna family from Aragón, one of whose members was Pope Benedict XIII. The town also has ski-lifts and former Olympic buildings.

 ←

The distinctive bell tower at the Església de Santa Eulàlia, Erill-la-Vall

 Tackling the slopes at Baqueira-Beret, one of Europe's top ski-resorts

25

Baqueira-Beret

 E5 ⓐ Lleida ⓘ Ski station; www.baqueira.es

This ski resort is one of Spain's best and most popular. There is reliable winter snow cover and a choice of over 100 pistes at altitudes from 1,520 m to 2,470 m (4,987 ft to 8,104 ft).

Baqueira and Beret were separate mountain villages before skiing became popular, but now form a single resort. The Romans took full advantage of the thermal springs located here; nowadays the springs are appreciated by tired skiers looking to relax after a day on the slopes.

Did You Know?

Baqueira-Beret is a favourite holiday destination of the Spanish royal family.

26

Berga and Serra del Cadí

ⓐ **F6** ⓐ C1411/E09 ⓘ C/Àngels 7; www. turismeberga.cat

The historic town of Berga, at the foot of the majestic Queralt mountain, is famous for La Patum, one of the wildest of Catalan fiestas. Just off the Calle Mayor, a street leads to the Iglesia de San Joan, built by the Knights Hospitallers in 1220. Worth seeing are the former houses of the aristocracy, such as the Modernist Casa Barons at Nos 9–11 Calle Mayor, and, opposite the church of San Joan, the Palacio de los Peguera. The palace was designed in 1905–8 by Ramon Cot. On its first floor is the Cal Negre café. Also on the main street is an 18th-century windmill – the Molino de la Sal. A spectacular walk leads up from the town to the sanctuary of Queralt, high up above Berga.

Some 60 km (37 miles) northwest of Berga, the Serra del Cadí has some of the best walking country in the eastern Pyrenees, and is home to the lonely village of Gosol, where Pablo Picasso spent several months painting in 1905.

STAY

Hotel El Ciervo
This homely Vielha hotel makes the perfect place to relax after a day on the slopes.

ⓐ **E5** ⓐ Plaza de San Orencio 3, Vielha ⓦ hotelelciervo.net

 €€€

Mas El Mir
A converted farmhouse just outside Ripoll where you can relax in peaceful, rustic luxury.

ⓐ **F6** ⓐ Ctra de les Llosses, Ripoll ⓦ maselmir.com

 €€€

Hostal La Plaça
This quiet spot in the Vall de Boí sits opposite a Romanesque church.

ⓐ **E6** ⓐ Plaza de la Iglésia, Vall de Boí ⓦ hostal-laplaza.com

 €€€

㉗
Cerdanya

🅰F6 ⓘPuigcerdà;
972 88 05 42

This large valley sits on the borders of Catalonia, France and Andorra. Ringed by peaks over 2,000 m (6,560 ft) high, Cerdanya is the largest valley in the Pyrenees. It is also bordered in the south by Catalonia's largest nature park – Cadí-Moixeró, which has a population of alpine choughs. From the popular observation point at Balcón de la Cerdanya extend views of the Cadí-Moixero mountain chain, La Tossa, and part of the northern axis of the Pyrenees. Because it is unusually sheltered, the valley has a special temperate microclimate, with balmy summers. The lush surrounding countryside is known for its dairy produce.

The border between Spain and France, agreed in 1659, runs right across the valley. Puigcerdà is the main town on the Spanish side, and Font-Romeu on the French side. One village, Llívia– which was the ancient capital of the region – is Spanish but encircled entirely by French territory.

> **Although Puigcerdà sits on a relatively small hill compared with the vast encircling mountains, it has fine views down the beautiful Cerdanya Valley.**

Among the sites of interest in the valley are Neolithic dolmens, in the little villages of Eina, Brangulí and Talltendre. In Talló there is the Via Ceretana – a Roman road, as well as a Romanesque cathedral. There are impressive churches in several villages, including Ix, Planés, Dorres, Guils, Talltorta, Tarteras, Mosoll and Bastanit. The village of Bellver still has its 13th-century town walls.

Cerdanya is a major winter sports area, especially around La Molina, one of the largest ski resorts in Catalonia. Other good resorts include Masella and Aransa.

㉘
Puigcerdà

🅰F6 🅰Girona ⓘPlaça Santa María; www.
puigcerda.cat

A popular ski centre in winter, and a magnet for walkers and climbers in summer, this is the main town on the Spanish side of the Cerdanya. It is set among hills at an altitude of 1,202 m (3,944 ft), next to the French border.

Although Puigcerdà sits on a relatively small hill compared with the vast encircling mountains (which rise to 2,900 m / 9,500 ft), it has fine views down the beautiful Cerdanya Valley.

The town was established in 1177 by Alfonso II, king of Aragón, and replaced the Roman settlement of Hix as the capital of Cerdanya. Its name derives from the Catalan word *puig* (hill).

In the town centre is the lovely Romanesque church of Sant Tomàs de Ventajo, which dates from the 10th century. The Torre del Campanar is all that remains of the town's parish church of 1288, which suffered damage during a fire. Its present appearance dates from a partial reconstruction in 1938, though the interior contains medieval fragments.

Steps outside Puigcerdà's town hall, offering views over the valley ↑

Andorra

↑ Magnificent carved friezes on the portal of the Monestir de Santa María in Ripoll

🅐F6 🅐Principality of Andorra 🅘Plaça de la Rotonda, Andorra la Vella; www.visitandorra.com

Legend has it that Charlemagne established Andorra in 805 to thank local people for their help in fighting the Saracens. For centuries, the principality fought for its independence from the Spanish dukedoms and France, which it gained in 1278. In 1993, it ratified its first-ever constitution.

Situated on the border between France and Spain, the principality occupies an area of 468 sq km (180 sq miles). It is divided into seven districts, characterized by typical mountain scenery and Mediterranean flora. The average altitude is 1,996 m (6,550 ft) above sea level, and the highest peak is Coma Pedrosa (2,946 m/9,665 ft). Winter sports play an important role, with ski centres in Arinsal, Pas de la Casa, Grau Roig and Soldeu.

Andorra is theoretically a constitutional monarchy, the ceremonial joint heads of state being the French Count of Foix (a title adopted by the French president) and the Spanish bishop of La Seu d'Urgell. The legislative branch of government is the General Council, comprising 28 elected members. The official language is Catalan, though French and Castilian are also spoken. Andorrans are a minority in their own country, accounting for barely 26 per cent of the population; the remainder is made up of Spanish, Portuguese and French.

For many years Andorra has been a tax-free paradise for shoppers, reflected in the crowded shops of the capital, Andorra la Vella. Almost every one of Andorra's 20,000 native residents owns a shop.

Andorra's charm lies not only in its beautiful landscapes, but also its Romanesque architecture. One of the oldest historic monuments is the Iglesia de Santa Coloma. It was built in the 9th century in a pre-Romanesque style, then remodelled several times thereafter. Of particular note is the 12th-century belfry with narrow double windows. The Iglesia de Santa Eulália in Encamp, to the east of the capital, is an example of Pyrenean pre-Romanesque religious architecture. The stone Iglesia de San Juan de Casello has a typical Lombardy-style belfry.

During festivals like Carnival and Easter (p50), Andorra's streets are filled with people dancing the traditional *sardana*, *marratxa* and *el contrapes*.

Ripoll

🅐F6 🅐Girona 🅘Plaça Abat Oliba; www.ripoll.cat

Ripoll is known as the "cradle of Catalonia", because it was the first part of Catalonia recovered from the Moors by Guifré El Pelós (Wilfred the Hairy), founder of the 500-year dynasty of the House of Barcelona. He made Ripoll his capital, and in 879 established here the Benedictine Monestir de Santa María, an important centre of culture and art. The monastery had a well-stocked library, a scriptorium and a highly regarded monastic school. Abbot Oliba (1008–46) raised a new double-aisled basilica, but this unfortunately suffered extensive damage during an earthquake in 1428. Romanesque cloisters, from the 12th to the 16th centuries, survive. The basilica was reconstructed during the 19th century.

Today, visitors can admire the splendid Romanesque portal, with Christ Pantocrator occupying a central position above the entrance, flanked by angels, apostles and the 24 elders of the Apocalypse.

EAT

Umami

Asian-fusion food served up as tapas-style plates in a buzzy, chic and modern restaurant.

 G6 **Av dels Reis Catolics 31, Olot** **972 27 65 71**

€€€

Borda Vella

This spectacular Andorra eatery, where the traditional and modern collide, is an absolute must.

 F6 **22 Avinguda Princep Benlloch, Encamp, Andorra** **bordavella.com**

€€€

El Molí

A great spot for a beer, but even better for a slap-up meal. Catalan food at its best.

 F6 **Plaça Sant Eudald 4, Ripoll** **restaurante-ripoll.com**

€€€

31

Sant Joan de les Abadesses

F6 **Girona** **Plaça de l'Abadia 9; www.santjo andelesabadesses.cat**

The beginnings of this pretty market town date back to the establishment of a monastery in 887. It was founded by Guifré el Pelós, first count of Barcelona, as a gift to his daughter, the first abbess. The Benedictine monastery was in operation until 1076, when its activities were suspended by a papal bull.

The monastery church is unadorned, except for a superb wooden calvary depicting the Descent from the Cross. Originally created in 1150, part of the calvary (one of the thieves crucified with Christ) was burnt in the Civil War and replaced with great skill. The monastery's museum contains a collection of beautiful Renaissance and Baroque altarpieces.

The town, which was once encircled by walls with 24 towers and six gates, is approached by the fine 12th-century Gothic bridge that arches over the Ter river.

32

Olot

G6 **Girona** **C/ Francesc Fàbregas 6; www.turismeolot.com**

This small market town, set in an odd landscape ringed by stumpy, extinct volcanoes and vast expanses of beech woods, lost most of its historic monuments during an earthquake in 1427. The buildings here today date largely from the 18th and 19th centuries.

In 1783, a Public School of Drawing was founded in Olot to train local craftsmen. In time, it became an important centre of religious art; there are some lovely sculptures in the Museu dels Sants, on Carrer de Joaquim Vayreda.

 ←

Sculpture in the Museu dels Sants (Museum of the Saints) in Olot

↑ The elegant pedestrian bridge leading into Sant Joan de les Abadesses

Much of the school's secular work can be seen in the **Museu Comarcal de la Garrotxa**, housed in an 18th-century hospice with a large patio and arcades. There are also exhibits illustrating the development of the provincial economy and crafts.

Museu Comarcal de la Garrotxa

 🏛 Calle Hospici 8 📞 972 27 11 66 🕙 10am–1pm & 3–6pm Tue–Fri, 11am–2pm & 4–7pm Sat, 11am–2pm Sun & public hols 🔒 1 & 6 Jan, 25 Dec

---

③③
Queralbs and Sanctuari de Núria

🅰 F6 🅰 Girona 🚉 ℹ Estació Vall de Núria; www.valldenuria.cat

For a lovely local day out, most people start in the little town of Ribes de Freser, in the Ribes valley. From here a delightful little rack railway leads up to the pretty village of Queralbs, home to the 12th-century Romanesque church of Sant Jaume, and on to the Sanctuari de Núria. There are some wonderful walks from Queralbs, and in winter, there is good skiing,

with a full suite of chairlifts operating busily.

At the top of the railway track is the Sanctuari de Núria, set amid lovely alpine meadows which spread across the hillsides. Located at an altitude of 1,967 m (6,453 ft), the shrine of Núria is an important place of pilgrimage. It was first mentioned in historical documents in 1162. St Gil, who sculpted the altar of the Virgin Mary of Núria, is said to have lived here in the 8th century; the feast of the Virgin is celebrated each year on 8 September. The shrine was extended in 1449, and again in 1640 and 1648. In 1883, it acquired a Neo-Romanesque church, completed in 1964.

In summer you can take a gondola ride up to a peak high above the shrine, with a jaw-dropping viewpoint over the entire valley. The youth hostel perched up here has a café.

---

③④
Vall de Camprodon

🅰 F6 🅰 C38, C26 ℹ Sant Roc 22, Camprodon; www.valldecamprodon.org

This long valley is home to several charming villages. Its main town is Camprodon; nearby is tiny Llanars, with its

Romanesque Església de Sant Esteve, a beautiful church which is tucked away in the old quarter among narrow winding streets. Setcases, further up the valley, is a famous and picturesque spot. Above it is Vallter, the easternmost ski resort in the Pyrenees.

↑ Independent shops in the streets of Camprodon, principal town of the Vall de Camprodon

A DRIVING TOUR
THE COSTA BRAVA

Length 135 km (84 miles) **Stopping-off points** L'Escala; Begur; Palamós; Tossa de Mar **Terrain** Some steep, hilly roads to Begur, but generally easy

In the northeasternmost corner of Spain, the Costa Brava ("wild coast") runs from the region of Empordà (Ampurdán), on the eastern cusp of the Pyrenees, down to Blanes in the south. This driving tour follows the coast, from arty Cadaqués to lively Lloret de Mar, and takes in a varied landscape of pine-backed sandy coves, golden beaches and crowded, modern resorts. Wine, olives and fishing were the mainstays of the area before the tourists came in the 1960s and the first part of this route takes in pretty little towns that seem almost untouched by tourism. The busiest resorts – Platja d'Aro and Tossa de Mar – are to the south, but there are also some unspoiled gems to be discovered on this stretch of the coast, including Sant Feliu de Guíxols and Palamós, which are still working towns behind the summer rush. Take a detour inland to explore medieval villages, such as Peralada, Peratallada and Pals.

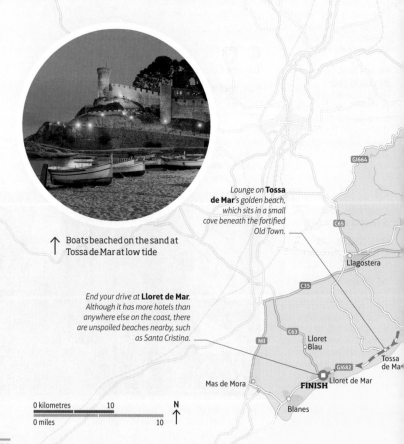

↑ Boats beached on the sand at Tossa de Mar at low tide

*Lounge on **Tossa de Mar**'s golden beach, which sits in a small cove beneath the fortified Old Town.*

*End your drive at **Lloret de Mar**. Although it has more hotels than anywhere else on the coast, there are unspoiled beaches nearby, such as Santa Cristina.*

Peralad

N26

C260

C31

GI664

C65

Llagostera

C35

NII

C63

Lloret Blau

GI682

Mas de Mora

FINISH Lloret de Mar

Tossa de Mar

Blanes

0 kilometres   10
0 miles   10

N ↑

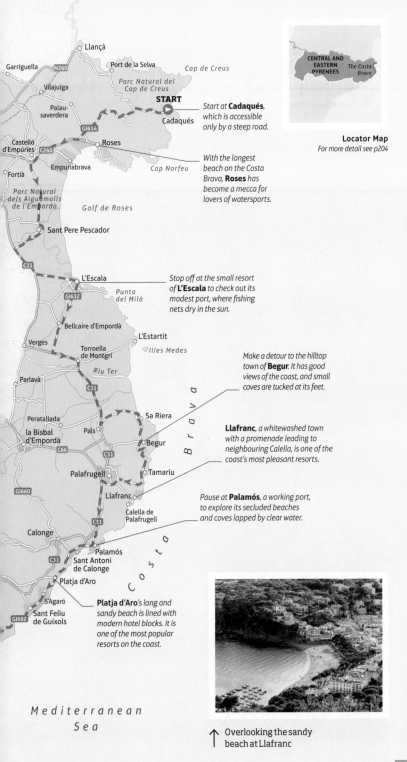

Llançà
Garriguella
Port de la Selva
Cap de Creus

Vilajuïga
N260
Parc Natural del
Cap de Creus

Palau-
saverdera
START
GI614
Cadaqués

Castelló
d'Empúries
C260
Roses

Fortià
Empuriabrava
Cap Norfeu

Parc Natural
dels Aiguamolls
de l'Empordà
Golf de Roses

Sant Pere Pescador
C31

L'Escala
Punta
del Milà
GI632

Verges
Bellcaire d'Empordà
L'Estartit
Torroella
de Montgrí
Illes Medes

Parlavà
Riu Ter
C31

Peratallada
Sa Riera
Pals

la Bisbal
d'Empordà
Begur
C66
C31

Palafrugell
Tamariu
GI660
Llafranc

Calonge
Calella de
Palafrugell
C31

Palamós
Sant Antoni
de Calonge
Platja d'Aro
S'Agaró
Sant Feliu
de Guíxols
GI682

Start at **Cadaqués**, *which is accessible only by a steep road.*

With the longest beach on the Costa Brava, **Roses** *has become a mecca for lovers of watersports.*

Stop off at the small resort of **L'Escala** *to check out its modest port, where fishing nets dry in the sun.*

Make a detour to the hilltop town of **Begur**. *It has good views of the coast, and small coves are tucked at its feet.*

Llafranc, *a whitewashed town with a promenade leading to neighbouring Calella, is one of the coast's most pleasant resorts.*

Pause at **Palamós**, *a working port, to explore its secluded beaches and coves lapped by clear water.*

Platja d'Aro's *long and sandy beach is lined with modern hotel blocks. It is one of the most popular resorts on the coast.*

Costa

Brava

Mediterranean
Sea

↑ Overlooking the sandy
beach at Llafranc

CENTRAL AND
EASTERN
PYRENEES
The Costa
Brava

Locator Map
For more detail see p204

229

NEED TO KNOW

Cycling the craggy Bárdenas Reales

BEFORE
YOU GO

Forward planning is essential to any successful trip. Be prepared for all eventualities by considering the following points before you travel.

AT A GLANCE

CURRENCY
Euro (EUR)

AVERAGE DAILY SPEND

SAVE	SPEND	SPLURGE
€80	€150	€200+

BOTTLED WATER	COFFEE	BEER	DINNER FOR TWO
€0.80	€1	€2.50	€40

ESSENTIAL PHRASES

Hello	Hola
Goodbye	Adiós
Please	Por favor
Thank you	Gracias
Do you speak English	¿Habla inglés?
I don't understand	No comprendo

ELECTRICITY SUPPLY

Power sockets are type F, fitting a two-prong, round-pin plug. Standard voltage is 230 volts.

Passports and Visas

EU nationals may visit for an unlimited period, registering with local authorities after three months. Citizens of the US, Canada, Australia and New Zealand can reside without a visa for up to 90 days. For those arriving from other countries, check with your local Spanish embassy or on the **Exteriores** website.
Exteriores
W exteriores.gob.es

Travel Safety Advice

Visitors can get up-to-date travel safety information from the **UK Foreign and Commonwealth Office**, the **US Department of State** and the **Australian Department of Foreign Affairs and Trade**.
Australia
W smartraveller.gov.au
UK
W gov.uk/foreign-travel-advice
US
W travel.state.gov

Customs Information

An individual is permitted to carry the following within the EU for personal use:
Tobacco products 800 cigarettes, 400 cigarillos, 200 cigars or 1 kg of smoking tobacco.
Alcohol 10 litres of alcoholic beverages above 22 per cent strength, 20 litres of alcoholic beverages below 22 per cent strength, 90 litres of wine (60 litres of which can be sparkling wine) and 110 litres of beer.
Cash If you plan to enter or leave the EU with €10,000 or more in cash (or the equivalent in other currencies) you must declare it to the customs authorities.
Limits vary if travelling outside the EU, so always check restrictions before travelling.

Insurance

It is advisable to take out an insurance policy covering theft, loss of belongings, medical

problems, cancellations and delays. EU citizens are eligible for free emergency medical care in Spain provided they have a valid **EHIC** (European Health Insurance Card).
EHIC
w ec.europa.eu

Vaccinations

No inoculations are necessary for Spain.

Money

Most urban establishments accept major credit, debit and prepaid currency cards. Contactless payments are common in cities, but it's always a good idea to carry cash for smaller items. ATMs are widely available throughout the country, although many charge for cash withdrawals.

Booking Accommodation

Northern Spain offers a diverse range of accommodation, including a system of government-run hotels called *paradors*. A useful list of accommodation can be found on the **Turespaña** website.

Throughout peak season (June–August) lodgings are soon fully booked and prices are high, so reserve in advance where possible. Rates are also higher during major fiestas.

Most hotels quote prices per room and meal prices per person without including tax (IVA).
Turespaña
w spain.info

Travellers with Specific Needs

Spain's **COCEMFE** (Confederación Española de Personas con Discapacidad Física y Orgánica) and **Accessible Spain** provide information and tailored itineraries, and companies such as **Tourism For All** offer specialist tours for those with reduced mobility, sight and hearing.

Spain's public transport system generally caters for all passengers, providing wheelchairs, adapted toilets, and ramps. Most trains and some buses can accommodate wheelchair users. Airports and major stations offer reserved car parking, as well as other facilities. Metro maps in Braille are available from **ONCE** (Organización Nacional de Ciegos).

Accessible Spain
w accessiblespaintravel.com
COCEMFE
w cocemfe.es
ONCE
w once.es
Tourism For All
w tourismforall.org.uk

Language

Castellano (Castilian) is Spain's primary language, but others are widely spoken across the north, most notably *català* (Catalan) in Catalonia; *galego* (Galician) in Galicia; and *euskara* (Basque) in the Basque Country. As a visitor, it is perfectly acceptable to speak Castilian wherever you are. English is widely spoken in the cities and other tourist spots, but the same cannot always be said for rural areas.

Closures

Lunchtime Many shops and some museums and public buildings may close for the siesta between 1pm and 5pm.
Monday Many museums, public buildings and monuments are closed all day.
Sunday While most points of interest are open on Sunday, churches and cathedrals are closed to the public during mass. Some public transport runs less frequently.
Public holidays Most museums, public buildings and many shops either close early or do not open at all.

PUBLIC HOLIDAYS

1 Jan	New Year's Day
6 Jan	Epiphany
Mar/Apr	Good Friday
1 May	Labour Day
15 Aug	Assumption Day
12 Oct	Spain's National Day
1 Nov	All Saints' Day
6 Dec	Spanish Constitution Day
8 Dec	Feast of the Immaculate Conception
25 Dec	Christmas Day

GETTING
AROUND

Whether you are visiting for a short city break or a rural country retreat, discover how best to reach your destination and travel like a pro.

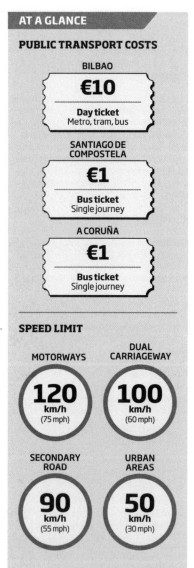

AT A GLANCE

PUBLIC TRANSPORT COSTS

BILBAO

€10

Day ticket
Metro, tram, bus

SANTIAGO DE COMPOSTELA

€1

Bus ticket
Single journey

A CORUÑA

€1

Bus ticket
Single journey

SPEED LIMIT

MOTORWAYS

120 km/h
(75 mph)

DUAL CARRIAGEWAY

100 km/h
(60 mph)

SECONDARY ROAD

90 km/h
(55 mph)

URBAN AREAS

50 km/h
(30 mph)

Arriving by Air

The two major airports for long-haul flights into Spain are located in Madrid and Barcelona. Other airports in Northern Spain offer international and domestic flights, the most useful of which are in A Coruña, Bilbao and Oviedo. European budget airlines fly to Spain all year round.

For information on getting to and from the main airports, see the table opposite.

Train Travel

International Train Travel

Spain's international and domestic rail services are operated by state-run **Renfe** (Red Nacional de Ferrocarriles Españoles). For international train trips, it is advisable to purchase your ticket well in advance. **Eurail** and **Interrail** sell passes (to European non-residents and residents respectively) for international journeys lasting from five days up to three months. Both passes are valid on Renfe trains.

Northern Spain is easily accessible from France. The main western route runs from Paris through Hendaye in the Pyrenees to San Sebastián. The eastern route from Paris runs via Cerbère and Port Bou to Barcelona, from where connections can be made to Northern Spain. Trains from London, Brussels, Amsterdam, Geneva, Zürich and Milan also reach Barcelona via Cerbère.

Northern Spain is accessible from Portugal via the Sud Express. It departs daily from Lisbon, terminating in the French border town of Hendaye, from where you can catch one of the regular services to a Spanish town or city. The Lusitania sleeper train also runs from Lisbon, via Entroncamento and Coimbra, to Madrid in around nine hours.

Journeys from other European countries will require a connection in France.

Eurail
W eurail.com
Interrail
W interrail.eu
Renfe
W renfe.com

GETTING TO AND FROM THE AIRPORT

Airport	Distance to city	Taxi fare	Public Transport
A Coruña	10 km (6 miles)	€15	Bus (25 mins)
Barcelona	14 km (9 miles)	€35	Rail (35 mins), bus (25 mins)
Bilbao	12 km (7 miles)	€26	Bus (30 mins)
Madrid	16 km (10 miles)	€30	Bus (20 mins), metro (30–40 mins)
Oviedo	45 km (28 miles)	€55	Bus (40 mins)

CAR JOURNEY PLANNER

Plotting the main driving routes according to journey time, this map is a handy reference for travelling between Spain's main cities by car. The times given reflect the fastest and most direct routes available. Tolls apply on *autopista* motorways (AP roads) but not on *autovías* (A roads).

••• Major road connections

A Coruña to Santiago de Compostela	1 hr	**Bilbao to Pamplona**	2 hrs
Barcelona to Girona	2.5 hrs	**Bilbao to Santander**	1.25 hrs
Barcelona to Valencia	4 hrs	**Bilbao to Santiago de Compostela**	6 hrs
Barcelona to Bilbao	6 hrs	**Madrid to Barcelona**	6 hrs
Bilbao to San Sebastián	1.25 hrs	**Madrid to Bilbao**	4.25 hrs
Bilbao to Burgos	1.75 hrs	**Madrid to Santiago de Compostela**	6.5 hrs
Bilbao to León	3.25 hrs	**Madrid to Valencia**	3.75 hrs

Domestic Train Travel

Renfe (p234) is the country's national rail operator, from whom you can buy tickets online or at the station. *Regionales y cercanías* (the regional and local services) are frequent and cheap. Along with regional companies like **FGC** (Ferrocarrils de la Generalitat) in Catalonia and **EuskoTren** in the Basque Country Renfe operates a good service throughout Spain. Intercity services link Northern Spain with the rest of the country. Madrid is just over six hours from A Coruña, and just over five hours from Bilbao by rail. Overnight trains are offered by Estrella (a basic service) to Madrid, and by Trenhotel (more sophisticated) to A Coruña and Vigo, in Galicia. Major train terminals pass luggage through scanners, so allow extra time for this.

EuskoTren
w euskotren.eus
FGC
w fgc.es

Long-Distance Bus Travel

Often the cheapest way to reach and travel around Northern Spain is by coach. **Eurolines** operates various routes throughout Europe and runs daily services to Madrid and Barcelona.

Within Spain itself, there is no national coach company, but private regional companies operate routes around the country. The largest of these is **Alsa**, which runs in all regions and has routes that cover most of the country.

Tickets and information for long-distance travel are available at all main coach stations as well as on the websites below, but note that it is not always possible to book tickets in advance.

Alsa
w alsa.es
Eurolines
w eurolines.com

Public Transport

Sightseeing and getting around in Northern Spain's towns and cities is best done on foot and by public transport. The majority of towns offer only a bus service, but larger cities operate multiple public transport systems, including metros or trams. **Bilbao**, **Santiago de Compostela**, **Santander** and **Pamplona** all have efficient transport systems. For up-to-date information about a city's public transport options, as well as ticket advice, check out their individual municipal websites.

Bilbao
w bilbao.eus
Pamplona
w pamplona.es
Santander
w santander.es

Santiago de Compostela
w santiagodecompostela.gal

Tickets

Public transport tickets are available at newsagents, but the best place to purchase is at stations themselves, either from ticket windows or automatic ticket machines. Tickets are sold as paper tickets or as a smart card which can either hold a season ticket or be topped up with cash and used pay-as-you-go.

Metro

Northern Spain's only metro system is the **Metro Bilbao,** serving Bilbao's city centre and outskirts. It is well run and a very useful alternative to overground transport. Tickets can be bought from machines in stations, or if you're staying for longer, you can buy a contactless *barik* card which you can top up to pay as you go. Up to 10 people can travel on the same card, and you can use it on all of Bilbao's public transport systems.

Metro de Bilbao
w metrobilbao.eus

Trams

Tram services are fairly uncommon in Northern Spain as most have been decommissioned. **Tranvías Coruña** runs a historical-style tram along the A Coruña promenade, aimed at sightseers. In the Basque Country, **EuskoTren** runs tram services in Bilbao and Vitoria, which are among the most modern in the country.

EuskoTren
w euskotren.eus
Tranvías Coruña
w tranviascoruna.com

Bus

Buses remain the most common mode of public transport throughout Spain, but they can sometimes follow an erratic timetable. Many services do not run after 10pm, although there are some night buses in the cities.

Local bus routes and timetables are posted at bus stops. Single tickets can be bought from the driver when you board the bus (always through the front doors), but in most cities multi-journey tickets *(bonobus* or *tarjeta)*, valid for 10 journeys on local buses, are preferable. You buy these in advance from bus offices, automatic machines or *estancos* (tobacconists). Advance tickets are cheaper, and save time when boarding the bus.

Taxis

Throughout Northern Spain, particularly in cities and towns, taxis are a reasonably priced way to get around if public transport isn't an option. Generally speaking, the journey starts with a flat fee and then increases depending on the distance travelled. Fares tend to be higher at night and also during the weekend and public holidays. Surcharges usually apply for trips to airports and bus and train stations.

Driving

If you drive to Spain in your own car, you must carry the vehicle's registration document, a valid insurance certificate, a passport or a national identity card and your driving licence at all times. You must also display a sticker on the back of the car showing its country of registration and you risk on-the-spot fines if you do not carry a red warning triangle and a reflective jacket with you at all times.

Spain has two types of motorway: *autopistas*, which are toll roads, and *autovías*, which are toll-free. You can establish whether a motorway is toll-free by the letters that prefix the number of the road: A = free motorway; AP = toll motorway.

Carreteras nacionales, Spain's main roads, have black-and-white signs and are designated by the letter N (Nacional) plus a number. Those with Roman numerals start at the Puerta del Sol in Madrid, and those with ordinary numbers have kilometre markers giving the distance from the provincial capital.

Carreteras comarcales, secondary roads, have a number preceded by the letter C. Other minor roads have numbers preceded by letters representing the name of the province, such as the LE1313 in Lleida.

In winter, especially in the Pyrenees and around Burgos, minor roads may be closed.

Car Hire

Popular car-hire companies in Spain are **Europcar**, **Avis** and **Hertz**. All have offices at airports and major train stations, and in bigger cities. Fly-drive, an option for two or more travellers where car hire is included in the cost of your air fare, can be arranged by travel agents and tour operators.

If you wish to hire a car locally for around a week or less, you will be able to arrange it with a local travel agent. A car for hire is known as a *coche de alquiler*.

Avis
W avis.com
Europcar
W europcar.com
Hertz
W hertz-europe.com

Rules of the Road

When using a car in Spain, drive on the right and use the left lane only for passing other vehicles. Most traffic regulations and warnings to motorists are represented on signs by easily recognized symbols. However, a few road rules and signs may be unfamiliar to some drivers from other countries.

If you have taken the wrong road, and it has a solid white line, you may make a U-turn as indicated by a *cambio de sentido* (change of direction) sign. At crossings, give way to all on-coming traffic, unless a sign indicates otherwise.

The legal blood-alcohol concentration (BAC) limit is 0.5 mg/ml and is very strictly enforced. It is compulsory to wear a seat belt in the front and rear seats of any private vehicle.

Boats and Ferries

Ferries connect Northern Spain to France, England and Ireland. All the important routes are served by car ferries. **Aferry** operates a regular connection between Saint-Nazare (Nantes) and Gijón. **Brittany Ferries** operates regular services connecting Plymouth, Portsmouth and Cork with Santander and Bilbao, and other European destinations. The *Pont-Aven* (Plymouth to Santander) and *Cap Finistère* (Portsmouth to Santander and Bilbao) leave two to three times weekly, with one- or two-night crossings available. Ferries are equipped with cabins, restaurants, cinemas and gyms, plus other facilities for passengers. Tickets are best purchased in advance online. Book early if you plan to travel in summer or around big public holidays.

Aferry
W aferryfreight.co.uk
Brittany Ferries
W brittany-ferries.co.uk

Cycling

Bicycles are becoming more common on Spanish streets, and an increasing number of northern cities maintain excellent cycling lanes. With Northern Spain's cooler temperate climate, cycling trips through the countryside are popular. There are pleasant, off-road stretches on the Camino de Santiago along which **Cycling Through the Centuries** operates eight-day guided tours. There are challenging routes through the Pyrenees for more adventurous riders: **Saddle Skedaddle** offers guided on-road and mountain bike rides through the Basque country and Catalonia.

Bicycles can be taken on board local trains (*cercanías*, after 2pm only), on all regional trains (*regionales*) with goods compartments and on all overnight long-distance trains (*largo recorrido*).

Cycling Through the Centuries
W cycling-centuries.com
Saddle Skedaddle
W skedaddle.com

PRACTICAL
INFORMATION

A little know-how goes a long way in Northern Spain. Here you will find all the essential advice and information you will need during your stay.

Personal Security

Violent crime is rare in Northern Spain, but visitors should avoid walking alone in poorly lit areas. Pickpocketing is common in the major cities. Take particular care at markets, popular sights and on public transport, and wear bags and cameras across your body, not on your shoulder. Contact your embassy if you have your passport stolen, or in the event of a serious crime.

Health

Seek medicinal supplies and advice for minor ailments from a pharmacy (*farmacia*), identifiable by a green or red cross. Each pharmacy displays a card in the window showing the address of the nearest all-night pharmacy.

Emergency medical care in Spain is free for all EU citizens. If you have an EHIC (*p233*), present this as soon as possible. You may have to pay after treatment and reclaim the money later.

For visitors coming from outside the EU, payment of medical expenses is the patient's responsibility, so it is important to arrange comprehensive insurance before travelling.

Smoking, Alcohol and Drugs

Smoking is banned in enclosed public spaces and is a fineable offence, although you can still smoke on the terraces of bars and restaurants.

Spain has a relaxed attitude towards alcohol consumption and, in cities, it is common to drink on the street outside the bar of purchase.

Recreational drugs are illegal, and possession of even a very small quantity can lead to an extremely hefty fine. Amounts that suggest an intent to supply drugs to other people can lead to custodial sentences.

ID

By law you must carry identification with you at all times in Spain. A photocopy of your passport should suffice. If stopped by the police you may be asked to report to a police station with the original document.

Local Customs

Regional pride is strong throughout Northern Spain. Be wary of referring to Catalans, Galicians and Basque people as "Spanish", as this can sometimes cause offence.

A famous Spanish tradition is the siesta, which sees many shops closing between 1pm and 5pm. This is not always observed by large stores or in very touristy areas.

Bullfighting

Attitudes towards *corridas* (bullfights) vary drastically throughout Northern Spain. The sport is banned in Catalonia, but Pamplona in Navarra is home to Spain's biggest bull-themed festival, San Fermín.

Supporters argue that the bulls are bred for the industry and would be killed as calves were it not for bullfighting, while organizations such as **ADDA** (Asociación Defensa Derechos Animal) organize protests throughout the country.

If you do decide to attend a *corrida*, bear in mind that it's better to see a big-name matador because they are more likely to make a clean and quick kill. The audience will make their disapproval evident if they don't.

ADDA
w addaong.org

Visiting Churches and Cathedrals

Most churches and cathedrals will not permit visitors during Sunday mass. Generally, entrance to churches is free, however a fee may apply to enter special areas, like cloisters.

Spain retains a strong Catholic identity. When visiting religious buildings ensure that you are dressed modestly, with knees and shoulders covered.

Mobile Phones and Wi-Fi

Free Wi-Fi is reasonably common in Northern Spain, particularly in libraries, large public spaces, restaurants and bars. Some places may charge for you to use their Wi-Fi.

Visitors travelling to Spain with EU tariffs are able to use their devices abroad without being affected by roaming charges. Users will be charged the same rates for data, calls and texts as at home.

Post

Correos is Spain's postal service. Postal rates fall into three price bands: Spain; Europe and North Africa; and the rest of the world.

Parcels must be weighed and stamped at Correos offices, which are open 8:30am–9:30pm Monday to Friday (outside the cities they close by 1–2pm on weekdays) and 9:30am–1pm on Saturday.

Letters sent from a post office usually arrive more quickly than if posted in a *buzón* (postbox). In cities, *buzóns* are yellow pillar boxes; elsewhere they are small, wall-mounted postboxes.

Correos
w correos.es

Taxes and Refunds

IVA in mainland Spain is usually 21 per cent, but with lower rates for certain goods and services. Under certain conditions, non-EU citizens can claim a rebate of these taxes. Present a form and your receipts to a customs officer at your point of departure.

Discount Cards

Some cities offer a visitor's pass or discount card that can be used for free or reduced-price entry to exhibitions, events and museums, and at participating restaurants. These are not free, so consider carefully how many of the offers you are likely to take advantage of before purchasing a card.

WEBSITES AND APPS

España
Spain's official tourism website
(*www.spain.info*).
Moovit
A route-planning app.
WiFi Map
Finds free Wi-Fi hotspots near you
(*www.wifimap.io*).

INDEX

D

F

G

H

PHRASE BOOK
SPANISH

IN AN EMERGENCY

Help!	¡Socorro!	soh-**koh**-roh
Stop!	¡Pare!	**pah**-reh
Call a doctor!	¡Llame a un médico!	**yah**-meh ah oon **meh**-dee-koh
Call an ambulance!	¡Llame a una ambulancia!	**yah**-meh ah **oonah** ahm-boo-**lahn**-a thee-ah
Call the police!	¡Llame a la policía!	**yah**-meh ah lah poh-lee-**thee**-ah
Call the fire brigade!	¡Llame a los bomberos!	**yah**-meh ah lohs bohm-**beh**-rohs
Where is the nearest hospital?	¿Dónde está el hospital más próximo?	**dohn**-deh ehs-**tah** ehl ohs-pee-**tahl mahs** prohx-ee-moh

COMMUNICATION ESSENTIALS

Yes	Sí	see
No	No	noh
Please	Por favor	pohr fah-**vohr**
Thank you	Gracias	**grah**-thee-ahs
Excuse me	Perdone	pehr-**doh**-neh
Hello	Hola	**oh**-lah
Goodbye	Adiós	ah-dee-**ohs**
Goodnight	Buenas noches	**bweh**-nahs noh chehs
Morning	La mañana	lah mah-**nyah**-nah
Afternoon	La tarde	lah **tahr**-deh
Evening	La tarde	lah **tahr**-deh
Yesterday	Ayer	ah-**yehr**
Today	Hoy	oy
Tomorrow	Mañana	mah-**nyah**-nah
Here	Aquí	ah-**kee**
There	Allí	ah-**yee**
What?	¿Qué?	keh
When?	¿Cuándo?	**kwahn**-doh
Why?	¿Por qué?	pohr-**keh**
Where?	¿Dónde?	**dohn**-deh

USEFUL PHRASES

How are you?	¿Cómo está usted?	**koh**-moh ehs-**tah** oos-**tehd**
Very well, thank you.	Muy bien, gracias.	mwee bee-**ehn grah**-thee-ahs
Pleased to meet you.	Encantado de conocerle.	ehn-kahn-**tah**-doh deh koh-noh-**thehr**-leh
See you soon.	Hasta pronto.	ahs-tah **prohn**-toh
That's fine.	Está bien.	ehs-**tah** bee-**ehn**
Where is/are ...?	¿Dónde está/están ...?	**dohn**-deh ehs-**tah**/ehs-**tah** tah/ehs-**tahn**
How far is it to ...?	¿Cuántos metros/ kilómetros hay de aquí a ...?	**kwahn**-tohs meh-trohs/kee-**loh**-meh-trohs **eye** deh ah-**kee** ah
Which way to ...?	¿Por dónde se va a ...?	pohr **dohn**-deh seh **bah** ah
Do you speak English?	¿Habla inglés?	ah-blah een-**glehs**
I don't understand	No comprendo	noh kohm-**prehn**-doh
Could you speak more slowly, please?	¿Puede hablar más despacio, por favor?	pweh-deh ah-**blahr mahs** dehs-pah-thee-oh pohr fah-**vohr**
I'm sorry.	Lo siento.	loh see-**ehn**-toh
What is the Wi-Fi password?	¿Cuál es la contraseña del wifi?	**kawl**-ehs lah kohn-trah-**sehn**-yah dehl **wee**-fee

USEFUL WORDS

big	grande	**grahn**-deh
small	pequeño	peh-**keh**-nyoh
hot	caliente	kah-lee-**ehn**-teh
cold	frío	**free**-oh
good	bueno	**bweh**-noh
bad	malo	**mah**-loh
enough	bastante	bahs-**tahn**-the
well	bien	bee-**ehn**
open	abierto	ah-bee-**ehr**-toh
closed	cerrado	thehr-**rah**-doh
left	izquierda	eeth-key-**ehr**-dah
right	derecha	deh-**reh**-chah
straight on	todo recto	toh-doh **rehk**-toh
near	cerca	**thehr**-kah
far	lejos	**leh**-hohs

up	arriba	ah-**ree**-bah
down	abajo	ah-**bah**-hoh
early	temprano	tehm-**prah**-noh
late	tarde	**tahr**-deh
entrance	entrada	ehn-**trah**-dah
exit	salida	sah-**lee**-dah
toilet	lavabos, servicios	lah-**vah**-bohs sehr-**bee**-thee-ohs
more	más	mahs
less	menos	**meh**-nohs

SHOPPING

How much does this cost?	¿Cuánto cuesta esto?	**kwahn**-toh **kwehs**-tah **ehs**-toh
I would like ...	Me gustaría ...	meh goos-ta-**ree**-ah
Do you have...?	¿Tienen...?	tee-**yeh**-nehn
I'm just looking, thank you.	Sólo estoy mirando, gracias.	soh-loh ehs-**toy** mee-**rahn**-doh **grah**-thee-ahs
Do you take credit cards?	¿Aceptan tarjetas de crédito?	ah-**thehp**-tahn tahr-**heh**-tahs deh **kreh**-dee-toh
What time do you open?	¿A qué hora abren?	ah keh oh-rah **ah**-brehn
What time do you close?	¿A qué hora cierran?	ah keh oh-rah thee-**ehr**-rahn
This one.	Este.	**ehs**-the
That one.	Ese.	**eh**-she
expensive	caro	**kahr**-oh
cheap	barato	bah-**rah**-toh
size, clothes	talla	**tah**-yah
size, shoes	número	**noø**-mehr-oh
white	blanco	**blahn**-koh
black	negro	**neh**-groh
red	rojo	**roh**-hoh
yellow	amarillo	ah-mah-**ree**-yoh
green	verde	**behr**-deh
blue	azul	ah-**thool**
antiques shop	la tienda de antigüedades	lah tee-**ehn**-dah deh ahn-tee-gweh-**dah**-dehs
bakery	la panadería	lah pah-nah-deh-**ree**-ah
bank	el banco	ehl **bahn**-koh
book shop	la librería	lah lee-breh-**ree**-ah
butcher's	la carnicería	lah kahr-nee-theh-**ree**-ah
cake shop	la pastelería	lah pahs-teh-leh-**ree**-ah
chemist's	la farmacia	lah fahr-**mah**-thee-ah
fishmonger's	la pescadería	lah pehs-kah-deh-**ree**-ah
greengrocer's	la frutería	lah froo-teh-**ree**-ah
grocer's	la tienda de comestibles	lah tee-**yehn**-dah deh koh-mehs-**tee**-blehs
hairdresser's	la peluquería	lah peh-loo-keh-**ree**-ah
market	el mercado	ehl mehr-**kah**-doh
newsagent's	el kiosko de prensa	ehl kee-**ohs**-koh deh **prehn**-sah
post office	la oficina de correos	lah oh-fee-**thee**-nah deh kohr-**reh**-ohs
shoe shop	la zapatería	lah thah-pah-teh-**ree**-ah
supermarket	el supermercado	ehl soo-pehr-mehr-**kah**-doh
tobacconist	el estanco	ehl ehs-**tahn**-koh
travel agency	la agencia de viajes	lah ah-**hehn**-thee-ah deh bee-**ah**-hehs

SIGHTSEEING

art gallery	el museo de arte	ehl moo-**seh**-oh deh **ahr**-the
cathedral	la catedral	lah kah-teh-**drahl**
church	la iglesia	lah ee-**gleh**-see-ah
	la basílica	lah bah-**see**-lee-kah
garden	el jardín	ehl hahr-**deen**
library	la biblioteca	lah bee-blee-oh-**teh**-kah
museum	el museo	ehl moo-**seh**-oh
tourist information office	la oficina de turismo	lah oh-fee-**thee**-nah deh too-**rees**-moh
town hall	el ayuntamiento	ehl ah-yoon-tah-mee-**ehn**-toh
closed for holiday	cerrado por vacaciones	thehr-**rah**-doh pohr bah-kah-cee-**oh**-nehs
bus station	la estación de autobuses	lah ehs-tah-thee-**ohn** deh owtoh-**boo**-sehs
railway station	la estación de trenes	lah ehs-tah-thee-**ohn** deh **treh**-nehs

STAYING IN A HOTEL

Do you have a vacant room?	¿Tienen una habitación libre?	tee-**eh**-nehn **oo**-nah ah-bee-tah-thee-**ohn** lee-breh
double room	habitación doble	ah-bee-tah-thee-**ohn** doh-bleh
with double bed	con cama de matrimonio	kohn kah-mah deh mah-tree-**moh**-nee-oh
twin room	habitación con dos camas	ah-bee-tah-thee-**ohn** kohn dohs **kah**-mahs
single room	habitación individual	ah-bee-tah-thee-**ohn** een-dee-vee-doo-**ahl**
room with a bath	habitación con baño	ah-bee-tah-thee-**ohn** kohn bah-nyoh
shower	ducha	**doo**-chah
porter	el botones	ehl boh-**toh**-nehs
key	la llave	lah **yah**-veh
I have a reservation.	Tengo una habitación reservada.	tehn-goh **oo**-na ah-bee-tah-thee-**ohn** reh-sehr-**bah**-dah

EATING OUT

Have you got a table for …?	¿Tienen mesa para …?	tee-**eh**-nehn **meh**-sah pah-**rah**
I want to reserve a table.	Quiero reservar una mesa.	kee-eh-roh reh-sehr-**bahr** **oo**-nah **meh**-sah
The bill, please.	La cuenta, por favor.	lah **kwehn**-tah pohr fah-**vohr**
I am a vegetarian	Soy vegetariano/a	soy beh-heh-tah-ree-**ah**-no/na
waitress/ waiter	camarera/ camarero	kah-mah-**reh**-rah/ kah-mah-**reh**-roh
menu	la carta	lah **kahr**-tah
fixed-price menu	menú del día	meh-**noo** dehl **dee**-ah
wine list	la carta de vinos	lah **kahr**-tah deh **bee**-nohs
glass	un vaso	oon **bah**-soh
bottle	una botella	oo-nah boh-**teh**-yah
knife	un cuchillo	oon koo-**chee**-yoh
fork	un tenedor	oon teh-neh-**dohr**
spoon	una cuchara	oo-nah koo-**chah**-rah
breakfast	el desayuno	ehl deh-sah-**yoo**-noh
lunch	la comida/ el almuerzo	lah koh-**mee**-dah/ ehl ahl-**mwehr**-thoh
dinner	la cena	lah **theh**-nah
main course	el primer plato	ehl pree-**mehr plah**-toh
starters	los entrantes	lohs ehn-tran **tehs**
dish of the day	el plato del día	ehl **plah**-toh dehl **dee**-ah
coffee	el café	ehl kah-**feh**
rare	poco hecho	**poh**-koh **eh**-choh
medium	medio hecho	**meh**-dee-oh **eh**-choh
well done	muy hecho	mwee **eh**-choh

MENU DECODER

asado	ah-**sah**-doh	roast
el aceite	ah-**thee**-eh-teh	oil
las aceitunas	ah-theh-**toon**-ahs	olives
el agua mineral	**ah**-gwa mee-neh-**rahl**	mineral water
sin gas/con gas	seen gas/kohn gas	still/sparkling
el ajo	**ah**-hoh	garlic
el arroz	ahr-**rohth**	rice
el azúcar	ah-**thoo**-kahr	sugar
la carne	**kahr**-neh	meat
la cebolla	theh-**boh**-yah	onion
la cerveza	thehr-**beh**-thah	beer
el cerdo	**therh**-doh	pork
el chocolate	choh-koh-**lah**-teh	chocolate
el chorizo	choh-**ree**-thoh	chorizo
el cordero	kohr-**deh**-roh	lamb
el fiambre	fee-**ahm**-breh	cold meat
frito	**free**-toh	fried
la fruta	**froo**-tah	fruit
los frutos secos	**froo**-tohs **seh**-kohs	nuts
las gambas	**gahm**-bahs	prawns
el helado	eh-**lah**-doh	ice cream
al horno	ahl **ohr**-noh	baked
el huevo	oo-**eh**-voh	egg
el jamón serrano	hah-**mohn** sehr-**rah**-noh	cured ham
el jerez	heh-**rehz**	sherry

la langosta	lahn-**gohs**-tah	lobster
la leche	**leh**-cheh	milk
el limón	lee-**mohn**	lemon
la limonada	lee-moh-**nah**-dah	lemonade
la mantequilla	mahn-teh-**kee**-yah	butter
la manzana	mahn-**thah**-nah	apple
los mariscos	mah-**rees**-kohs	seafood
la menestra	meh-**nehs**-trah	vegetable stew
la naranja	nah-**rahn**-hah	orange
el pan	**pahn**	bread
el pastel	pahs-**tehl**	cake
las patatas	pah-**tah**-tahs	potatoes
el pescado	pehs-**kah**-doh	fish
la pimienta	pee-mee-**yehn**-tah	pepper
el plátano	**plah**-tah-noh	banana
el pollo	**poh**-yoh	chicken
el postre	**pohs**-treh	dessert
el queso	**keh**-soh	cheese
la sal	sahl	salt
las salchichas	sahl-**chee**-chahs	sausages
la salsa	**sahl**-sah	sauce
seco	**seh**-koh	dry
el solomillo	soh-loh-**mee**-yoh	sirloin
la sopa	**soh**-pah	soup
la tarta	**tahr**-tah	pie/cake
el té	teh	tea
la ternera	tehr-**neh**-rah	beef
las tostadas	tohs-**tah**-dahs	toast
el vinagre	bee-**nah**-greh	vinegar
el vino blanco	**bee**-noh **blahn**-koh	white wine
el vino rosado	**bee**-noh roh-**sah**-doh	rosé wine
el vino tinto	**bee**-noh **teen**-toh	red wine

NUMBERS

	Spanish	Pronunciation
0	cero	**theh**-roh
1	uno	**oo**-noh
2	dos	dohs
3	tres	trehs
4	cuatro	**kwa**-troh
5	cinco	**theen**-koh
6	seis	says
7	siete	**see**-eh-the
8	ocho	**oh**-choh
9	nueve	**nweh**-veh
10	diez	dee-**ehth**
11	once	**ohn**-theh
12	doce	**doh**-theh
13	trece	**treh**-theh
14	catorce	kah-**tohr**-theh
15	quince	**keen**-theh
16	dieciséis	dee-eh-thee-**seh-ees**
17	diecisiete	dee-eh-thee-see **eh**-the
18	dieciocho	dee-eh-thee-**oh**-choh
19	diecinueve	dee-eh-thee-**nweh**-veh
20	veinte	**beh**-een-the
21	veintiuno	beh-een-tee-**oo**-noh
22	veintidós	beh-een-tee-**dohs**
30	treinta	**treh**-een-tah
31	treinta y uno	treh-een-tah ee **oo**-noh
40	cuarenta	kwah-**rehn**-tah
50	cincuenta	theen-**kwehn**-tah
60	sesenta	seh-**sehn**-tah
70	setenta	seh-**tehn**-tah
80	ochenta	oh-**chehn**-tah
90	noventa	noh-**vehn**-tah
100	cien	thee-**ehn**
101	ciento uno	thee-**ehn**-toh **oo**-noh
102	ciento dos	thee-**ehn**-toh **dohs**
200	doscientos	dohs-thee-**ehn**-tohs
500	quinientos	khee-nee-**ehn**-tohs
700	setecientos	seh-teh-thee-**ehn**-tohs
900	novecientos	noh-veh-thee-**ehn**-tohs
1,000	mil	meel
1,001	mil uno	**meel oo**-noh

TIME

one minute	un minuto	oon mee-**noo**-toh
one hour	una hora	oo-na oh-**rah**
half an hour	media hora	meh-dee-a **oh**-rah
Monday	lunes	**loo**-nehs
Tuesday	martes	**mahr**-tehs
Wednesday	miércoles	mee-**ehr**-koh-lehs
Thursday	jueves	hoo-**weh**-vehs
Friday	viernes	bee-**ehr**-nehs
Saturday	sábado	**sah**-bah-doh
Sunday	domingo	doh-**meen**-goh

BASQUE

IN AN EMERGENCY

Help!	Lagundu!	lah-goon-doo!
Stop!	Gelditu!	gehl-dee-too!
Call a doctor!	Sendagile bati deitu!	sehn-dah-gee-leh bah-tee deh-ee-too!
Call an ambulance!	Anbulantzia bati deitu!	ahn-boo-lahn-tzee-ah bah-tee deh-ee-too!
Call the police!	Poliziari deitu!	poh-lee-zee-ah-ree deh-ee-too!
Call the fire brigade!	Suhiltzaileei deitu!	suh-eel-tzah-ee-leh-eh-ee deh-ee-too!
Where is the nearest hospital?	Non dago ospitalerik gertuena?	nohn dah-goh ohs-pee-tah-leh-reek gehr-too-eh-nah?

COMMUNICATION ESSENTIALS

Yes	Bai	bah-ee
No	Ez	ehs
Please	Mesedez	meh-seh-dehs
Thank you	Eskerrik asko	ehs-keh-reek ahs-koh
Excuse me	Barkatu	bahr-kah-too
Hello	Kaixo	kah-ee-sho
Goodbye	Agur	ah-goor
Good night	Gabon	gah-bohn
Morning	Goiza	goh-ee-sah
Afternoon	Arratsaldea	ah-rah-tsahl-deh-ah
Evening	Arratsaldea	ah-rah-tsahl-deh-ah
Yesterday	Atzo	ah-tzoh
Today	Gaur	gah-oor
Tomorrow	Bihar	bee-ahr
Here	Hemen	eh-mehn
There	Hor	ohr
What?	Zer?	zehr?
When?	Noiz?	noh-ees?
Why?	Zergatik?	zehr-gah-teek?
Where?	Non?	nohn?

USEFUL PHRASES

How are you?	Zer moduz?	zehr moh-dooz?
Very well, thank you.	Ondo, eskerrik asko	ohn-doh, ehs-keh-reek ahs-koh
Pleased to meet you.	Pozten nau zu ezagutzeak	pohz-tehn nah-oo zoo eh-zah-goo-tzeh-ahk
See you soon.	Gero arte	geh-roh ahr-teh
That's fine.	Ados	ah-dohs
Where is/are ...?	Non dago/daude ...?	nohn dah-goh/dah-oo-deh ...?
How far is it to...?	Ze tarte dago hemendik ...-ra?	seh tahr-teh da-goh eh-mehn-deek ... -rah?
Which way to...?	Nondik joaten da ...-ra?	nohn-deek joh-ah-tehn dah ... -rah?
Do you speak English?	Ingelesez badakizu?	een-geh-leh-sehs bah-dah-kee-zoo?
I don't understand	Ez dut ulertzen	ehs doot oo-lehr-tzehn
Could you speak more slowly, please?	Mantsoago hitz egin dezakezu, mesedez?	mahn-tsoh-ah-goh ee-tz eh-geen deh-sah-keh-zoo, meh-seh-dehs?
I'm sorry.	Barkatu	bahr-kah-too
What is the Wi-Fi password	Za der WiFi pasahitza?	zehr dah wee-fee pah-sah-eet-zah

USEFUL WORDS

big	Handia	ahn-dee-ah
small	Txikia	txee-kee-ah
hot	Beroa	beh-roh-ah
cold	Hotza	oh-tzah
good	Ona	oh-nah
bad	Txarra	txah-rah
enough	Nahikoa	nah-ee-koh
well	Ondo	ohn-doh
open	Zabalik	sah-bah-leek
closed	Itxita	ee-txee-tah
left	Ezkerra	ehs-keh-rah
right	Eskuina	ehs-koo-ee-nah
straight on	Zuzen	zoo-zehn
near	Gertu	gehr-too
far	Urrun	oo-roon
up	Goian	goh-ee-ahn
down	Behean	beh-eh-ahn
early	Goiz	goh-eez
late	Berandu	beh-rahn-doo
entrance	Sarrera	sah-reh-rah
exit	Irteera	eer-teh-eh-rah
toilet	Komunak	koh-moo-nahk
more	Gehiago	geh-ee-ah-goh
less	Gutxiago	guh-txee-ah-goh

SHOPPING

How much does this cost?	Zenbat balio du honek?	zehn-baht bah-lee-oh. duh oh-nehk?
I would like...	... gustatuko litzaidake	... guhs-tah-too-koh lee-tzah-ee-dah-keh
Do you have?	Ba al daukazue ...-rik?	bah ahl dah-oo-kah-zoo-eh ... -reek?
I'm just looking.	Begiratzen nago, besterik ez.	beh-gee-rah-tzehn nah-gob, behs-teb-reek ebs
Do you take credit cards?	Txartelik onartzen al duzue?	txahr-teh-leek ohn-nahr-tzehn ahl doo-zoo-eh?
This one.	Hau	ah-oo
That one.	Hori	oh-ree
expensive	Garestia	gah-rehs-tee-ah
cheap	Merkea	mehr-keh-ah
size, clothes	Neurria, arropa	neh-oo-ree-ah, ah-roh-pah
size, shoes	Neurria, oinetazkoak	neh-oo-ree-ah, oh-ee-neh-tahz-koh-ahk
white	Zuria	zoo-ree-ah
black	Beltza	behl-tzah
red	Gorria	goh-ree-ah
yellow	Horia	oh-ree-ah
green	Berdea	behr-deh-ah
blue	Urdina	oor-dee-nah
antiques shop	Antigoaleko gauzen denda	ahn-tee-goh-ah-leh-koh gah-oo-zehn dehn-dah
bakery	Okindegia	oh-keen-deh-gee-ah
bank	Bankua	bahn-koo-ah
book shop	Liburu-denda	lee-boo-roo dehn-dah
butcher's	Harategia	ah-rah-teh-gee-ah
cake shop	Gozotegia	goh-zoh-teh-gee-ah
chemist's	Farmazia	far-mah-zee-ah
fishmonger's	Arrandegia	ah-rahn-deh-gee-ah
greengrocer's	Frutategia	froo-tah-teh-gee-ah
grocer's	Janari-denda	jah-nah-ree dehn-dah
hairdresser's	Ile-apaindegia	ee-leh ah-pah-een-deh-gee-ah
market	Azoka	ah-zoh-kah
newsagent's	Kioskoa	kee-ohs-koh-ah
post office	Postetxea	pohst-eh-txeh-ah
shoe shop	Zapata-denda	zah-pah-tah dehn-dah
supermarket	Supermerkatua	soo-pehr-mehr-kah-too-ah
tobacconist	Tabako-denda	tah-bak-koh dehn-dah
travel agency	Bidaia-agentzia	bee-dah-ee-ah ah-ghehn-tzee-ah

SIGHTSEEING

art gallery	Arte-galeria	ahr-teh gah-leh-ree-ah
cathedral	Katedrala	kah-teh-drah-lah
church	Eliza	eh-lee-zah
garden	Lorategia	loh-rah-teh-gee-ah
library	Liburutegia	lee-boo-roo-teh-gee-ah
museum	Museoa	moo-seh-oh-ah
tourist information office	Turismo bulegoa	too-rees-moh boo-leh-goh-ah
town hall	Udaletxea	oo-dhal-eh-txeh-ah
closed for holiday	Oporretan gaude	oh-poh-reh-tahn gah-oo-deh
bus station	Autobus-geltokia	ah-oo-toh-boos gehl-toh-kee-ah
railway station	Tren-geltokia	trehn gehl-too-kee-ah

NUMBERS

0	Zero	zeh-roh
1	Bat	baht
2	Bi	bee
3	Hiru	ee-roo
4	Lau	lah-oo
5	Bost	bohst
6	Sei	seh-ee
7	Zazpi	zahz-pee
8	Zortzi	zohr-tzee
9	Bederatzi	beh-deh-rah-tzee
10	Hamar	ah-mahr

GALICIAN

IN AN EMERGENCY

English	Galician	Pronunciation
Help!	¡Axuda!	ah-shu-dah
Stop!	¡Detéñase!	deh-teh-nyah-seh
Call a doctor!	¡Chamen a un médico!	chah-mehn ah oon meh-dee-koh
Call an ambulance!	¡Chamen a unha ambulancia!	chah-mehn ah oon-ah ahm-boo-lahn-thee-ah
Call the police!	¡Chamen á policía!	chah-mehn ah poh-lee-thee-ah
Call the fire brigade!	¡Chamen ós bombeiros!	chah-mehn ohs bohm-beh-ee-rohs
Where is the nearest hospital?	¿Onde está o hospital máis próximo?	onh-deh ehs-tah oh ohs-pee-tahl mah-ees prohx-ee-moh

COMMUNICATION ESSENTIALS

English	Galician	Pronunciation
Yes	Sí	see
No	Non	nohn
Please	Por favor	pohr fah-bohr
Thank you	Gracias	grah-thee-ahs
Excuse me	Desculpe	Dehs-kool-peh
Hello	Ola	oh-lah
Goodbye	Adeus	ah-deh-oos
Good night	Boas noites	boh-ahs noh-ee-tehs
Morning	Mañá	mah-nya
Afternoon	Tarde	tahr-deh
Evening	Serán	seh-rahn
Yesterday	Onte	ohn-teh
Today	Hoxe	oh-sheh
Tomorrow	Mañá	mah-nya
Here	Aquí	ah-khee
There	Alí	ah-lee
What?	¿Que?	keh
When?	¿Cando?	kahn-doh
Why?	¿Por que?	pohr-keh
Where?	¿Onde?	ohn-deh

USEFUL PHRASES

English	Galician	Pronunciation
How are you?	¿Como está vostede?	koh-moh ehs-tah bohs-teh-deh
Very well, thank you.	Moi ben, gracias.	moh-ee behn grah-thee-ahs
Pleased to meet you.	Encantado de coñecelo.	ehn-kahn-tah-doh deh koh-nye-teh-loh
See you soon.	Ata pronto.	ah-tah prohn-toh
That's fine.	Está ben.	ehs-tah behn
Where is /are...?	¿Onde está/ están...?	ohn-deh ehs-tah/ ehs-than
How far is it to...?	¿Canto hai de aquí a...?	kahn-toh eye deh ah-kee ah
Which way to...?	¿Cal é o camiño para ir a...?	kahl eh oh kah-mee-nyo pah-ra eer ah
Do you speak English?	¿Fala inglés?	fah-lah een-glehs
I don't understand	Non comprendo.	nohn kohm-prehn-doh
Could you speak more slowly?	¿Podería falar máis a modo	poh-deh-reeah fah-lahr mah-ees ah-moh-doh
I'm sorry.	Síntoo.	seen-toh-oh
What is the Wi-Fi password?	Cal é o contrasinal wifi?	kahl eh oh kon-trah-see-nah wifi?

USEFUL WORDS

English	Galician	Pronunciation
big	grande	grahn-deh
small	pequeno	peh-keh-noh
hot	quente	kehn-teh
cold	frío	free-oh
good	bo	boh
bad	malo	mah-loh
enough	abondo	ah-bohn-doh
well	ben	behn
open	aberto	ah-behr-toh
closed	pechado	peh-cha-doh
left	esquerda	ehs-kehr-dah
right	dereita	deh-reh-ee-tah
straight on	cara adiante	kah-rah ah-dee-ahn-teh
near	preto	preh-toh
far	lonxe	lohn-sheh
up	arriba	ah-ree-bah
down	abaixo	ah-bah-ee-shoh
early	cedo	theh-doh
late	tarde	tahr-deh
entrance	entrada	ehn-trah-dah
exit	saída	sah-ee-dah
toilet	baño	bah-nyo
more	máis	mah-ees
less	menos	meh-nohs

SHOPPING

English	Galician	Pronunciation
How much does this cost?	¿canto custa?	kahn-toh koos-tah
I would like...	quero...	keh-roh
Do you have	¿teñen...?	teh-nyehn
I'm just looking.	estou a mirar.	ehs-toh-oo ah mee-rahr
Do you take credit cards?	¿aceptan tarxetas de crédito?	ah-thep-tan tahr- sheh tahs deh kreh-dee-toh
What time do you open?	¿a que hora abren?	ah keh oh-rah ah-brehn
What time do you close?	¿a que hora pechan?	ah keh oh-rah peh-chahn
This one.	este.	ehs-teh
That one.	ese.	eh-seh
expensive	caro	kah-roh
cheap	barato	bah-rah-toh
size, clothes	talla	tah-yah
size, shoes	número	noo-meh-roh
white	branco	brahn-koh
black	negro	neh-groh
red	vermelo	behr-meh-yoh
yellow	amarelo	ah-mah-reh-loh
green	verde	behr-deh
blue	azul	ah-thool
antiques shop	tenda de antigüidades	tehn-dah deh ahn-tee-gwih-dah-dehs
bakery	forno	fohr-noh
bank	banco	bahn-koh
book shop	librería	lee-breh-ree-ah
butcher's	carnicería	kahr-nee-theh-ree-ah
cake shop	pastelería	pahs-teh-leh-ree-ah
chemist's	farmacia	fahr-mah-thee-ah
fishmonger's	peixería	pey-sheh-ree-ah
greengrocer's	froitería	froh-ee-teh-ree-ah
grocer's	tenda	tehn-dah
hairdresser's	barbería (men)/ perruquería (women)	bahr-beh-ree-ah/ pehr-roo-keh-ree-ah
market	mercado	mehr-kah-doh
newsagent's	quiosco de prensa	kee-ohs-koh deh prehn-sah
post office	correos	kohr-reh-ohs
shoe shop	zapatería	thah-pah-teh-ree-ah
supermarket	supermercado	soo-pehr-mehr-kah-doh
tobacconist	estanco	ehs-tahn-koh
travel agency	axencia de viaxes	ah-shehn-thee-ah deh bee-ah-shehs

SIGHTSEEING

English	Galician	Pronunciation
art gallery	galería de arte	gah-leh-ree-ah deh ahr-teh
cathedral	catedral	kah-teh-drahl
church	igrexa	ee-greh-shah
garden	xardín	shar-deen
library	biblioteca	bee-blee-oh-teh-kah
museum	museo	moo-seh-oh
tourist information office	oficina de turismo	oh-fee-thee-nah deh too-rees-moh
town hall	casa do concello	kah-sah doh kohn-theh-yoh
closed for holiday	pechado por vacacións	peh-chah-doh pohr bah-kah-thee-ohns
bus station	estación de autobuses	ehs-tah-thee-ohn deh ah-oo-toh-boo-sehs
railway station	estación de trens	ehs-tah-thee-ohn deh trehns

NUMBERS

	Galician	Pronunciation
0	cero	theh-roh
1	un	oon
2	dous	doh-oos
3	tres	trehs
4	catro	kah-troh
5	cinco	theen-koh
6	seis	sayhs
7	sete	seh-teh
8	oito	oh-ee-toh
9	nove	noh-beh
10	dez	dehth

ACKNOWLEDGMENTS

The publisher would like to thank the following for their kind permission to reproduce their photographs:

Key: a-above; b-below/bottom; c-centre; f-far; l-left; r-right; t-top

123RF.com: Guillermo Avello 213cla; Iakov Filimonov 8cla, 26tl; Pabkov 167br, 226-7t; Igor Plotnikov 22t; tichr 85tl; Tonobalaguer 10clb, 185tl.

4Corners: Francesco Carovillano 19tl, 174-5; Hans-Georg Eiben 87tl; Olimpio Fantuz 82-3t, 86b; Reinhard Schmid 58-9, 188b; Luigi Vaccarella 140bl.

akg-images: Hervé Champollion 92tr.

Alamy Stock Photo: AGAMI Photo Agency / Oscar Diez 209crb; AGE Fotostock / Gonzalo Azumendi 28cr, 145b, 223t, / Bruno Almela 28br, / Tolo Balaguer 190bl, / F. J. Fdez. Bordonada 186t, / David Herraez Calzada 184b, / Rafael Campillo 172b, / Juan Carlos Cantero 80b, / Facto Foto 4, 117clb, / Fernando Fernández 79cla, / FSG 222bl, / María Galán 82bl, / Javier Larrea 20crb, 32t, 114-5t, 154bl, 158clb, 165tl, 165tr, 168b, 169tr, 211tr, 214clb, / David Miranda 33br, 85clb, 104-5b, 124bl, / Juan José Pascual 129tr; AJF 111tl; Jerónimo Alba 44-5b, 53tr, 115tr, 161crb; Andreas Altenburger 69tr; Kiko Alvarez 39cl; Lasse Ansaharju 128-9b; Arcaid Images / Nicholas Kane 135tc; Archive PL 170t, 170cl; Juan Aunion 53cb; Aurelian Images 136bl; Christian Bertrand 50crb; Bildarchiv Monheim GmbH / Markus Bassler 180tc; Eduardo Blanco 198bl, 220tr; blickwinkel / Trapp 209crb (Asp Viper); Tatiana Boyle 160b; Michael Brooks 153cra; Pau Buera 51cl; Nano Calvo 11br; Cavan / Aurora Photos / David Santiago Garcia 194t; James Cheadle 108-9b; Timo Christ 78-9b; Classic Image 76t, 214b, 225tl; Ian G Dagnall 18, 49bl, 106t, 117br 146-7, 155cra, 156br; DCarreño 89br, 90bl, 91t, 183bl, 195br, 197t; Dleiva 190-1t; Peter Eastland 143bc; EFE News Agency / David Aguilar 8clb; Factofoto 138-9t; Alexei Fateev 216-7b; FLPA 209br; David Forster 42-3t; Maria Galan 39crb; Nick Gammon 192-3b; Ainara Garcia 51clb; David Gato 50cra, 51tr, / *Campesinos de Gandia* by Hermen Anglada © DACS 2019 108tl; Stéphane Gautier 38-9b; Kevin George 137cra; Javier Gil 48-9t, 112bl; GL Archive 55t, 126bc; Víctor Gómez 110clb; Paul Christian Gordon 30-1cla, 50cl, 197br; Monica R. Goya 125br; Granger Historical Picture Archive / NYC 54tl, 56-7t; Matt Griggs 207clb; hemis.fr / Ludovic Maisant 35clb, / René Mattes 210bl, / Bertrand Rieger 22cr, 166br, / Arnaud Späni 125cra; Heritage Image Partnership Ltd / Index / A. Noé 56bc; Historic Collection 84cr; Image Professionals GmbH / Quadriga Images 46tl; imageBROKER / Christian Handl 13cr, 141tr; Ivoha 67tr, 92bl, 93br,

180br; Jack Cox in Spain 103bl; Jon Arnold Images Ltd 16c, 60-1, 150t; Lanmas 54br; Gloria Latorre & Álvar Montes 34tl; Cro Magnon 187bl, 188clb; Stefano Politi Markovina 168tr; Marshall Ikonography 53cla; Francisco Martinez 125t; Melba Photo Agency 215tr, 230-1; Mikel Bilbao Gorostiaga- Nature & Landscapes 11cr, 43bl; Mikel Bilbao Gorostiaga- Travels 17bl, 130-1, 173t; Tim Moore 103cl, 196bl; Miguel Moya 47br; Juan Carlos Muñoz 127br; Eric Nathan 72t; National Geographic Image Collection / Tino Soriano 116-7t; Nature Photographers Ltd / Paul R. Sterry 221cra; Nature Picture Library / Jose B. Ruiz 122tr; Alberto Paredes 117crb; Photo12 / Archives Snark 56tl; Pictorial Press Ltd 56bl; The Picture Art Collection 145clb, 193br; Prisma Archivo 52t, 52bc, 53br, 54bl, 55cra, 55clb; Campillo Rafael 35tr; M Ramírez 24cr, 31tl, 123bl; Rolf Hicker Photography 19cb, 202-3; Jordi Salas 227br; Science History Images / Photo Researchers 55tl; Carmen Sedano 219tr; Travelscape Images 153t; Fabrizio Troiani 178-9t; Lucas Vallecillos 22crb, 30cra, 46-7b, 49crb, 73tr, 150bc, 226bc; Marcos Veiga 51tl; Sebastian Wasek 206-7t; WENN Rights Ltd 57cb; Jan Wlodarczyk 80clb; World History Archive 56cla; Cristian Zaharia 212-3b.

AWL Images: Marco Bottigelli 34-5b; Matteo Colombo 159tl.

Bodegas Muga: 24t.

Bridgeman Images: © Look and Learn 54cb.

Depositphotos Inc: ly0712 20bl; mathes 182t.

Dorling Kindersley: Dorota Jarymowicz / Mariusz Jarymowicz 111tr, 125cr.

Dreamstime.com: Absente 75cra; Aidart 33cla; Alex7209 57bc; Dolores Giraldez Alonso 97tr; Amartphotography 170-1b; Zeynur Babayev 53tl; Jesus Ignacio Murguizu Bacaicoa 45cl; Mircea Bezergheanu 41cl; Marina Bombina 85b

Penguin Random House

Main Contributors Ben Ffrancon Davies,
Patricia Harris & David Lyons,
Agnieszka Drewno, Zuzanna Jakubowska,
Renata Szmidt, Carlos Marrodán Casas

Senior Editor Ankita Awasthi Tröger

Senior Designer Tania Da Silva Gomes

Project Editor Lucy Sienkowska

Project Art Editor Dan Bailey

Designers Ankita Sharma, Vinita Venugopal,
Priyanka Thakur, Jordan Lambley

Factchecker Lynnette McCurdy Bastida

Editor Louise Abbott

Proofreader Kathryn Glendenning

Indexer Hilary Bird

Senior Picture Researcher Ellen Root

Picture Research Marta Bescos,
Sumita Khatwani, Rituraj Singh, Vagisha Pushp

Illustrators Michał Burkiewicz, Paweł Marczak

Cartographic Editor James Macdonald

Cartography Rajesh Chhibber, Animesh Pathak
and Magdalena Polak

Jacket Designers Maxine Pedliham,
Bess Daly, Dan Bailey

Jacket Picture Research Susie Watters

Senior DTP Designer Jason Little

DTP Designer Rohit Rojal

Producer Rebecca Parton

Managing Editor Hollie Teague

Art Director Maxine Pedliham

Publishing Director Georgina Dee

**The information in this
DK Eyewitness Travel Guide is checked regularly.**
Every effort has been made to ensure that this book
is as up-to-date as possible at the time of going to
press. Some details, however, such as telephone
numbers, opening hours, prices, gallery hanging
arrangements and travel information, are liable to
change. The publishers cannot accept responsibility
for any consequences arising from the use of this
book, nor for any material on third party websites,
and cannot guarantee that any website address
in this book will be a suitable source of travel
information. We value the views and suggestions
of our readers very highly. Please write to: Publisher,
DK Eyewitness Travel Guides, Dorling Kindersley,
80 Strand, London, WC2R 0RL, UK, or email:
travelguides@dk.com

First edition 2007

Published in Great Britain by Dorling Kindersley Limited,
80 Strand, London, WC2R 0RL

Published in the United States by DK Publishing,
1450 Broadway, Suite 801, New York, NY 10018

Copyright © 2007, 2020 Dorling Kindersley Limited
A Penguin Random House Company
20 21 22 23 10 9 8 7 6 5 4 3 2 1

A CIP catalog record for this book
is available from the British Library.

A catalog record for this book is available
from the Library of Congress.

ISSN: 1542 1554
ISBN: 978 0 2414 0862 9

Printed and bound in China.

www.dk.com